SCOTT WALKER

The Rhymes of Goodbye

SCOTT WALKER

The Rhymes of Goodbye

New Edition, Revised and Updated

Lewis Williams

Plexus, London

All rights reserved including the right
of reproduction in whole or in part in any form
Copyright © 2006, 2019 by Lewis Williams
Published by Plexus Publishing Limited
26 Dafforne Road
London SW178TZ
www.plexusbooks.com
www.rhymesofgoodbye.com

British Library Cataloguing in Publication Data
A catalogue record for this book is available from the British Library.

ISBN-13: 978-085965-558-3

The right of Author's name to be identified as author of
this work has been asserted by him in accordance with
the Copyright, Designs and Patents Act, 1988

Printed and manufactured in Great Britain by Bell and Bain Ltd, Glasgow
Original book design by Rebecca Martin.
Cover and interior for this new, revised and updated edition
redesigned by Martin Bushell.

Contents

'Yes, there are people in the world
who do not love Scott Walker.
But what must their hearts be like?'

Stuart Maconie, *New Musical Express*

A Note to the Reader of the 2019 Edition

This revised edition of *Scott Walker: The Rhymes of Goodbye* comes 13 years after the original edition was published in 2006. Needless to say, the world has changed a great deal in that time. We have lost not only Scott Walker himself, who died in March 2019 – the one celebrity death that upset me more than any other ever has done – but also his fellow Walker Brother, John Maus, in 2011, and a number of others who were mentioned in the first edition of this book. Among these notable figures were Angela Morley, who died in 2009, and the great David Bowie, whom we lost in 2016.

It is also difficult to ignore the difference in Scott Walker's musical output from 2006 onwards. I would argue that this difference lies not so much in the quality of his art but rather in the quantity he produced during this later period. Having grown accustomed to gaps of 11 years between album releases in the years preceding the first publication of this book, Scott's work rate after 2006 seems positively prolific in comparison.

After releasing *The Drift* in 2006, Scott wrote and recorded one dance soundtrack, two film soundtracks and a collaborative album with experimental metal band Sunn O))), not to mention composing an original score for a production for the Royal Opera House and publishing a collection of his lyrics. All the commercially available recorded outputs from these activities are covered by new song entries *(293-340)* in this new edition of *The Rhymes of Goodbye*. During this period after 2006 and up until his death, Scott also became far more comfortable talking about his art. One of his final radio interviews with his friend Jarvis Cocker in 2017 found him very open and relaxed compared to the impression he gave of a rabbit caught in the headlights when he was interviewed on TV around the time of the release of *Climate of Hunter* all those years ago in 1984.

The way we listen to music today has also changed significantly. Despite Scott's continued hope that listeners would buy his music in physical form – so that they could read his lyrics – downloading and streaming are the way a lot of us access music today. Fortunately, though, many more of the Scott and Walker Brothers albums have become available since 2006. In 2006 the album that is *Scott 5* in all but name, *'Til the Band Comes In*, was criminally out of print; now it is more readily available, whether one chooses to listen to it via streaming or as part of a recently available CD set of his first five solo albums. Likewise, any difficulty there was in obtaining Walker Brothers material was put aside with the release of the *Everything Under the Sun* box set that effectively comprised all the band's studio output, including 12 previously unheard, unreleased tracks – four of which, for reasons that I'll explain, hold particular interest. All 12 of these tracks are also covered by new song entries in this 2019 revised edition *(63-74)*. In this new edition, I have updated everything that I found to be out of date and have added important new pieces of information in places where I thought appropriate and of interest to the reader.

Lewis Williams, April 2019

Introduction

No one had a recording career quite like that of Scott Walker. So who was he? The lead singer with the Walker Brothers, the group who, for a significant part of the 1960s, held the pop world in their hands; scoring a string of hits, including the number ones 'Make It Easy on Yourself' and 'The Sun Ain't Gonna Shine Anymore'; breaking a million hearts in the process. The reluctant pop idol. The man behind a series of fashion-defying solo records which, behind their numeric titles, hid a world of popular music, so strange and beautiful, that still stands up today as some of the greatest ever recorded. The existentialist who took the Jacques Brel song 'Jackie' – with its lyric of 'bordellos' and 'authentic queers and phoney virgins' – into the singles chart, in the days when censorship ruled the broadcasting world. The so-called 'crooner' of standards with his own BBC TV show. The popular artist who seemed unstoppable in 1968, but who, by the end of the following year, was unable to even make the charts. The possessor of one of the greatest singing voices of all time, who later saw himself as having prostituted his art for most of the 1970s. The avant-garde artist of the modern era whose records defy categorisation, and who in the 1980s, 1990s and early 2000s used 'that voice' so sparingly that he released just one album roughly every ten years. The answer is all of these.

The dark and intense world of Scott Walker's first modern album, 1995's *Tilt*, belongs to a different universe than the records he sang on in the Sixties, both with the Walker Brothers and as a solo artist. A journey spanning light years had taken place – from literal lyrics of romantic loss to fractured poetry, embracing topics such as the Nazi Holocaust, arms deals and murder; from orchestral pop to a mix of industrial noise and orchestral anti-pop. Such disparity has led some commentators to talk of two Scott Walkers[1] - avant-garde artist versus popular singer. But that is to over-simplify. Back in the late Sixties, we could have spoken of two Scotts – the singer of romantic middle-of-the-road ballads, who admired and sought to emulate Jack Jones, and the serious singer-songwriter whose compositions were influenced by classical music and lyrically inspired by the Belgian songwriter Jacques Brel, existentialist authors Jean-Paul Sartre and Albert Camus, and Russian poet Yevgney Yevtushenko. Yet neither of these two Scotts prepared us for *Tilt*'s 'shock of the new'. Were there then three Scott Walkers? Add to this list the 'voice for hire' and would-be country music singer of the mid-Seventies, and we might be left thinking of a half-dozen or so alternate identities.

But it is not simply the diversity of his output that made Scott's recording career unique. In terms of embracing differing musical styles, other artists have demonstrated greater versatility. In their comparatively brief eight-year recording career, the Beatles proved themselves capable of embracing every musical style from pop to folk, from rock'n'roll to psychedelia, including neo-music hall ('When I'm Sixty Four') and avant-garde sound collage ('Revolution No. 9') along the way. David Bowie, throughout his remarkable recording career, embraced folk rock, heavy metal, glam rock, blue-eyed soul, electronica, stadium rock and even, on 1997's *Earthling*, drum and bass. But Scott Walker's career is rendered unique by a number of factors. There is the quantum distance that exists between the records for which he probably still remains best known – 'The Sun Ain't Gonna Shine Anymore' or his biggest selling solo hit single, 'Joanna' – and his trio of modern albums, *Tilt*, *The Drift* and *Bish Bosch*. Since 1978, Scott's recorded output was marked by an extraordinary resolve not to relive former glories. It showed itself both in the long periods of infrequency of that output and its sheer uncompromising nature. With *Tilt*, he released one of his most significant records at a point 30 years into his recording career. Music critic Ian MacDonald has described a process which, he says, will sooner or later happen to every pop/rock artist. The artist's creative vitality will decline, losing its 'expressive force' and 'the crucial element of habit-transcending surprise'.[2] This, MacDonald says, happened to both Paul McCartney and John Lennon. And the thesis would certainly seem to apply generally. However good the latest record from McCartney, Dylan, Brian Wilson, the Rolling Stones, Elton John or Stevie Wonder, it is not going to possess the same potency as the artist's classic early records. Perhaps Scott Walker was the unique exception to this rule.[3] Despite the fact that it came following a long break from recording, *Tilt* possesses an expressive force and an ability to surprise that is truly remarkable for a pop/rock artist in his fifties (as he was at the time of its recording). And it's but one aspect of a career that's both unique and compelling.

Our journey through all things Walker is a musical one. *The Rhymes of Goodbye* is not a biography. Noel Scott Engel (the man known in public as Scott Walker) did, since the end of the Sixties, successfully manage to keep his private life a reasonably well-kept secret. For example, the biography that appeared in the mid-Nineties (*A Deep Shade of Blue* (Virgin 1994)) was full of anecdotal material from his acquaintances, but, as its authors acknowledged, the man himself, his closest friends and family were each unwilling to contribute.[4] Would our lives be particularly enriched by knowing where Scott Walker lived, with whom he lived, what he had for breakfast, or what he did on Tuesday mornings? I would suggest not, but we can certainly be enriched by his music. *The Rhymes of Goodbye* is a commentary both on his music as a solo artist and with the Walker Brothers. Personal circumstances are mentioned – where they are mentioned at all – only in passing.

This book is divided into five easy pieces. All recordings released under the names of the Walker Brothers or Scott Walker are covered. The only recordings intentionally omitted from our consideration are those made by Scott prior to the release of the Walker Brothers' first single, 'Pretty Girls Everywhere'. None of these are of outstanding quality. But ironically, whilst some better Scott Walker records have never been released on CD, there always seems to be a place for the availability of the vastly less interesting recordings he made in his pre-Walker Brothers days. The likes of *Looking Back with Scott Walker* or *In the Beginning* contain demo recordings made as a teenager in the Fifties and are best avoided. They have nothing in common with either his Walker Brothers or solo records, giving no real indication of 'that voice' or the greatness to come.

The book's first part covers the Walker Brothers' Sixties recordings, from their first single, 'Pretty Girls Everywhere', onwards. The origin of the Walker Brothers can be traced back to California in the early 1960s, and the moment when guitarist and vocalist John Maus invited jobbing bass player (Noel) Scott Engel to join him and his sister Judy in a musical trio. Whilst that particular trio was shortlived, John and Scott subsequently regrouped calling themselves the Walker Brothers, and ultimately secured both a residency at a club in Hollywood's Sunset Strip and a recording contract with Mercury Records. Two singles into their contract, the Walker Brothers, their permanent line up now completed by drummer Gary Leeds, decided at his suggestion to relocate to the UK, at that time the undoubted centre of the pop world. Not only did they meet with commercial success that exceeded their expectations, but the first three singles they recorded there rank as three of the greatest pop singles of all time. 'The Sun Ain't Gonna Shine Anymore', in particular, is assured of a classic status that has undoubtedly outlived its creators. These records aside, latter-day Scott Walker fans investigating the Walker Brothers will find out what their original fans already knew – that there was much more to the group than just the hit singles. Spread across LP tracks, EPs and B-sides were a wealth of riches, including early Scott Walker-penned classics such as 'You're All Around Me', 'Archangel' and 'Mrs Murphy', and stunning performances on non-originals such as 'In My Room' and 'Where's the Girl'. If the Walker Brothers made a mistake in the Sixties, it was to follow up 'The Sun Ain't Gonna Shine Anymore' with a series of A-sides cast in a very similar mould, and to confine their musical experimentation and development to more obscure tracks. Change not only mattered in the mid-Sixties pop world, it was essential in order to retain a place in its upper echelons. Faced with declining singles sales, and increasing differences between Scott and John over what they wanted from the group, the Walker Brothers split up at the end of April 1967.

The book's second part covers 'what Scott did next', the series of solo records released between 1967 and 1970. Never comfortable with his role as a pop idol, Scott was feeling constrained by what was expected of him. In the mid-Sixties, pop music – yet to undergo its transformation into rock music – wasn't supposed to be serious. True, both Bob Dylan and the Beatles had shown that pop's lyrical landscape could be expanded. (The Beatles had shown that a lyric concerned with loneliness and death and set to a string arrangement could top the pop charts – although 'Eleanor Rigby' was issued as a double A-side with the chirpy 'Yellow Submarine'.) But the general direction they were taking was tangentially opposed to that in which Scott Walker wanted to travel. The drug influences in, say, Bob Dylan's 1966 LP *Blonde on Blonde* or the Beatles' *Revolver* that same year are obviously apparent. In the Beatles' case, their music brilliantly anticipated and helped define the mood of the times, as psychedelia became the next big thing. To Scott, the whole psychedelic/flower-power/love and beads scene was nothing but phoniness. The honesty of the music he wanted to make had little in common with what was to become the late Sixties counterculture. Fortuitously, he found what he much later called 'the key to unlock' what he wanted to do at exactly the right time – the songs of Jacques Brel, and in particular their sympathetic translation into English by Mort Shuman. Scott was the first to record these Brel-Shuman lyrics, and his recordings remain their definitive English language versions. Had the LPs he recorded after the Walker Brothers' split just left us with these Brel covers that would still have been quite an achievement. But Brel was more than just a songwriter whose songs he could do justice to. In Brel, he found the inspiration to take his own songwriting to stellar heights. Jacques Brel's songs exhibited an honesty virtually unheard of in the pop songs of the day – a 'warts and all' depiction of life, not afraid to mention death, drunkenness or sex without love, reflecting the truth that losing one's girl was not the only cause of misery worth singing about. Some of the songs that Scott wrote and recorded on his first two solo LPs openly display their debt to Brel. But his gift for romance, poetry and melody lifts the likes of 'Montague Terrace (in Blue)' and 'The Girls from the Streets' from being exercises in Brel-worship to works of art in their own right. By *Scott 3*, the obviousness of the Brel influence was gone, leaving Scott's songwriting to its own devices and bequeathing us some of the most beautiful and unique tracks ever recorded in popular music.

The other remarkable thing about the first three solo LPs is that they achieved the seemingly impossible – commercial success whilst flying in the face of fashion and the prevailing mood of the times. *Scott*, *Scott 2* and *Scott 3* might be thought of as cult records today, but all three went to the Top Three of the album charts, with *Scott 2* even taking the Number One spot. Something had to give. The follow up proper to *Scott 3*, entitled (*quelle surprise*) *Scott 4*, failed to sell, and the same disappointing commercial fate met its successor, *'Til the Band Comes In*. The reasons for their commercial failure are examined in this book, but it wasn't due to their quality. *Scott 4* is widely regarded as the younger Scott's masterpiece, and it wouldn't be wrong to think of *'Til the Band Comes In* as *Scott 5*. These are the five LPs upon which Scott's reputation justly rests, the records that moved Julian Cope to subtitle the anthology LP he compiled *The God-Like Genius of Scott Walker*.[5] He had a point.

The third part of *The Rhymes of Goodbye* covers Scott's wilderness period: five LPs recorded between 1969 and 1974 that feature not one single Scott Walker composition. Included in this section is the LP that was actually released in between *Scott 3* and *Scott 4*, *Scott Walker Sings Songs from His TV Series*. The reason for messing with the chronology in this manner is twofold. Firstly, the

TV Series LP features no Walker (or Engel) originals. Secondly, it's a lost LP to the extent that it's one of those Scott preferred you not to listen to; he blocked its reissue on CD and described it as 'useless'. This was self-revisionism. Scott's fondness for material one might call middle of the road was an integral – if inclined to come across as somewhat schizophrenic – part of his 1960s persona. *Scott* and *Scott 2* both feature, in addition to Brel and Engel compositions, material previously recorded by the likes of Tony Bennett and Matt Monro. No one was pointing a gun to Scott's head to force him to record these songs for the LPs he called his 'obsession'. Moreover, the audio soundtrack that survives to the TV series itself reveals Scott to be fairly gushing in his praise of many of these songs. The *TV Series* LP – which, if taken on its own, would be a gross misrepresentation of Scott Walker's work – nevertheless compiles some superb performances in a genre which, at the time, was an integral part of his art.

The commercial failure of *Scott 4* and *'Til the Band Comes In* undoubtedly affected Scott badly. The four solo albums released subsequently saw him abandon songwriting completely. Exactly how much of this was due to record company pressure and how much was due to his own decision is subject to speculation. But we can safely say that, by 1975, Scott and his erstwhile band-mates were signed to a comparatively sympathetic record company. All the same, more original material was not immediately forthcoming. These four 1970s solo albums find Scott performing songs from a variety of different sources: songs from films on 1972's *The Moviegoer*; an eclectic pop selection on 1973's *Any Day Now*; country music on 1973's *Stretch* and 1974's *We Had It All*. None of them managed to re-ignite his record sales, and they remain all but lost today. *The Moviegoer* and *Any Day Now* have to date never been reissued on CD. *Stretch* and *We Had It All* were given an unheralded reissue on a single, very badly packaged CD in 1997. Often unfairly maligned, not least by the singer himself, these albums should not be dismissed out of hand. The brilliance of Scott Walker was often as an interpreter of other people's songs, as 'The Sun Ain't Gonna Shine Anymore' and many other tracks ably prove. Including the *TV Series* LP in our considerations, all five of Scott's lesser LPs feature his superb voice in abundance and have plenty to recommend them. Indeed, one of the themes of this book is that, to a greater or lesser extent, all of Scott's lost LPs deserve to be found.

The fourth part of *The Rhymes of Goodbye* covers the Walker Brothers' Seventies reunion. In 1975, with all three erstwhile brothers' careers at a low ebb, they took the step of reforming the group that originally made them stars. By the beginning of the following year, the strong comeback single 'No Regrets' put Scott, John and Gary back in the Top Ten of the singles chart for the first time in years. Further chart success failed to follow, and the momentum of the reunion was lost. The two albums of country-tinged adult pop that the Seventies Walker Brothers recorded, 1975's *No Regrets* and 1976's *Lines*, are not without their highlights, but neither LP is particularly convincing as a whole. In 1978 though, with their career going nowhere fast, the Walker Brothers ended their reunion with a release no one could have predicted. The self-penned LP *Nite Flights* is by far the darkest Walker Brothers product. With snarling rock guitar, death disco arrangements and nightmare lyrics of torture and enslavement, it tore the rulebook to shreds. The album sounds so unlike anything else recorded by the Walkers in the Sixties or the Seventies that, were it not for the distinctiveness of Scott's voice, it might be mistaken for an entirely different group. It also presented, apparently out of nowhere, a new and uncompromising Scott Walker. The time, it seemed, was right for him to awaken from his songwriting hibernation, and the masterful quartet of songs he contributed to *Nite Flights* was both a return to form and, at the same time, a step in an entirely new direction that set the agenda for the remarkable solo records to follow.

Part five of this book deals with all those post-*Nite Flights* recordings. From 1978 onwards there was to be no re-treading of old ground. No regrets? It seems Scott Walker had a few – chief among those being having ever allowed himself to compromise on the grounds of popular appeal. It became clear that the latter-day Scott Walker would only record the albums that he himself wanted to make. For a long period during the 1980s, 1990s and early 2000s the record releases were, to say the least, infrequent. Released in 2006, *The Drift* was Scott Walker's first album for eleven years and it was preceded by just two other albums released since *Nite Flights*: 1984's *Climate of Hunter* and 1995's *Tilt* – amounting to a total of three albums in 28 years! In the wake of *The Drift* and Stephen Kijak's documentary film, *Scott Walker: 30 Century Man*, also released in 2006, Scott Walker never quite disappeared from view in the same way again. A spate of projects occupied the years from 2006 onwards, including film and dance soundtracks, guest contributions and two studio albums: *Bish Bosch* in 2012 and *Soused* in 2014, recorded with the band Sunn O))). These albums, along with his others from the post-1978 era, sound, in their different ways, so unlike anything else in the pop/rock universe that they defy simple description. With lyrics that left narrative form far behind – whether with the 'honed down'-till-their-essence-alone-remains approach of *Climate of Hunter* or the 'verbal diarrhoea' of the dark, time-bending, bathetic *sui generis* world of *Bish Bosch*'s lyrics – the albums are apt to come across as inscrutability itself. Whilst it's as much an oversimplification to say there are just two kinds of Scott Walker fan as it is to say there were only two Scott Walkers, there are definitely those for whom these albums are a journey too far from that which made them fans in the first place. But none of the albums, from *Climate of Hunter* to *Bish Bosch*, are as impenetrable as it might first appear. There are lyrical and musical points of entry to these records. In particular, the loose trilogy of *Tilt*, *The Drift* and *Bish Bosch* reward the repeated listenings necessary to appreciate them. They are astonishing records, and those on which Scott Walker's modern reputation stands.

Before we go on to look at that career in detail, it will be useful to add a few notes on the book's format.

Each officially released track under discussion is given a number, in roughly chronological release date order.[6] The main exceptions are the previously unreleased tracks dealt with at the end of the section of the book that they relate to, while, as noted, the tracks from the *TV Series* LP appear out of chronological order in Part Three.

Alternative titles are sometimes given where a song has been known by more than one title.

The writing credits are as given on the original record label. Thus Scott Walker compositions appear variously listed as by Scott Engel, S. Engel, Engel, N. S. Engel, Walker and Scott Walker – all should be taken to refer to the same man. John Walker compositions appear variously listed as by Maus, J. Maus, J. J. Maus and John Walker, or under the pseudonym A. Dayam. Gary Walker's compositions (all two of them) are credited to G. Leeds. In a small number of cases the song-writing credit given on the record label is known to be incorrect and a correction has been made – in such cases this is mentioned in the text.

If applicable, the year and the format (A-side/B-side/LP/EP/CD) in which the track originally obtained a British release is listed.

Notes on current availability are included in respect of selected entries only, mainly in Part Three in respect of the lost Scott Walker albums that you won't find in their entirety on CD or streaming services. All Walker Brothers' A-sides, B-sides and EP tracks can now be found on the *Everything Under the Sun* box set, so those tracks *are* easily found today. Where a track is not currently commercially available, this fact is noted.

Throughout the book, the convention of song titles in 'quotation marks' and LP or EP titles in *italics* is followed. This is of particular importance, as No Regrets, Lines, Nite Flights and Tilt are both song titles and LP titles.

1. For example, Richard Cook in the 1995 BBC2 *Late Show* segment on Scott Walker. The same idea is used by Jeremy Reed to open his curious book *Another Tear Falls* (Creation Books 1998), see p.7.

2. Ian MacDonald, *Revolution in the Head* (second revised edition, Pimlico 2005) p.36.

3. Perhaps David Bowie comes closest in this regard. He certainly recorded some great albums late in his career, but whether *Heathen* or *The Next Day*, for example, can be said to be career-defining for him in the way that *Tilt* was for Scott Walker is open to debate.

4. Mike Watkinson and Pete Anderson, *A Deep Shade of Blue* (Virgin Books 1995) p.254. All subsequent page references to *A Deep Shade of Blue* are to the paperback edition.

5. In 1981, at a time when Scott's classic solo LPs were out of print and seriously hard to obtain, long-term fan Julian Cope – then the lead singer of The Teardrop Explodes – compiled an anthology for the independent Zoo label entitled *Fire Escape in the Sky: The God-Like Genius of Scott Walker*.

6. Numbering differs from that given in the first edition of *The Rhymes of Goodbye* due to the addition of previously unreleased Walker Brothers tracks in Part Two.

part one
The Walker Brothers
1965 - 1967

The Walker Brothers released three LPs, ten singles and two EPs in the UK between 1965 and their split in 1967. Happily, the tracks from all these records are now easily found, with them all being included on the *Everything Under the Sun* 5-CD box set.

1965

1. Pretty Girls Everywhere (Church/Williams)
Original release: single A-side 1965

Hardly an essential item, the Walker Brothers' first single doesn't have too much in common with the successes that followed it. For one thing, in place of majestic heartbreak or any deep emotion, 'Pretty Girls Everywhere' finds John and Scott singing a cheerful ditty that is slight in the extreme. There are, you guessed it, pretty girls everywhere, and the lyric does nothing more than tell us where the singers have found them - on the beach, in the park (long after dark) and at the rodeo on horses![1] 'Pretty Girls Everywhere' had originally been a US Top Ten R&B chart and Top 40 pop hit for its co-composer Eugene Church in 1958. For the Walker Brothers' version, the song is given more of a contemporary 'beat' feel and a brassy arrangement to replace the call and response backing vocals of the original. The result is not a bad record, just not a great or original one and not a success. It is John's rather than Scott's voice that dominates the record. In retrospect, given Scott's outstanding vocal talent, that might seem odd - a bit like having Jimi Hendrix in your group and having him play the drums on your debut single. But the instatement of Scott Walker as the A-side lead singer had yet to occur – it had to wait but a short while, until 3 'Love Her', the second single. In 1964, when this track was recorded in America before the group's relocation to the UK, and even before Gary joining, John was very much the Walker Brothers' leader. It was from his assumed surname of Walker that they took their name.[2] It was with him as lead singer and guitarist that the group secured both a residency at Gazzari's Club on Sunset Strip and a recording contract, and went on to secure appearances on the US TV pop programme *Shindig*. Scott at that time was happy to generally confine himself to playing the bass and providing harmony vocals. The *Shindig* footage that survives from 1964 shows the Walker Brothers in a very different light to the mean and moody image of the following year. Performing as a two-piece, John and Scott do not come across as the epitome of Sixties cool they were soon to become. Instead they sport matching narrow ties, matching pre-Beatle quiffed hair-dos, matching jackets or V-necked pullovers, generally grin their heads off[3] and hardly look like a band ready to conquer the mid-Sixties pop world. All that was to change.

2. Doin' the Jerk (Scott Engel)
Original release: single B-side 1965

The B-Side to *1* 'Pretty Girls Everywhere' and the track that has the distinction of being the first Scott Walker-penned song that the Walker Brothers recorded. Unfortunately, none of Scott's future poetic vision or melodic talent is apparent here. Instead, 'Doin' the Jerk' is pretty much an exercise in songwriting by numbers – a paean to a dance craze, the Jerk, which, like the Monkey, the HitchHike and the Wah-Watusi, had its brief moment in the early Sixties and was immortalised in song. According to Scott's lyric, the Jerk (which is rhymed with work repeatedly) is the 'greatest dance' which all the 'hippies' love.[4] Given a similar brassy arrangement to 'Pretty Girls Everywhere', the track is a pleasant enough period piece, but anybody expecting to detect the direction of Scott's later songwriting, or hear a prototype for, say, *106* 'Plastic Palace People' is going to be disappointed.

The Walker Brothers are captured for posterity performing (for which read miming to) 'Doin' the Jerk' in the 1965 film *Beach Ball*. The tag line to that film, 'Those surf ridin', skin divin', sky jumpin', drag racin', beach bashin' boys and their bikini beauties . . . in a blast of a beach brawl!', should be enough to warn readers that it's one of those films that gives bland commercialism a bad name. Their extremely brief appearance captures them pre-Gary, performing with a drummer who doesn't really look the part of a surrogate brother to John and Scott. If nothing else, the film appearance marks the start (albeit an inauspicious one) of Scott Walker's career-long association with music for or from films.

'Pretty Girls Everywhere'/'Doin' the Jerk', whilst it did achieve some local success in California, failed to chart in the UK when it was given a belated British release in early 1965.

3. Love Her (Mann/Weil)
Original release: single A-side 1965

Once again recorded in America, prior to the group's relocation to Britain, but this time things were different. The first big difference was the presence of arranger Jack Nitzsche. Nitzsche's eclectic career as an arranger, musician, composer and producer would later include key contributions to the music of the Rolling Stones and Neil Young, and the scores to such films as *Performance*, *The Exorcist*, *One Flew Over the Cuckoo's Nest* and *9½ Weeks*. But at the time of 'Love Her' his CV was already singularly impressive. Nitzsche had played a key role in the building of Phil Spector's famous 'wall of sound',[5] providing the arrangement for 'He's a Rebel' by the Crystals and such indisputable Spector classics as 'Be My Baby' by the Ronettes and 'Da Doo Ron Ron' by the Crystals.

By late 1964/early 1965, with the public beginning to tire of his girl group sound, Spector's hottest act was the Righteous Brothers. And it was the Righteous Brothers who by all accounts were on Nitzsche's mind when he was invited to arrange the Walker Brothers' second single. The Righteous Brothers' most successful record, 'You've Lost That Lovin' Feeling', had been recorded in late 1964. Spector had married his wall of sound production technique to the vocals of two 'brothers' who weren't really brothers[6] and recorded a break-up song written by Mann and Weil. The arrangement for that record wasn't undertaken by Nitzsche, who had been busy on another project at the time, so Spector asked somebody else instead. Whether piqued by this or not, Nitzsche would marry a wall of sound arrangement to the vocals of two 'brothers' who weren't really brothers and record a break-up song written by Mann and Weil.

That song, 'Love Her', elevates the Walker Brothers' second single way above their first. Husband and wife songwriting team Barry Mann and Cynthia Weil were one of a number of gifted songwriters working out of New York's Brill Building in the early Sixties. Although their most successful and celebrated song will always be 'You've Lost That Lovin' Feeling', their songwriting credits and co-credits include the diverse likes of 'On Broadway' (a hit for the Drifters), 'Here You Come Again' (a hit for Dolly Parton) and 'We Gotta Get Out of This Place' (a hit for the Animals). Not least among their achievements is the gem that is 'Love Her'. They truly do not write them like this anymore. For one thing there is Cynthia Weil's beautiful, almost unbelievably tender lyric. Yes, it's a break-up song, and the singer has lost his girl, but unlike any song written today, the lyric doesn't have the singer sing about himself or 'diss' his ex. Instead, he asks his girlfriend's new beau to 'love her like I should have done, and be the guy that I couldn't be.' Previously recorded by the Everly Brothers as an unassuming B-side, 'Love Her' was a fine choice of song to bring out into the light.

But what makes 'Love Her' a special record is not just the song (which had been recorded before) or the wall of sound arrangement (of which many had been recorded before) but the voice of Scott Walker. Scott's role as the lead singer of the Walker Brothers seems to have happened more by accident than design. Legend has it that producer Nick Venet felt the track would benefit from a deeper singing voice, and asked which of the 'brothers' sang the lowest. Step forward Scott Walker, and one of the greatest voices in popular music. Apparently coming out of nowhere,[7] Scott's rich baritone intoned every word of 'Love Her' without overloading the song with emotion, as so many pop epics of the time were wont to do. Classic as 'You've Lost That Lovin' Feeling' is, the Righteous Brothers' vocals verge on the hysterical – particularly towards the end, where each 'baby', 'please' or 'bring it on back' is sung in a more histrionic fashion than the preceding one. In contrast, Scott's vocal on 'Love Her' is dignity itself. The first great Walker Brothers record had been made and, incredibly enough, the next three singles would be even better.

4. The Seventh Dawn (Ortolani/Webster)
Original release: single B-side 1965

The B-side to *3* 'Love Her', and humble fare in comparison to its A-side. The song, like a number of other Walker recordings to follow, comes from a film – in this case the 1964 British film *The Seventh Dawn*. Music for the song was written by the prolific Italian film composer Riz Ortolani, with words by Hollywood lyricist Paul Francis Webster of 'Love Is a Many Splendored Thing' and 'Secret Love' fame. Webster was also responsible for the lyrics to *149* 'The Hills of Yesterday', 'Days of Love' and 'Tender Is the Night', later performed by Scott on his TV series, and *67* 'The Shadow of Your Smile', which the Walker Brothers recorded but did not release.

Although recorded with the same production and arrangement team as its A-side, 'The Seventh Dawn' finds the Walker Brothers performing in a vocal style harking back to the white vocal harmony groups of the early Fifties. Add to this the syrupy Mantovani-style strings at the end, and the fact that 'The Seventh Dawn' is not the strongest song in the world, and the track does not stand the test of time well, sounding dated today in a way that other Walker Brothers records do not. This is a track deserving of its B-side status.

5. Make It Easy on Yourself (Burt Bacharach/Hal David)
Original release: single A-side 1965

In the mid-Sixties Gary Leeds made at least two very good decisions. The first was to join the Walker Brothers and become Gary Walker. The second was to persuade the group to relocate themselves to the UK. In the mid-Sixties Britain was the centre of the pop universe. America had fallen head over heels for the Beatles in 1964, and a so-called 'British Invasion' of the US charts followed, with an unprecedented number of British acts making it big in America. For a small island, Britain gave the world a remarkable outpouring of talent in the mid-Sixties, also including the Rolling Stones, the Kinks, the Who, the Animals, the Hollies and many others. The UK became important in all areas of pop culture, including fashion, art and cinema. In 1966, America's *Time* magazine made things official by declaring London to be *the* swinging city. The tide only turned back in America's favour with the advent of the psychedelic era. Gary Leeds had toured Britain as part of singer P. J. Proby's backing band and had been impressed with what he found there. He rightly felt that the Walker Brothers' best chance of success was to relocate themselves to London, where the action was. Also persuaded by factors other than commercial logistics – avoidance of being drafted into the US military and, in Scott's case, an early love of European culture – the group moved to London in February 1965. Chart success followed fairly quickly, with the US-recorded single 'Love Her' entering the UK singles chart in April and achieving a respectable peak at Number Twenty.[8] But it was the British follow-up single that established the group as a major pop phenomenon.

The Walker Brothers' British record label was Philips. Home of the largely forgotten Four Pennies and Frankie Vaughan, and celebrated ivory tinkler Winifred Atwell, it didn't sound like the hippest place to be – but being with Philips was to prove fortuitous both for the Walker Brothers and Scott as a solo artist. In the mid-Sixties, Philips' most important recording artist was Dusty Springfield, and the same people who helped make her records great helped to make the Walkers' records great. Their first British records boasted the services of arranger Ivor Raymonde, engineer Peter Olliff and producer Johnny Franz. Raymonde – who among many other things co-wrote Dusty's hit 'I Only Want to Be with You' would leave Philips in 1966, to have his musical director's shoes filled in the Walker world by the talents of Reg Guest, Wally Stott and Peter Knight. Recording engineer Olliff and producer Franz stayed the course though, working with the Walker Brothers until their split in 1967 and continuing to work with Scott as a solo artist until he left Philips in 1972. Franz was Philips' Head of Artists and Repertoire, in those days a role that could encompass record production as well as selecting the artists and the repertoires they would record,[9] though there's no suggestion he dictated to the Walkers what songs they would record. Rather the process seems to have been one of friendly collaboration, with Johnny Franz and Scott Walker striking up a close friendship. Between the two of them, they made the perfect choice for the Walker Brothers' first British-recorded single.

Bacharach and David's 'Make It Easy on Yourself' had been recorded before. Jerry Butler had recorded it as a US hit single in 1962, and Dionne Warwick, the singer generally regarded as the definitive vocalist for Bacharach and David's Sixties output, released her version in 1963. But the song had not been a hit in the UK before. Given that the British public had recently demonstrated their appreciation of Bacharach and David by putting both Sandie Shaw's '(There's) Always Something There to Remind Me' and Cilla Black's version of 'Anyone Who Had a Heart' at Number One, 'Make It Easy on Yourself' was a good choice on paper alone. But of course it was more than that. Composer Burt Bacharach and lyricist Hal David's songwriting had gone from strength to strength since they first began collaborating in 1957. By the early Sixties they were writing increasingly sophisticated and classy pop songs, of which 'Make It Easy on Yourself' is a fine example. For the Walker Brothers' recording of the song, the wall of sound approach of 3 'Love Her' is developed via an even more extravagant arrangement, with swirling strings, reverb-laden drums and a heavenly choir opening the track. However, a number of things save it from coming across as a mere copying of the Spector template. Firstly, even had it been the intention

23

to deliberately replicate the Phil Spector wall of sound, differences in studio technology, budget and musicians' union rules between the Gold Star and Philips studios would always have left the British record sounding different. Secondly, Ivor Raymonde's arrangement, particularly in its more classical elements, is truly distinctive – as just listening to the first few seconds is enough to tell you. Finally, there is Scott Walker's magnificent voice. A lot clearer in the mix than it had been on 'Love Her', Scott's vocal is allowed to truly shine, making Hal David's unbelievably altruistic love song his own.

The Walker Brothers could lay claim to having recorded the definitive version of 'Make It Easy on Yourself', and also one of the greatest pop singles of all time. The record went to Number One in the British charts, but that is only part of the story. Gary had been right about the Walker Brothers being able to make it big in the UK, but no one could have predicted the adulation the group inspired. Their image undoubtedly contributed. With John and Scott having dropped the quiffs and matching lounge outfits of the *Shindig* days, the Walkers came across as fresh and exciting. Here were three good-looking, long-haired Americans, with two singers both impossibly tall and handsome from which fans could choose their favourite heartthrob. A fully-fledged Walker-mania accompanied the group wherever they went, with scenes of mass frenzy comparable to those inspired by the Beatles or the Rolling Stones. The Walker Brothers had arrived and they were *bone fide* pop idols.

6. But I Do (Robert Guidry/Paul Gayten)
Original release: single B-side 1965

The B-side to 5 'Make It Easy on Yourself' and a cover of a song that was a Top Ten hit on both sides of the Atlantic for Clarence 'Frogman' Henry in 1961. Given that up-tempo chirpy is not a style for which the Walker Brothers are renowned, their version of 'But I Do' succeeds remarkably well. Henry's original is very much in the Fats Domino or Big Bopper style of Fifties rock 'n' roll, complete with honking saxophone and gravelly vocal. For the Walker Brothers' update the song is given a big arrangement, stepped up a pace and transformed into a much more sophisticated proposition. Sung as a duet by Scott and John, but with a fair proportion of the lyric handed over to the female backing singers, the result is a stylish B-side. Curiously, the lyric is not the tale of happiness that a cursory listen to either version would have you believe, but a tale of lost love and sleepless nights. Scott does capture a little of this pathos in the song's middle eight, which he sings solo.

7. My Ship Is Coming In (Joey Brooks)
Original release: single A-side 1965

Sandwiched in between their two Number One singles, the Walker Brothers' fourth single is often unfairly overlooked. Perhaps this is because those DJs who do occasionally still play them tend, with a typical lack of imagination, to concentrate on the Number Ones 5 'Make It Easy on Yourself' and 19 'The Sun Ain't Gonna Shine Anymore'. This is a real shame, because 'My Ship Is Coming In', which reached Number Three in the British singles chart, is certainly the equal of at least the former.

'My Ship Is Coming In' was a new song and a fortunate find for the Walker Brothers. The original had been recorded earlier in the year by US soul singer Jimmy Radcliffe, with the writing credit going to his songwriting partner Joey Brooks. But the original, as with Radcliffe's other records, didn't achieve the commercial success it deserved. Radcliffe's biggest ever success remains a lowly Number 40 UK chart hit, his recording of the Bacharach and David song 'Long After Tonight Is All Over', which has become a Northern Soul classic.

The Walker Brothers rescued 'My Ship Is Coming In' from obscurity and their version is sublime. Another towering production, distinctive introduction and superlative lead vocal by Scott make it so. But what makes it so special is, unlike any of the other truly great Walker Brother records, its sheer joyous optimism. Scott didn't have to be in misery to sound great. There may have been dreams that haven't come true, bad times and shabby dresses, but these are for the past. And because of the lyric's acknowledgement of these bad times, and because Scott sings it beautifully enough to melt hearts at twenty paces, the romantic optimism shines through, the antithesis of anything bland. The pop kids who fell for the Walker Brothers and bought their records by the shed-load were not buying disposable rubbish (as might be said of some latter-day boy bands) but extremely classy pop records that sound as wonderful today as they did over 50 years ago.

8. You're All Around Me (Engel/Duncan)
Original release: single B-side 1965

The B-Side of 7 'My Ship Is Coming In' and the first great Walker Brothers B-side. 'You're All Around Me' was co-written by Scott and the British singer-songwriter (Miss) Lesley Duncan.[10] As only his second writing credit for the Walker Brothers, it marked a quantum leap forwards in his songwriting from the banality of 2 'Doin' the Jerk'. True, the theme of 'You're All Around Me' is hardly original – the singer has lost his girl and is missing her – but there is enough poetry, romance, depth of feeling and melody to lift it well above the norm. Performed against another epically grand Ivor Raymonde arrangement, Scott's homage to his lost love, who is gone but all around him 'in this city's lonely places, this crowded sea of faces', is just gorgeous. As if it wasn't staggering enough that he could, at the age of only 22, sing as he did, he could also (co-) write great songs. Too good to be left as a B-side, the track was also included on the Walker Brothers' debut LP. Speaking of which . . .

Take It Easy with the Walker Brothers LP 1965

9. There Goes My Baby (Nelson/Patterson/Treadwell)

Original release: *Take It Easy with the Walker Brothers* 1965 LP

The Walker Brothers' debut LP, released in December 1965.

Hot on the heels of *7* 'My Ship Is Coming In', the Walkers' debut LP was released in time for Christmas 1965. Unlike the album that followed it, *Take It Easy with the Walker Brothers* comes across as a rather odd and disjointed collection of songs. For one thing, they end up sounding positively schizophrenic – heartbroken one minute, dancing in the street the next, then heartbroken, then dancing, heartbroken, in love, heartbroken . . . But whilst it isn't as strong an LP as its two successors, it's still worth saying a few words in defence of its selections. Firstly, what was expected from an LP changed very quickly in a very short time between 1965 and the end of the Sixties. In 1965, nobody expected pop LPs to contain only the artist's own compositions, to possess a unifying concept, or to be free of filler tracks. Bob Dylan's and the Beatles' largely self-written and somewhat thematic LPs were the pioneering exception rather than the rule.[11] To judge *Take It Easy with the Walker Brothers* in 1965 terms, it's a very good LP despite having no unifying mood and some weaker tracks on it. More so than the albums that followed it, it includes tracks that were an integral part of the Walkers' stage act. And it's worth bearing in mind, if only because it makes the album's successes more remarkable, that the LP would have been recorded extremely quickly. The Walker Brothers might have been able to get away with more extravagance later in their career, such as the location recording of the cinema organ for *42* 'Archangel', but for their debut album, recording would have been strictly governed by the 'four tunes in a session' work ethic at Philips.[12]

UK chart protocol in the Sixties had it that singles shouldn't be included on LPs. However, an exception to this rule appears to have been allowed in the case of debut albums – for example, the Beatles' debut album was allowed the singles 'Please Please Me' and 'Love Me Do', and the Who's debut LP was allowed to include 'My Generation' and 'The Kids Are Alright'. For the Walker Brothers' debut, the already released B-side *8* 'You're All Around Me' and single *5* 'Make It Easy on Yourself' were included along with ten new songs. These new songs comprise numbers *9* to *18* in our list.

First of these is the album's second track, 'There Goes My Baby'. The Drifters originally recorded this song, and it marked an interesting and pivotal moment in that band's history. In 1958 the Drifters' manager, George Treadwell (the Treadwell of the writing credit), took the unusual step of sacking the entire band and replacing them whilst retaining the Drifters' name. The new band's old manager was the splendidly named Lover Patterson (the Patterson of the writing credit). One of the new band's members, Benjamin Nelson (the Nelson of the writing credit), had come up with the song and, on the back of it, became the group's lead singer. He changed his name to Ben E. King and the rest, as they say, is history. In 1959 'There Goes My Baby' was the first US hit for the Drifters' new line-up, their first hit with Leiber and Stoller as producers and on which they used a string section, and the first taste of success for Ben E. King.

For the Walker Brothers' version of 'There Goes My Baby', the doo-wop introduction used to open the original is wisely dropped and the song is given the big British wall of sound treatment. It's certainly a strong track, but is it better than the original? Composer King's sublime vocal on the Drifters' version makes it too close to call.

10. First Love Never Dies (Morris/Seals)
Original release: *Take It Easy with the Walker Brothers* 1965 LP

A song dating from 1961, written by Bob Morris and Jimmy Seals of the instrumental group the Champs. The first person to record the song was Jerry Fuller, who at the time of the song's composition was touring with the Champs as a featured vocalist. Released on a single A-side in 1961, Fuller's version sank into obscurity. That failure didn't seem to harm either his or the composers' careers. Fuller went on to be a successful songwriter and producer – his credits include the song *222* 'Lines', as covered by the reformed Walker Brothers in the Seventies. Jimmy Seals later found considerable success as one half of the duo Seals and Croft.

'First Love Never Dies' was an excellent choice of song to rescue from obscurity. It's hard to imagine it ever being handled better than it is by Scott and arranger Ivor Raymonde. Against a majestic backing track, Scott mourns the loss of his first love and begs her to return, with a passion and dignity that really tug at the heartstrings. One of the album's definite highlights.

11. Dancing in the Street (Stevenson/Gaye)
Original release: *Take It Easy with the Walker Brothers* 1965 LP

Following three Scott-dominated lost love songs on the album, John Walker returns to the lead vocal role that was once his for a cover of the Motown classic 'Dancing in the Street'.

12. Lonely Winds (Pomus/Shuman)
Original release: *Take It Easy with the Walker Brothers* 1965 LP

Another song like *9* 'There Goes My Baby', previously recorded by the Drifters in their heyday, but a less wise choice. Although written by songwriting greats Doc Pomus and Mort Shuman, 'Lonely Winds' is hardly the greatest song in the world, and not suited to the Walker Brothers' style or Scott's voice at all. Times were moving fast in the world of pop in the Sixties (consider the Beatles' passage from 'Help!' to the completely out-there 'Tomorrow Never Knows' in the space of eighteen months), and 'Lonely Winds', with its girl singers, 'little bitty girlie' and cheesy instrumental break, must have sounded dated even in 1965. It comes across as album filler.

13. The Girl I Lost in the Rain (David Gates)
Original release: *Take It Easy with the Walker Brothers* 1965 LP

In the mid-Sixties, David Gates was a songwriter and producer working in Los Angeles. He later went on to form the group Bread, recording his own songs including 'Make It with You', 'Everything I Own' and *185* 'If'. A product of his jobbing songwriter days, 'The Girl I Lost in the Rain' was recorded by Phil Spector session musician Leon Russell and released as a single, under the alias C. J. Russell, in 1963.

An excellent vehicle for Scott's romantic balladeering, 'The Girl I Lost in the Rain' succeeds superbly. The track has even been cited by John Walker as one of his favourite Walker Brothers recordings.[13] Vocal and arrangement capture a melancholy of almost cinematic quality. One can picture the heartbroken man walking through the rain-soaked city streets at night. At the end of the track, the instrumentation falls away briefly to leave Scott's voice virtually *a cappella* and drenched in reverb – a trick that would later be used to greater effect at the end of the more ambitious *53* 'Orpheus'.

14. Land of 1,000 Dances (C. Kenner)
Original release: *Take It Easy with the Walker Brothers* 1965 LP

Side two of the Walker Brothers' debut album opens with another song that formed a key part of their stage act – the song they used to open each show. It has an interesting history. Written by the largely uncelebrated New Orleans R&B singer-songwriter Chris Kenner, its memorable hook, 'na, na, na, na, na', wasn't added until a group called Cannibal and the Head Hunters invented it for their recording of the song. For that they received no writing credit, but on latter-day credits for the song one A. Domino (AKA Fats Domino) appears not because he had anything to do with writing the song, but because he wouldn't record it unless Kenner agreed to give him a credit. The song's most celebrated version (by Wilson Pickett) wasn't recorded until 1966, after the Walker Brothers' version.

Given that up-tempo dance numbers aren't what the Walkers are celebrated for, their version of 'Land of 1,000 Dances' is a very good one. Footage that survives of them performing this song, on a German TV programme in 1966, indicates how the group came across live. The footage reveals three distinct personalities: Gary, a little bemused by it all perhaps, but obviously pleased to be a part of it; John, by this time sporting extremely long hair, a flamboyant blouse-like top and extremely tight trousers, playing the part of the showman and enjoying every minute of it; by way of contrast, the more conservatively dressed Scott looks extremely uncomfortable, moves with a lack of grace, and looks like a man who'd rather be doing anything other than performing in front of an audience.

15. Love Minus Zero (Bob Dylan)
Original release: *Take It Easy with the Walker Brothers* 1965 LP

No two artists cast a longer shadow over pop music in the Sixties than the Beatles and Bob Dylan. It was they, more than anyone else, who proved that pop acts could write and record their own material, and in the mid-Sixties just about everybody wanted to record their songs. For their part, the Walker Brothers avoided committing any Beatles songs to vinyl (although 'I'm a Loser', *83* 'Yesterday' and apparently 'We Can Work It Out' were performed live or on TV appearances). But they did record this one Dylan song. Perhaps chosen because it's Dylan at his most melodic, and the closest thing to an I-love-you song on the album, this really isn't the Walkers at their best. The problem is a mis-match of styles. Dylan's song needs the jangly charm of its original version for it to work, not the earnestly grandiose approach of the Walker Brothers. Dylan's wordy, abstract lyric, with its dime-store bohemianism, just doesn't suit the gravitas of Scott's delivery or the arrangement. Even the decision not to sing Dylan's more abstract third and fourth verses doesn't save Scott's vocal from coming across as uncharacteristically pompous. It's telling that when Scott later wrote a song which he saw as inspired by his own beatnik/bohemian past, the resulting *114* 'It's Raining Today' sounds like nothing of the sort. More of that later. For now, it's sufficient to note that Scott Walker wisely steered clear of recording any more Bob Dylan songs for the next 30 years.

16. I Don't Want to Hear It Anymore (R. Newman)
Original release: *Take It Easy with the Walker Brothers* 1965 LP

Randy Newman was a songwriter with whom Scott could feel more at home. Before going on to record his own albums later in the Sixties, Newman was a staff songwriter at Metric Music in Los Angeles. Among his output from this period were – along with more conventional pop fare – some seriously classy, poignant songs, most notably the gorgeous 'I've Been Wrong Before' (a hit for Cilla Black in 1965, also recorded that same year by Dusty Springfield), 'I Think It's Going to Rain Today' (also recorded by Dusty, among many others), *191* 'Just One Smile', and this song.

'I Don't Want to Hear It Anymore' had been recorded previously by Jerry Butler – the same man who got there first with *5* 'Make It Easy on Yourself'. But that doesn't make the Walker Brothers' version superfluous. Not only does Scott make the song his own, producing one of the album's undoubted highlights, but Newman's narrative lyric certainly provided further inspiration. 'I Don't Want to Hear It Anymore' is the song of the heartbroken young man in room 149, who hears the never-ending gossip of his neighbours about his unfaithful girlfriend through walls that are much too thin. Its *dramatis personae* approach, where the neighbours are quoted in the lyric, finds a definite reflection in Scott's own later 'bedsit drama' compositions, especially *46* 'Mrs Murphy'.

Later recorded by Dusty Springfield on her 1969 *Dusty in Memphis* LP, it's one of many songs recorded by both Scott Walker (and/or the Walker Brothers) and Dusty.

17. Here Comes the Night (Pomus/Shuman)
Original release: *Take It Easy with the Walker Brothers* 1965 LP

The second Pomus/Shuman track on the first LP, and this time not a song previously recorded by the Drifters but by Ben E. King as a solo artist. The Walker Brothers' version succeeds better than *12* 'Lonely Winds', but the song's style isn't particularly suited to them and it remains one of the album's lesser tracks.

Doc Pomus and Mort Shuman were one of the great songwriting teams of the rock'n'roll era, and the two songs of theirs that the Walkers chose to record are hardly representative of their towering achievements. During a nine-year songwriting partnership Pomus and Shuman wrote over 500 songs, including 'Save the Last Dance for Me', 'Sweets for My Sweet', 'A Teenager in Love' and numerous hits for Elvis, such as 'His Latest Flame', 'Suspicion' and 'Viva Las Vegas'. In the mid-Sixties, Pomus and Shuman went their separate ways. Mort Shuman moved to Paris, where he would brilliantly translate the lyrics of Jacques Brel into English – thereby playing a key role in Scott Walker's solo career.

18. Tell the Truth (Pauling)
Original release: *Take It Easy with the Walker Brothers* 1965 LP

The first LP ends with the raucous, up-tempo 'Tell the Truth', mainly sung by John. Originally recorded by early R&B group the Five Royales, the Walker Brothers probably knew the song from Ray Charles' recording of it.

1966

19. The Sun Ain't Gonna Shine Anymore (B. Crewe/B. Gaudio)
Original release: single A-side 1966

The Walker Brothers' most famous and celebrated song was brought to the group by John. The song's writers, Bob Crewe and Bob Gaudio, were behind the success of Frankie Valli and the Four Seasons, Crewe being the group's producer and Gaudio a member of the band. Between them they wrote such songs as 'Sherry', 'Big Girls Don't Cry', 'Walk Like a Man' and 'Rag Doll', which established the Four Seasons as one of America's most successful male vocal groups. Inspired by nothing more significant than a grey day weather-wise, they wrote 'The Sun Ain't Gonna Shine Anymore' for Frankie Valli to sing. Valli recorded the song as a solo single A-side in 1965. It went nowhere fast. According to Crewe, about a month after the Valli version had been released, he ran into John Walker in London and gave him a copy with the advice, 'I think you ought to jump on this.'[14] The Walker Brothers did so.

The Walkers' version of 'The Sun Ain't Gonna Shine Anymore' simply outdoes the original by a country mile. With a towering Spector-esque production, a stunning Ivor Raymonde arrangement and Scott's superlative lead vocal, they made the song their own. As Scott puts more emotion than seems humanly possible into the simple word 'on' ('I can't go oo-oo-oo-oo-ooon'), it's more like the sound of the end of the world than a rainy day. The group knew they had something special. It's telling that 'The Sun Ain't Gonna Shine Anymore' was one of the few tracks where an extra session was permitted by Philips, apparently at Scott's request to make sure the record was as perfect as it could be. (An alternate unreleased version of 'The Sun Ain't Gonna Shine Anymore', which is slightly slower and rather less dramatic than the released version, can now be heard on the *Everything Under the Sun* box set.)

In John's words, the record was 'a killer, just an absolute killer'.[15] Even Scott, in less guarded moments, had been known to acknowledge the record's greatness. It became the Walker Brothers' most successful single, reaching Number One in the British chart and staying there for four weeks. Like 'Make It Easy on Yourself', it even crossed the Atlantic and became a US hit also.

The perfect marriage between artist and song, 'The Sun Ain't Gonna Shine Anymore' remains an unconditional classic, one of the greatest pop singles ever, period. It would only ever be folly for anybody to think they could improve upon it in any way. This hasn't stopped the likes of Cher and David Essex from recording it, but needless to say, their versions don't bear comparison.

As a coda, the record was also assured of its place in popular legend, as it was reputedly playing on the jukebox in the Blind Beggar pub when East End gangster Ronnie Kray shot fellow villain George Cornell. The story may or not be apocryphal, but it is recounted in his brother Reggie Kray's autobiography as follows: '. . . Ron and Ian [Barrie] walked into the saloon bar. Cornell was sitting at the end of the bar . . . a record was playing peculiarly enough entitled "The Sun Ain't Gonna Shine Anymore" . . . Ron drew a Luger gun out of his right hand overcoat pocket, levelled it at Cornell's head and fired . . . the sequel to the story is that the record had jammed at the same time as the bullet hit Cornell in the forehead, and kept repeating "the sun ain't gonna shine anymore."'[16]

20. After the Lights Go Out (John Stewart)
Original release: single B-side 1966

The B-side to *19* 'The Sun Ain't Gonna Shine Anymore' – as if the A-side wasn't enough, the B-side is truly great too. Written by Scott's friend from the California days, John Stewart, 'After the Lights Go Out' paints a more brooding and intimate portrait of lost love than its A-side. Opening with a bass line that vividly portrays the song's narrator pacing the floor of his room, and the rasping percussive sound of a guiro that seems to represent the grating torment of his mind, the track builds into a full orchestral sound and the result is a minor masterpiece. The singer, alone in his 'silent little room', is tormented by a world seen through 'the shadow of his mind', where everything, even the pigeon on the windowsill, reminds him of his loss. Scott turns in a superb vocal, laced with just a hint of brooding menace. Whether or not it was due to a personal affinity between John Stewart and Scott Walker,[17] Stewart's lyric suits Scott perfectly and foreshadows some of his personal compositions to come, such as *34* 'I Can See It Now' and *88* 'Montague Terrace (in Blue)'.

I Need You EP 1966

21. I Need You (Goffin/King)
Original release: *I Need You* EP 1966

The first of only two EPs released by the Walker Brothers in the Sixties, I Need You *topped the EP charts.*

In the Sixties there were 45s, LPs and EPs, and in between *19* 'The Sun Ain't Gonna Shine Anymore' and its follow-up came an EP comprising four new Walker Brothers recordings. Like their first LP in microcosm, the *I Need You* EP is something of a mixed bag, consisting of two great and two not-so-great tracks. The lead song falls into the former category. Carole King and Gerry Goffin were, like Mann and Weil, a husband and wife songwriting team working out of New York's Brill Building in the Sixties. Even more successful than Mann and Weil, Goffin and King were responsible for such slices of perfect pop as 'Up on the Roof ', 'One Fine Day' and 'Will You Still Love Me Tomorrow'. 'I Need You' was one such impeccable pop song. It had been previously recorded by US R&B singer Chuck Jackson as a single in 1964.[18] For the Walker Brothers' version, 'I Need You' was given the towering orchestral pop treatment and a superb lead vocal by Scott.

22. Looking for Me (Randy Newman)
Original release: *I Need You* EP 1966

As with *16* 'I Don't Want to Hear It Anymore', a song from the pen of Randy Newman. But unlike the former, this really does come across as the work of a jobbing songwriter. 'Looking for Me' is a *West Side Story*-like tale of street fighting gangs, wherein the singer faces trouble because he's stolen 'Eddie's girl'. It was just too corny and dated a song to suit the Walker Brothers' increasingly sophisticated sound. The original version of the song was an obscure US single released in 1964 by Vic Dana, a singer whose main claim to fame resides in taking 'Red Roses for a Blue Lady' into the US Top Ten in 1965.

Scott Walker would go on to rediscover Randy Newman in later years, recording *183* 'Cowboy', *191* 'Just One Smile' and *200* 'I'll Be Home'. The reformed Seventies Walker Brothers would also record the Newman songs *225* 'Have You Seen My Baby' and *245* 'Marie'.

23. Young Man Cried (J. Franz/S. Engel)
Original release: *I Need You* EP 1966

The EP's other great track, written by Scott with producer Johnny Franz. Along with *22* 'Looking for Me', it marked the introduction of Reg Guest as musical director to fill the shoes of the departing Ivor Raymonde, who left Philips to go to Decca in 1966. A stalwart of the British recording industry, Guest was no stranger to the Walker Brothers, having played keyboard parts on their singles. Guest admired Scott's talent. Scott admired Guest's talent. And their mutual admiration society would bear remarkable fruit, up to and including the recording of Scott's 1968 solo LP, *Scott 2*. The first great track to come out of their collaboration, 'Young Man Cried' is a superbly grandiose ballad. Lyrically it seems a transitional recording, with some lines coming across as pure poetry of the type that Scott would develop on his solo LPs. But the line about the cat on the pillow 'wondering where the girl's gone' appears to be directly inspired by Leiber and Stoller's *35* 'Where's the Girl'.[19]

24. Everything's Gonna Be Alright (Mitchell)
Original release: *I Need You* EP 1966

Like some of the tracks on the first LP, 'Everything's Gonna Be Alright' is an attempt to capture the more up-tempo feel of the Walker Brothers' live performances on vinyl. In this case, the accompaniment is provided by their stage backing band, the Quotations. 'Everything's Gonna Be Alright' was written by Memphis soul man Willie Mitchell and released by him as a single in 1966. More an excuse for a soul workout than a song, John and Scott belt out Mitchell's insubstantial lyric about a shotgun wedding with some gusto, but this remains one of the least memorable tracks recorded by the Walkers in the Sixties.

25. (Baby) You Don't Have to Tell Me (Pete Antell)[20]
Original release: single A-side 1966

How do you follow up a record like *19* 'The Sun Ain't Gonna Shine Anymore'? If you've released a single that is a culmination of those that went before it, and which in the public's ears virtually defines your sound, what do you do next?

At different points in 1966, two American groups seemed poised to present a serious challenge to the Beatles' UK pop supremacy. In the spring, the Walker Brothers held the Number One spot for four weeks with a record that seemed to be played everywhere, inspiring mass frenzy wherever they went. In the winter, the Beach Boys made Number One with 'Good Vibrations' and actually beat the Beatles to the title of world's best group in the NME's year-end poll.[21] But despite all this, by the following year both groups looked like old news for a surprisingly similar reason – the failure to follow up their biggest singles to date with something that showed any signs of development. The Beach Boys, for their part dogged by internal disagreement,[22] were reduced to releasing an old 1965 track as their UK follow-up to 'Good Vibrations'. The Walker Brothers followed up 'The Sun Ain't Gonna Shine Anymore' with a record cast very much in the same mould, but obviously its inferior. That's not to say that '(Baby) You Don't Have to Tell Me' is a bad record, or that any of the Walkers' subsequent Sixties singles are bad records (they aren't). But it didn't demonstrate any significant change of style or breaking of new ground. Change not only mattered in the Sixties pop world, it was essential in order to stay on top of the game. In 1966-67, so many British groups, like the Beatles, the Rolling Stones, the Kinks, the Small Faces, the Hollies and the Who, were approaching their artistic peak. Each single these groups released was a big artistic step forward.[23] By contrast the Walker Brothers, at least in terms of single A-sides, stuck with their tried and tested sound and sold in predictably decreasing numbers.

A cover version of an obscure American original, '(Baby) You Don't Have to Tell Me' was written by New York songwriter Pete Antell and released as a single by singer Bobby Coleman. The Walkers' version, whilst certainly a good record, offered nothing fresh or distinctive enough to sell itself to anyone but the faithful.

It reached the relatively disappointing position of Number Thirteen in the British singles chart in the summer of 1966.

26. My Love Is Growing (J. Stewart/R. Van Leeuwen)[24]
Original release: single B-side 1966

The B-Side to *25* '(Baby) You Don't Have to Tell Me', a little reward for those who did take the trouble to buy that single. The song stemmed from extracurricular activity that Scott was involved with in 1966, co-producing some tracks for Dutch band the Motions with his friend John Stewart. The authorship of 'My Love Is Growing' is co-credited to Stewart and Robbie Van Leeuwen, the guitarist with the Motions. The Motions' version of 'My Love Is Growing' appears on their 1966 LP, *Their Own Way*. Van Leeuwen later went on to form the band Shocking Blue and write their massively successful hit 'Venus', which reached Number One in the US charts. Not quite the match for that song, 'My Love Is Growing' is pleasing enough. Whilst ostensibly a straight love song, it includes enough melodrama in lines like 'don't know how I lived before' and 'don't know what I'm gonna do, if you tell me that we're through' to make Scott's lead vocal a worthwhile proposition.

Portrait 1966 LP

27. In My Room (Prieto – English lyrics by Pockriss/Vance)
Original release: *Portrait* 1966 LP

Even the cover exudes a certain class. The Walker Brothers' second and most consistently strong LP, Portrait was released in September 1966.

If the Walker Brothers' follow-up single to *19* 'The Sun Ain't Gonna Shine Anymore' was a creative letdown, the same cannot be said of their second LP,

Portrait. Released in the autumn of 1966, *Portait*'s rich palette offered twelve new tracks that found them at their consistent best. Even the record's cover exudes a certain class. It's worth noting that the Walkers' faces were so well known in 1966 that only the album's title appears on the front of the original LP, without the band's name – this in the days before Pink Floyd and Led Zeppelin turned the anonymous album cover into an art form. The first few seconds of side one, track one were enough to tell the listener that this was no ordinary pop LP. In fact the opening of the LP is more Bach than beat, a musical phrase from 'Toccata and Fugue' introducing one of the greatest tracks the Walker Brothers ever committed to vinyl. 'In My Room' started life as a Spanish language ballad, '*El amor*', written by J. Prieto. The song was given English lyrics by a pair of American songwriters one might least expect to find in the Walker discography. The two most famous songs Paul Vance and Lee Pockriss wrote are 'Catch a Falling Star' and 'Itsy Bitsy Teeny Weeny Yellow Polka Dot Bikini' – hardly Scott Walker material! 'In My Room' had previously been recorded by the American singer Verdelle Smith,[25] but without a great deal of commercial success. As they had done with 'The Sun Ain't Gonna Shine Anymore', the Walkers rescued a perfect song from obscurity at the perfect time. The greatness of their version of 'In My Room' lay in how they made it their own. Or rather, Scott Walker's own. For despite it not being his own composition, 'In My Room' is Scott's definitive brooding young man song. Others Scott recorded, such as *20* 'After the Lights Go Out', *23* 'Young Man Cried' or *39* 'Another Tear Falls', share the same lyrical theme as 'In My Room' – the singer has lost his love, and nothing can keep his mind from that fact. But nowhere is the portrayal of his brooding any darker, deeper or more menacing than it is on 'In My Room'. Yes, the words of the song are certainly part of the equation (and perhaps it's the fact that it's the singer's wife, not merely his girlfriend, that he's lost which ups the emotional ante). But what makes the track is Scott Walker's masterful vocal, and the magnificent Reg Guest arrangement against which it's heard. One can only speculate as to whether this song, perhaps a little too dark for radio audiences, would have fared better than *25* '(Baby) You Don't Have to Tell Me' as a follow-up to 'The Sun Ain't Gonna Shine Anymore'. Certainly it would have demonstrated a development of the Walker Brothers' sound, and it's worth noting that the Beatles, who continued to dominate the UK pop scene for the remainder of the Sixties, did so not by underestimating their audience but by developing beyond the boundaries of its expectations. On hearing *Portrait* for the first time, the NME's Keith Altham recorded his verdict on 'In My Room' on the album's original sleeve notes – it sounded to him like a 'potential single'. Perhaps it should have been released that way.

28. Saturday's Child (S. Engel)
Original release: *Portrait* 1966 LP

Only the fourth Scott Walker composition to appear on a Walker Brothers record. Described on the album's sleeve notes as 'a party time number', 'Saturday's Child' is proof positive that the Walkers were capable of making great records whilst embracing a more up-tempo, upbeat sound. But to call this 'a party time number' is to tell only half the story. Scott's lyric is no whoop of happiness. In fact, it might even be described as his take on 'Nineteenth Nervous Breakdown', both his and the Stones' heroines having lived too much in too few years. Scott's party girl is left heartbroken, friendless and crying. As such, 'Saturday's Child' does mark a broadening of his lyrical canvas and a step, albeit a tentative one, in the direction of the 'portraits' or 'miniatures' in song to be found on his solo LPs.

29. Just for a Thrill (L. Armstrong/D. Raye/M. Williams)
Original release: *Portrait* 1966 LP

The strongest vocal performance by John on a Walker Brothers record, a bluesily effective rendition of a song he undoubtedly knew from Ray Charles' 1959 version.

30. Hurting Each Other (Udell/Geld)
Original release: *Portrait* 1966 LP

A song that later proved to be a hit in waiting, 'Hurting Each Other' was subsequently recorded by the Carpenters and became a huge American single for them in 1972. With words by Peter Udell and music by Gary Geld, the song had been published in 1965. Other artists who recorded it before the Walker Brothers included a group called Chad Allen and the Expressions and fading teen idol Jimmy Clanton. The Walkers' version is an exercise in their famous big sound. The song is strong, the lyric romantic ('closer dear are we than the simple letters A and B are' indeed!), Ivor Raymonde's arrangement is distinctive (with its resonating cymbals, swelling orchestration and Spector-esque sleigh bells) and Scott's vocal is terrific. In sum total, it's anything but an ordinary Walker Brothers record.

31. Old Folks (Robison/Hill)[27]
Original release: *Portrait* 1966 LP

Scott's take on a jazz standard. 'Old Folks' had been written in 1938 by Willard Robison with a lyric by Dedette Lee Hill and recorded many times, including versions by Charlie Parker, Donald Byrd and Mel Torme. Scott performs the song against a very gentle, understated arrangement, which presents his vocal in an unusually naked setting and makes the track something of a treasure. It's conceivable that some might find the song a little too cornily sentimental, but the lyric is not without its charm (especially the line about the failed fishing trip: 'the whale got way, looks like we warm up the steak'). But if nothing else, 'Old Folks' marked another broadening of the Walker Brothers' lyrical landscape, taking in the subject of old age and, in the song's final verse, death. Not the common currency of pop music in the Sixties, but themes that the still young Scott Walker would return to again and again in his solo work.

The 'free signed portrait' included with the original vinyl edition of Portrait.

32. Summertime (Gershwin)

Original release: *Portrait* 1966 LP

The third song on side one of *Portrait* to date from the 1930s, surprising for a Sixties pop act. The Walker Brothers certainly seem to have been pursuing their own agenda, rather than overtly pandering to the tastes of the day. Gershwin's 'Summertime' was written in 1934 for the opera *Porgy and Bess*, and is one of the most covered songs of all time. The addition of the Walker Brothers to the long list of cover artists is in no way superfluous though. 'Summertime' closes side one of *Portrait* in wonderfully epic style. As the album's original sleeve notes hint, one might have expected two men in their early twenties (as John and Scott were) to mutilate Gershwin's classic. But instead they turn in sublime performances against an extremely classy arrangement that starts gently and then sours, taking in a memorable sax break along the way. 'Summertime' is also the best example of a true Walker Brothers track, with both singers taking solo lead lines as well as singing in harmony.

33. People Get Ready (Curtis Mayfield)

Original release: *Portrait* 1966 LP

For some strange reason, the US R&B vocal group the Impressions never made much of an impression on the UK charts. This was certainly not due to lack of talent on the part of the band, who originally included Jerry Butler[28] prior to his departure to pursue a solo career. Thereafter the group was dominated by the songwriting talents of Curtis Mayfield, notching up a string of American hit singles of which the evangelical 'People Get Ready' is a sublime example and was a US Top Twenty hit in 1965.[29] Handled in much grander fashion than the gentle original, the Walker Brothers' version, with its dramatic arrangement and Scott's lead vocal, whilst not eclipsing the original, is a worthy cover version and a great track. Almost enough to turn atheists into believers.

34. I Can See It Now (Engel/Franz)
Original release: *Portrait* 1966 LP

The second of only three songs ever with a joint writing credit for Scott and producer Johnny Franz. 'I Can See It Now', whilst minor in comparison to Scott's later songwriting achievements, is a fine song, interestingly arranged and beautifully sung. Its lost love lyric, whilst short (the third verse is an exact repeat of the second), is touching, given a subtle twist as it's directed at the second person 'you' rather than recounted in the first person. Although one can't help feel that the 'you' in question is really the singer trying to lift himself out of his own gloom.

35. Where's the Girl (Leiber/Stoller)
Original release: *Portrait* 1966 LP

The stand-out track on side two of *Portrait*. As with others of this period, Scott takes the song of another artist and turns it into his own. 'Where's the Girl', like *19* 'The Sun Ain't Gonna Shine Anymore' and *27* 'In My Room', sounds like it could have been written for him alone to sing. The songwriting team of Jerry Leiber and Mike Stoller were practically founding fathers of the rock/pop era, having written 'Hound Dog', 'Jailhouse Rock', 'Poison Ivy' and 'Love Potion #9', to name but a small selection of their hit songs. 'Where's the Girl' had previously been recorded by that man again, Jerry Butler, released as a US single in 1963. Singer Dorsey Burnette had also released his version that same year, and others would follow. However, what makes the Walker Brothers' version so special is how Scott's vocal fills the song with beauty and desolation. It isn't just the sound of a pop singer interpreting someone else's song very well. Such is the power of Scott's voice that it sounds as if his world is in pieces, and he finds even the trivial devastating ('who'd have thought that one nylon stocking could ever bring tears to these eyes?'). This is the sound of heartbreak, and in the face of this any retrospective accusations of sexism[30] or corniness are just churlish.

36. Living Above Your Head (Sanders/Black/Vance)
Original release: *Portrait* 1966 LP

Another cover version of a song by a group with plenty of chart success in their native USA, but none in the UK. Jay and the Americans are not remembered for being either particularly hip or for writing their own material, but the self-composed 'Living Above Your Head', the title song of their 1966 LP, is rather good. (The songwriting credit is to group members Marty Sanders, Jay Black and Kenny Vance.) The Walker Brothers' arrangement is obviously closely modelled on the original version. But the bigger Walkers sound and Scott's voice make the cover worthwhile, and, like *28* 'Saturday's Child', prove that they could do 'upbeat' convincingly.

37. Take It Like a Man (Leiber/Stoller)
Original release: *Portrait* 1966 LP

John takes lead vocal on a composition previously recorded by Gene Pitney in 1962. One can't help but be amused by the thought that John is in some way directing these pull-yourself-together-man lyrics at Scott. As so many of Scott's performances seemed to announce the end of the singer's world upon losing his love, as if in response to *19* 'The Sun Ain't Gonna Shine Anymore', this song's lyric answers, 'the sun's gonna shine with or without her'.

38. No Sad Songs for Me (T. Springfield)
Original release: *Portrait* 1966 LP

The *Portrait* LP ends with John and Scott duetting to lovely effect on Tom Springfield's 'No Sad Songs for Me'. He was, of course, Dusty Springfield's brother,[31] who with her and Tim Field comprised the early Sixties folk group the Springfields. The Springfields recorded the original version, although its first release seems to have been on a 1964 compilation album after that group split up. A folky version of the song was also recorded by the Four Pennies at around the same time as the Walker Brothers' version. The Walkers gave the song a laidback, classy arrangement, also notable for its classical opening bars (which Scott seems to have closely recalled when it came to composing *138* 'Prologue'). The track is also, like *32* 'Summertime, a true Walker Brothers collaboration, rather than a featured vocal by Scott or John. It's a fitting end to a fine LP that, unless you're one of those people who finds *31* 'Old Folks' just a bit too corny, doesn't have a single bad track on it. A commercial and critical success, *Portrait* reached Number Three in the British album chart and stayed on the chart for 23 weeks. It remains the Walker Brothers' most consistent LP, including those that the reformed group would release in the Seventies.

39. Another Tear Falls (Bacharach/David)
Original release: single A-side 1966

As was the dictate of UK chart protocol in the Sixties, no singles were taken from the *Portrait* LP. Instead, for their next single the group took the unimaginative step of returning to the Bacharach and David songbook, which had given them so much success with *5* 'Make It Easy on Yourself'. And therein they discovered a largely unheralded gem. 'Another Tear Falls' dated from 1962, previously recorded by Gene McDaniels and featuring in the British film *It's Trad Dad*, but failing to trouble the charts on either side of the Atlantic. The Walker Brothers' version is undoubtedly a great record, but one set very much in the classic Walker mould – Scott singing of lost love against a dramatic arrangement. And that was its problem. With nothing new or different to offer to a wider audience, it sold, like the previous single, only to the faithful. It reached a disappointing peak of Number Twelve in the British singles chart, at a time when the Walker Brothers needed a record to re-establish them in the upper reaches of the Top Ten.

40. Saddest Night in the World (John Maus)
Original release: single B-side 1966

The B-Side of *39* 'Another Tear Falls', a truly lovely and touching ballad. And given Scott's lead vocal, the surprise here is the writing credit for one John Maus – that is John Walker, making this John's finest hour to date, even though he let Scott do the singing. But the lyric was perfect for Scott, a gorgeously romantic and gentle tale of lost love, compassionately arranged and, at just over two minutes long, over all too quickly.

41. Deadlier than the Male (S. Engel/J. Franz)
Original release: single A-side 1966

The third and final song with authorship credited to Scott and Johnny Franz, the theme tune to the film of the same name. The 1966 British film *Deadlier than the Male* was one of many modelled on the successful formula of the James Bond films.

Left: A great night out at the Slough Adelphi was promised by this 1966 flyer, advertising one of the Walkers' headlining live appearances. Above: Philips' trade advert for Portrait, *1966.*

Unfortunately it's not a great film in itself. *Deadlier than the Male* would have very much liked to be *Goldfinger*, but it comes across more like a bad, overlong episode of one of those ITC TV shows like *Man in a Suitcase*. The best thing about the film is the Walker Brothers' theme tune. Despite opening with James Bond/John Barry-esque descending strings and brass, once underway the song is proof that Scott didn't have to be particularly profound or deep to come up with a great track – as is the case even with some of the tracks on the LP that's always portrayed as lyrically obscure, *Scott 4*.[32] In the case of 'Deadlier than the Male', the lyric is simply a development of the film's paraphrased Kipling title,[33] but there is enough poetry in the lyric and strength in the delivery, melody and arrangement to save this from coming across as disposable. Unfortunately, with the film itself being a letdown, little promotion for the single,[34] and competition in the shape of a simultaneous EP release from the Walker Brothers themselves (see *43-46* below), the single only managed to reach a peak of Number 34 in the British singles chart.

42. Archangel (S. Engel)
Original release: single B-side 1966

The B-Side of *41* 'Deadlier than the Male',[35] and really quite special. 'Archangel' is often rightly singled out as a turning point in Scott Walker's songwriting career. Certainly it marked his most ambitious and original (and most uniquely Scott) recording to date. According to Reg Guest,[36] Scott told him, 'I want it like Sibelius' Seventh Symphony.' We can safely assume that Sibelius didn't write his Seventh Symphony to be played on the organ in the Leicester Square Odeon, but it was exactly that instrument that was recorded on location to form the opening to 'Archangel'. The resulting track is quite possibly over the top, but brilliant. Opening with a 'church organ' (actually the cinema organ) playing what sounds like the chimes of doom, we expect to find ourselves in a Gothic horror film. Instead, the organ fades to the background and Scott's voice booms out, 'Silence, to hear once more her footsteps down the shadow corridor.' Only he could create something so gorgeously overblown, and downright romantic, around a concept as simple as someone waiting for his lover to return home. The singer variously watches young couples and the children playing from his window, but faces fear from 'the darkest day' and gloom from 'the tears of time all day', until, against the backdrop of a trademark big Walker Brothers sound, his 'Archangel rides in on the moon'. A fantastically good record.

Solo John, Solo Scott 1966 EP

43. Sunny (B. Hebb)
Original release: *Solo John, Solo Scott* 1966 EP

In a really curious move, at the same time as Philips released *41* 'Deadlier than the Male' as a single, they also released an EP of four new tracks entitled *Solo John, Solo Scott* – two tracks sung by Scott and two by John. As Scott already sang lead on all the singles, if the intention was to showcase John then it misfires because his tracks are hardly exciting. And 'Sunny' had already been in the 1966 charts three times!

44. Come Rain or Come Shine (Mercer/Arlen)
Original release: *Solo John, Solo Scott* 1966 EP

The second of John's tracks was more than likely inspired by Ray Charles' version on his immodestly titled 1959 LP, *The Genius of Ray Charles*.

45. The Gentle Rain (M. Dubey/L.Bonfa)
Original release: *Solo John, Solo Scott* 1966 EP

As if in answer to John's weather-related titles, Scott's first track on the *Solo John, Solo Scott* EP was 'The Gentle Rain', a song written for the 1966 film of the same name. By Scott's high standards this is a fairly ordinary track, but with 'that voice', unaccompanied for parts of the song, he still manages to rain on John's parade.

The Solo John, Solo Scott *EP showcased both of the Walker Brothers' singers. But Scott stole the show with 'Mrs Murphy', an early 'portrait' or 'miniature'.*

46. Mrs Murphy (Scott Engel)
Original release: *Solo John, Solo Scott* 1966 EP

The undoubted highlight of the *Solo John, Solo Scott* EP, a self-penned composition marking another step on the road to the 'portraits' or 'miniatures' in song to be found on his solo LPs. Perhaps inspired in part by Randy Newman's *16* 'I Don't Want to Hear It Anymore', it's also a tale of the gossiping neighbours quoted in the song's lyric. However, the world in miniature created in 'Mrs Murphy' is very much Scott's own vision, a world of twitching net curtains with a very defined cast of characters. Mr. Wilson flirts with Mrs. Murphy as they gossip about Mrs. Johnson, who, it seems does more than flirt with the young man at number 22. The rumours are true, as the last lines of the song show, but it's really saying as much about the unfulfilled lives of gossipers like the titular Mrs. Murphy. The song is a portrait of hypocritical pleasure, extramarital affairs, relationship age differences, illegitimate births, and the languid, daydreaming young man in number 22. All this is in a lyric comprising just twelve lines which, accompanied by Reg Guest's sympathetic arrangement, makes 'Mrs Murphy' a minor masterpiece.

1967

47. Stay with Me Baby (Ragovoy/Weiss)
Original release: single A-side 1967

The Walker Brothers' penultimate single, released in early 1967, a cover version of a song that had been a Top Twenty US R&B hit and a minor US pop hit for soul singer Lorraine Ellison the previous year. Co-written by Ellison's arranger-producer Jerry Ragovoy, 'Stay with Me Baby' is a fine song that the Walkers' version does justice to. However, times were changing faster in the Sixties pop world than anybody in their camp probably realised at the time. There was, of course, the burgeoning psychedelic/flower-power scene which would reach its zenith in 1967's 'summer of love'. At around the same time as the Walker Brothers released 'Stay with Me Baby', the Beatles released their perfectly English take on psychedelia, 'Penny Lane'/'Strawberry Fields Forever'. But the notion that the Walkers' success was on the wane because they didn't suddenly don kaftans, wear flowers or talk about chemically expanding their minds is apt to be overplayed. In fact, psychedelia didn't really dominate the upper reaches of the charts until the summer of 1967. More pertinent is that 'Stay with Me Baby' was cast in exactly the same mould as the previous Walker Brothers singles – Scott's lead vocal on a sorrowful ballad, performed against the trademark wall of sound orchestral backing. With nothing novel or exciting enough to recommend it to any but the faithful, who it seems were now diminishing in number, it reached only Number 26 in the British singles charts.

48. Turn Out the Moon (Scott Engel)
Original release: single B-side 1967

The B-Side to *47* 'Stay with Me Baby' and a Scott Walker composition, apt to be overlooked in favour of those immediately preceding it (*42* 'Archangel' and

46 'Mrs Murphy') and succeeding it (*51* 'Experience', *53* 'Orpheus' and *59* 'Genevieve'). 'Turn Out the Moon' appears to be an attempt to write a song in the Walker Brothers style, maybe a single A-side. It's a ballad of love lost, building to a dramatic arrangement, and even its title appears to be a development of their most celebrated moment – if the sun ain't gonna shine anymore, then the next logical step might be to turn out the moon as well. However, it has plenty to lift it above the act of writing to a formula. In place of the epic feel of a Walkers' A-side, its arrangement, though in places grandly orchestral, retains a haunting, wistful quality. Its lyric also includes poetic touches such as 'starless mornings' that are pure Scott. Moreover, the lyric is darker than it might first appear. When one considers the meaning of the song's main refrain, the inescapable conclusion is that, if the singer is not actually composing his suicide note in song, he is at least contemplating the act. If the sun ceasing to shine is a sign that happiness has gone from your world, then is to turn out the moon – and, the lyric adds, the stars in the sky – to say leave me with darkness, nothingness and death? Given that the refrain, towards the end of the song, is preceded by the singer's declaration that he is through living a life without his love, this interpretation seems hard to avoid.

Images 1967 LP

49. Everything Under the Sun (B. Crewe/G. Knight)
Original release: *Images* 1967 LP

The Walker Brothers' third and final Sixties LP, *Images*, was released in March 1967. By this time the official announcement of the group's split was imminent. With a string of singles that were comparative flops behind them, a touring schedule that Scott clearly hated every minute of, and artistic and personal differences between Scott and John growing ever wider, to have persevered any longer would have been merely to prolong the agony. *Images*, given that it's the sound of the group splitting up, is a uniquely interesting and, in places, wonderful LP. For whilst it opens and closes with two tracks that are very much Walker Brothers in style, the intervening tracks mainly find Scott and John increasingly pursuing their own respective agendas. In John's case, this meant finding one more standard to demonstrate his laidback bluesy voice, but also pursuing his own songwriting in two impressive compositions. In Scott's case, this meant pursuing the two agendas that would dominate the first part of his solo career. Firstly, his romantic balladeering side that would later be reflected in some of the tracks on the *Scott* and *Scott 2* LPs, his biggest solo single *112* 'Joanna', and in all of the *Scott Walker Sings Songs from His TV Series* LP. And secondly, the pursuance of his own songwriting without particular regard for commercialism. *Images* features Scott's two most *outré* works to date, *51* 'Experience' and *53* 'Orpheus', along with what is arguably his most perfectly realised composition of the Walker Brothers era, *59* 'Genevieve'. As if to confirm that the Walkers as a band were over, *Images* even ends on an apposite note of goodbye.

First though, back to track one. 'Everything Under the Sun', with its alternating lead vocal lines between Scott and John, sounds truly like the Walker Brothers as opposed to solo Scott or solo John, but given the song's pedigree that shouldn't be surprising. Like *19* 'The Sun Ain't Gonna Shine Anymore', it was co-written by Four Seasons producer Bob Crewe. The song had already been given a wall of sound treatment by the man himself, Phil Spector, in its original 1965 version by the Ronettes.[37] Wisely omitting the 'sh-doops' of the backing singers on the original version, the Walkers' version is a classy recording of a fine song. The up-beat mood and I-love-you lyric separate it from what might be seen as their standard fare, the sorrowful ballad. 'Everything Under the Sun' would probably have made a better choice for a single A-side than *47* 'Stay with Me Baby'. But it provides *Images* with a strong opening number.

Left: This 1967 concert flyer shows Jimi Hendrix as one of the Walkers' support acts on their final tour – a juxtaposition that in retrospect seems just bizarre. Above: Philips' trade advert for Images, *1967.*

50. Once upon a Summertime (Legrand/Marney/Mercer)
Original release: *Images* 1967 LP

The pop-group feel disappears completely for the album's second track. Instead, in what is in effect a solo track, Scott sings this gorgeously romantic ballad unaided against a gentle piano-led accompaniment. 'Once upon a Summertime' began life as the French language song '*La valse des lilas*' (literally, the waltz of the lilacs), composed in the mid-Fifties by Michel Legrand and Eddie Marnay. English lyrics were later added by Johnny Mercer,[38] having little in common with the original French other than a shared melancholy loss-of-love theme – the flower stalls, street cafés, feeding pigeons and chiming vespers are all Mercer's own. Its first recording appears to have been by jazz singer Blossom Dearie in 1958. Others have recorded the song since then, but it's hard to imagine it ever being recorded to better effect than it is on Scott's version.

51. Experience (S. Engel)
Original release: *Images* 1967 LP

If *50* 'Once upon a Summertime' showed one side to Scott Walker that would play a significant part in his solo career, then 'Experience' showed a very different side – Scott the songwriter, unafraid to be completely out of step with the prevailing mood of the times. In fact 'Experience' is so *outré* it sounds like nothing else before or since. Part cabaret, part oompah knees-up, part social critique, the result is truly invigorating. And whilst the lyric might appear to be a puzzle wrapped in an enigma, Scott was, back in those days, quite happy to explain what it all meant. 'Experience', according to its author, is to do with 'parents giving their children advice on things they know nothing about, as they've never experienced them anywhere past their TV screens.'[39] And armed with this information, 'Experience' does make more or less straightforward sense. The 'hero' is the father opening his box of 'worldly . . . wise' advice for his children. But the 'hero' is also sardonically described as self-assured, complacent, stubborn, empty and, finally, an ant. With his life comprising an early marriage and a pursuit of material possessions through his busy job at the plant, the implication is that the father has no worldly or wise advice to give. Put like this, 'Experience' is almost Scott's take on a song like 'My Generation'. But the fact that, in his hands, such subject matter ends up sounding more like a German drinking song than an angry-young-man rant is just one of the things that makes Scott Walker so special.

52. Blueberry Hill (A. Lewis/L. Stock/V. Rose)
Original release: *Images* 1967 LP

'Blueberry Hill' will always be best remembered for Fats Domino's cheery 1956 hit version. For his reading of the song, John Walker slows it down to a crawl. Sandwiched in between Scott's two most *outré* compositions to date, it sounds curiously out of place.

53. Orpheus (S. Engel)
Original release: *Images* 1967 LP

Beautifully, compassionately arranged with mournful brass and strings that dance like ballerinas and then attack like bees, 'Orpheus' is musically the shape of things to come. More three-minute classical symphony than three-minute Spector-style pop symphony, it foreshadows many sublime moments on the *Scott* LPs. Lyrically speaking, why the song should be named 'Orpheus' is not obvious. The lyric is certainly no retelling of the famous story of Orpheus, descending to the underworld to return his dead wife, Eurydice, to the world of the living, but failing and thereafter foreswearing the love of women. Scott's Orpheus does anything but foreswear the love of women. Instead, he bed-hops from married lover to married lover, from Mrs. Bleer to Mrs. Brown in a lyric of, for its time, explicit metaphor. The singer's promise to his married lover is 'to harpoon you like a whale'. Scott's Orpheus lives for today, smokes, has married lovers whom he leaves when he pleases, and comes across more like an enigmatic Alfie than a figure from Greek mythology. However, there is more to Scott's Orpheus than brash confidence; his 'harpoon' is, self-deprecatingly, really a 'bent and rusty nail'. And though he might try to live for the moment, yesterday is not always a sound that can be drummed out. In both *51* 'Experience' and 'Orpheus', the existentialist subtext is fairly clear.[40] The emphasis is on living life with action, freedom and decisiveness. The implication in 'Experience' is that the children of the song should live their own lives, make their own decisions of their own free choice, and not follow the narrow-minded advice of the song's parents. The narrator in 'Orpheus' is obviously a man of action (at least in the bedroom), making his own decisions and exercising his own freedom in spite of, not in blind obedience to, society's moral code. But of course existentialism is not the same thing as hedonism. The narrator acknowledges, albeit in a small way, that anxiety and even tenderness have a part to play in existence, as well as freedom of action. And it is these touches that prevent 'Orpheus' coming across as a song of cocksure swaggering.[41] Why then take the song title from Greek mythology? There are plenty of cultural references Scott could have been paying homage to – perhaps, Tennessee Williams' play *Orpheus Descending*, [42] or Jean Cocteau's film *Orpheus*. Or perhaps it is an allusion to the mythological Orpheus's celebrated charm. Either way, 'Orpheus' is a wonderfully significant track from its opening strain to its ending, with Scott's lonely, reverb-drenched voice warning that we might all be driven 'round the bend'.

54. Stand by Me (Ben E. King/J. Leiber/M. Stoller)[43]
Original release: *Images* 1967 LP

Along with *52* 'Blueberry Hill', the most disposable track on the *Images* LP. Unlike the boundary-testing *51* 'Experience' and *53* 'Orpheus', 'Stand by Me' is very much a return to the tried and tested Walker Brothers sound. Not normally a bad thing, but what makes it so uninteresting is that Ben E. King's original version is so sublime, so obviously the definitive version, that a cover would have to pull something fairly special out of the bag to make its existence worthwhile. On this count it fails to deliver. It both models its arrangement closely on the

Ben E. King original, and at the same time crushes all of the delicate beauty out of it with a steamrolling wall-of-sound approach that simply doesn't suit the song. Perhaps not quite as artistically pointless as David Essex covering 'The Sun Ain't Gonna Shine Anymore', but close.

55. I Wanna Know (J. Maus)
Original release: *Images* 1967 LP

Side two of *Images* opens with a pleasant surprise, the first of two strong John Walker compositions. John's 'I Wanna Know' is a breezy pop song of the type not normally associated with the Walker Brothers, and even features a veritable freakbeat-style guitar solo.

Just saying goodbye – the Walker Brothers pictured shortly before the break-up of the band in 1967. Left to right: Gary, Scott and John.

56. I Will Wait for You (Gimbel/Legrand)
Original release: *Images* 1967 LP

Abandoning the pop-group feel entirely, Scott's take on 'I Will Wait for You' takes up where *50* 'Once upon a Summertime' left off in nearly every way. Like that song, it's a Michel Legrand tune that began life with a French language lyric, '*Je ne pourrai jamais vivre sans toi*' (literally, 'I Will Never Be Able to Live Without You'), as featured in the remarkable 1964 French musical film *Les parapluies de Cherbourg* ('The Umbrellas of Cherbourg').[44] Scott sings the English lyric, which

49

in this case is from the pen of Norman Gimbel, beautifully. And with lines as incredibly romantic as 'for a thousand summers I will wait for you,' another wonderful track is assured.

Images was the final Walker Brothers LP of their 1960s heyday. Scott (centre) and John (left) pursued their separate musical agendas to the extent that a split seemed inevitable.

57. It Makes No Difference Now (Pattacini/English lyrics N. Newell)
Original release: *Images* 1967 LP

After two songs on *Images* that were originally written in French (*50* and *56*) comes further evidence of Scott's increasingly Eurocentric outlook. The work of Italian composer Iller Pattacini, with an English lyric added by Norman Newell, 'It Makes No Difference Now' is a gorgeous song which Scott's voice and Reg Guest's arrangement more than do justice to. Once again, it's an extremely romantic loss-of-love lyric which this time includes a particular line – 'the crowd will see me smile but I'm pretending' – which, taken out of the context of the song, seems to pretty well sum up Scott Walker's feelings about his pop-star role in the Walker Brothers.

58. I Can't Let It Happen to You (J. Maus)
Original release: *Images* 1967 LP

Two great Scott moments on side two of *Images* are followed by John Walker's finest. This wistful ballad is genuinely touching, beginning with just an acoustic guitar and building into a haunting arrangement complete with a melancholy trumpet solo.

59 Genevieve (S. Engel)
Original release: *Images* 1967 LP

Scott Walker's most perfectly realised, coherent and tender composition from the original Walker Brothers era. Scott seems to have been justifiably proud of the song – it being just about the only Walkers song he seemed happy to sing after the group split. He performed it on his first TV special in August 1968, enigmatically introducing it with the words, 'This is for someone I used to know.' 'Genevieve' is a tale of lost love, but a complex one. For one thing, it is the singer who is preparing to leave the title character, not Genevieve who has left the singer. About Genevieve, the lyric tells us very little specifically, other than she is pretty, but the words still create a tangible impression of her spirit: 'Genevieve, love hangs on a string, pretty thing, love shines in the sky for you.' The song is as much about the singer, who has tried to make Genevieve's dreams come true but who has also whispered lies, and who it seems wants to love but can't, the romantic outsider who might have stepped from the pages of Barbusse, Camus or Sartre. Against an arrangement that is almost baroque, with a vocal that is sublime, a simple phrase like 'love hangs on a string' manages to convey so much. Evoking both the plaything world of Genevieve and the fact that love is not easy – a difficult thing to find and a difficult thing to keep, it dangles on a string just out of reach, a fragile string that may break at any time. Everything about the track shines, right up to and including another forgivable use of the reverb/ *a cappella* ending gimmick previously heard on *13* 'The Girl I Lost in the Rain' and *53* 'Orpheus'.

60. Just Say Goodbye (Clark / Hatch / Delanoe)
Original release: *Images* 1967 LP

After what are effectively solo tracks, *Images* ends with a return to the more familiar Walkers group sound on a splendidly apposite note of farewell. 'Just Say Goodbye' was originally recorded by Petula Clark (the Clark in the writing credit) the previous year. The Hatch of the writing credit was Tony Hatch, who would go on to co-write Scott's biggest selling solo single *112* 'Joanna'. In their hands the song becomes classic Walker Brothers, without even a hint of kitsch MOR-ness. It's simply a joy to hear Scott sing romantic lines like 'the memory of you will always make me cry,' and 'oh my love, my own true love, oh where did we go wrong?' It's also a fitting allegory for the group's demise, as Scott announces, 'Let me walk away, there's nothing more to say,' and 'Leave me on my own to face the world alone.' A fitting end to a strong and diverse LP.

The *Images* LP was a critical and commercial success, almost managing to sell as well as its predecessors and reaching Number Six in the British album charts in the spring of 1967. Perhaps the Walkers were simply ahead of their time in being an album rather than a singles band from late 1966 to early 1967.

61. Walking in the Rain (Mann / Spector / Weill)
Original release: single A-side 1967

After a final British tour, having just toured Japan and Australia, the Walker Brothers called it a day at the end of April 1967. As a portent of things to come, and as a juxtaposition that in retrospect seems just bizarre, one of the support acts was the Jimi Hendrix Experience. Hendrix would of course go on to become the archetypal rock star, and an icon for the late Sixties counterculture with which the Walker Brothers and Scott shared no affinity. In the face of what was, by May 1967, the soon-to-explode flower-power/summer of love/psychedelic scene, a final Walkers single was released. And whilst on *Images* they had shown plenty of diversity and development, the single released in its wake showed no such qualities. Not that 'Walking in the Rain' is a bad record, just that it showed a complete lack of imagination in rehashing their unchanging single A-side sound in by now rapidly changing times. To underscore this point, it was a cover version of a US hit for Phil Spector's protégés, the Ronettes. That the Walker Brothers' trademark sound was indebted to Spector is something no one can deny, but to actually copy a Spector classic right down to the rainy sound effects was to show a singular lack of imagination. Whilst the *Images* LP makes for an elegant epitaph, 'Walking in the Rain', released by Philips after the group had split up, is more of a cardboard tombstone. The Walker Brothers were so much more than Spector copyists.

62 Baby Make It the Last Time (S. Engel/K. E. Duncan/M. Nicholls)
Original release: single B-side 1967

The B-side to *61* 'Walking in the Rain'. Whilst all the Walker Brothers' singles since *5* 'Make It Easy on Yourself' featured good, if not great, B-sides, the final single lets the side down on this score too. 'Baby Make It the Last Time' is that rarest of beasts, a really dull Walkers record, a slight song that offers nothing to make it interesting or memorable. Even the Scott Walker co-writing credit doesn't help matters. Scott, it seems, must have been saving his artistic energies for the greatness that was to come during his solo career.

Extras

The above tracks *1-62* comprise all those given an official UK release during the group's original lifetime, but, of course, there is now more Walker Brothers material available to us that was not available to fans at the time.

The extras below comprise the 12 previously unreleased Walker Brothers songs given a release on the *Everything Under the Sun* box set (*63-74 below*), one track that received a US but not a UK release at the time (*75*), and the curio that is the live LP, *The Walker Brothers in Japan* (*76-86*).

63. Lazy Afternoon (John LaTouche/Jerome Moross)
Original release: not applicable, recorded 26 March 1966

In July 2006, shortly after the publication of the original edition of *The Rhymes of Goodbye*, the long-promised Walker Brothers box set was eventually released. Comprising five CDs, it did 'what it said on the tin' and compiled the Walker Brothers' entire studio output from both their Sixties heyday and their Seventies reunion days, missing only one track released during the group's lifetime *75* 'Don't Fight It'. The box set certainly compensated for this omission though, with the inclusion of 12 previously unreleased Walker Brothers songs, along with previously unheard, alternate versions of *19* 'The Sun Ain't Gonna Shine Anymore' and *22* 'Looking for Me'. And those 12 songs were very popular with dedicated fans, as the Sixties Walker Brothers were almost unique amongst all other notable artists of the period in that they had not before had any of their unreleased recordings exposed by either bootleg or official release. Walker Brothers fans had long known of a list of titles that were said to exist in the vault. Now here were 12 of them available at last. These songs ranged from contemporary cover versions to standards to four tracks of officially unknown composition that may or may not be early Scott Walker compositions.

'Lazy Afternoon' can be said to fall into the category of standards, it being a song from the 1954 Broadway musical *The Golden Apple* that had been covered by at least 25 different artists by the time Scott Walker came to record his vocal for the Walker Brothers' unreleased version in the mid-Sixties. Barbra Streisand later came to record what is probably regarded as the most well-known version in the 1970s. The song is a gentle celebration of the sights and sounds of nature in the titular afternoon and a laid-back invitation from the singer to spend the afternoon together. Of course, Scott Walker singing standards was never a bad thing, and this track is no exception to that rule.

64. In the Midnight Hour (Steve Cropper/Wilson Pickett)
Original release: not applicable, recorded 25 April 1966

A creditable cover of the then contemporary and now classic Wilson Pickett track, which in fairness to all concerned was never going to surpass the greatness of the now iconic Stax original.

65. A Song for Young Love (Bill Post/Doree Post)
Original release: not applicable, recorded 27 April 1966

A cover of a 1962 track by the Lettermen and the title track of their album which reached America's Top Ten in the same year. Scott and John's close-harmony vocals on the song's gently romantic lyric follow those of the Lettermen.

66. Let the Music Play (Burt Bacharach/Hal David)
Original release: not applicable, recorded 27 April 1966

'Let the Music Play' finds the Walker Brothers taking a previously unheard further dip into the Bacharach and David songbook. And, like *5* 'Make It Easy on Yourself' and *39* 'Another Tear Falls', these are great songs given powerful lead vocals and epic arrangements. True, there's nothing revelatory here, but nothing to complain about either, and this is definitely one of the best of the previously unreleased tracks.

67. The Shadow of Your Smile (Johnny Mandel/Francis Webster)
Original release: not applicable, recorded 27 May 1966

'The Shadow of Your Smile' might now be called a standard, but its first recording was in April 1965, making it fairly contemporary at the time Scott came to sing it for the Walker Brothers' version. The song featured in the 1965 movie starring Richard Burton and Elizabeth Taylor *The Sandpipers* and went on to win that year's Academy Award for Best Original Song (incidentally beating other nominees including 'I Will Wait for You' as also recorded by the Walker Brothers (56)). 'The Shadow of Your Smile' went on to be recorded by literally hundreds of different artists, against which I would wager Scott's take, though unreleased at the time, would more than stand up against most of them.

68. Hang On for Me (unknown/unconfirmed Scott Walker)
Original release: not applicable, recorded 16 June 1966

Here things do get very interesting as there are four tracks included on the *Everything Under the Sun* box set for which the compilers could not find composer credits, begging the question of whether any or all of them were previously unheard Scott Walker compositions. John Maus conjectured that they probably were.[45] The man himself, of course, did not add any comment, but in an interview with Jarvis Cocker in 2017 he did recall how the Philips four-tunes-in-a-session work ethic extended to songs of his own composition.[46] These were still viewed as secondary or fillers for albums or B-sides. By the mid-Sixties, the Beatles may have enjoyed the luxury of time and space in the studio to develop the recording of their own songs, but the same was not true for Scott Walker as a member of the Walker Brothers. It may very well be, as Scott's songwriting skills developed as rapidly as they did in his solo career and the burgeoning Brel influence came into play, that he simply chose not to return to the unreleased compositions he had been working on with the Walker Brothers, and so they became entirely forgotten.

Of 'Hang On for Me' it could be said that it is derivative of so much that can be found elsewhere in the Walker Brothers canon, which, if it is indeed a Scott Walker composition, perhaps helps explain why he never returned to it. It's not hard to find the themes of lost love, goodbyes, rain and so on in other songs recorded by the Walker Brothers, but that said, lines like 'Our faces like lost children' and 'We loved yesterday' strike me as pure Scott. And its derivativeness notwithstanding, 'Hang On for Me' is really rather wonderful – certainly the best of the four uncredited tracks, and I might go so far as to say a gothic pop masterpiece, albeit one that Scott was quite understandably ready to leave behind him as he took the giant steps towards the genius of his first solo records.

69. I Got You (I Feel Good) (James Brown)
Original release: not applicable, recorded 29 June 1966

Whereas a live Walker Brothers version of 'I Got You (I Feel Good)' from an off-air recording of their June 1966 TV appearance on *The London Palladium Show* had long circulated amongst fans, the studio version remained unreleased until 2006. It is, of course, a cover of the James Brown original that went on to become a classic and one of its author's signature songs. And as with *64* 'In the Midnight Hour', I think I can say in fairness to all concerned that the Walker Brothers version was never going to surpass the greatness or significance of its composer's original recording.

70. I Got Lost for a While (unknown/unconfirmed Scott Walker)
Original release: not applicable, recorded 5 August 1966

'I Got Lost for a While' is the second of those songs of unknown/unconfirmed authorship. Like a number of others of the previously unreleased tracks, whilst it is of course presented on the box set as being a Walker Brothers track, this is a track with a Scott lead vocal and no apparent sign of John's (or Gary's) involvement. Thematically, 'I Got Lost for a While' is virtually identical to *68* 'Hang On for Me', right down to its lyrical reference to rain and being from the perspective of a lover asking to be taken back, but the whole is a little less inspired and heartfelt. Also, whilst 'Hang On for Me' tipped a nod to the Walker Brothers own oeuvre, 'I Got Lost for a While', with its laid-back tempo and brassy arrangement, wears its Burt Bacharach influence on its sleeve. None of which is to say this is a bad track – it isn't at all – just one where again it's understandable that Scott chose to leave it behind.

71. A Fool Am I (Testa/Carraresi/Callendar)
Original release: not applicable, recorded 26 August 1966

Originally an Italian language song (*'Dimmelo, parlami'* – Tell Me, Talk to Me), 'A Fool Am I' was given its English lyric by the late Peter Callander, the man responsible for many a pop hit lyric.[47] In its English language form, the song was recorded by Cilla Black earlier in 1966 and then very few others. Interestingly, the lyric as Scott sings it here is substantially different to that sung by Cilla Black. Cilla's version, and presumably the official lyric, is from the point of view of someone who considers themselves a fool for loving someone they know is really no good. But the lyric as Scott sings it has been almost completely rewritten by somebody (I would guess Scott himself) so as to be completely 'Walkerised'; it's now a song of simple lost love – another Walker Brothers song where Scott's girlfriend has left him. And, of course, we know that songs of lost love are, for the most part, what the Walker Brothers did to great effect – this song, which might be described as being like a lesser version of *27* 'In My Room', included.

72. Wipe Away My Tears (unknown/unconfirmed Scott Walker)
Original release: not applicable, recorded 15 November 1966

Perhaps the weakest of the four songs of unknown/unconfirmed authorship, 'Wipe Away My Tears' styles itself after the up-tempo dance side of the Walker

Brothers, as opposed to their brooding ballads side, which defined their artistic and commercial success. Complete with girl backing singers, 'Wipe Away My Tears' offers up a not unpleasant serving of vintage blue-eyed R&B. But with repeated lines like 'I can't hear you no more / And baby you're such a bore', if this is of Scott's authorship, it might just about be said that it is a step up from *2* 'Doin' the Jerk' but a million miles away from 'Montague Terrace (in Blue)'.

73. Lost One (unknown/unconfirmed Scott Walker)
Original release: not applicable, recorded 15 March 1967

Despite instrumentation that is so sweet and chirpy it might stand as a constant threat to the listener's enjoyment, and despite the unfinished feel to it, 'Lost One' is a track that deserved to be found. The melody line and the lyric are both fairly gorgeous and, again if this is Scott's authorship, then the song sees its author on the road to greatness with lyrics like 'Walk around the hallowed ground / Search the ruins of his heart' and 'Touch the rose that never grows / Dying sadly on its own'. Nevertheless, its chirpy musical feel, at least as it was recorded here, and the unreserved optimism of its lyrical conclusion ('Never designate your life to any fate / You'll find you go where you belong') would hardly have made it the best of fits on the *Scott* LP.

74. Me About You (Gary Bonner/Alan Gordon)
Original release: not applicable, recording date not known

This track is something of a mystery. It appears on the *Everything Under the Sun* box set, sequenced as though it were a Walker Brothers track released in 1967, and yet not declared as a previously unreleased track. However, it does not seem to have appeared on any previous Walker Brothers release from 1967 or otherwise. It is a cover version of a song first recorded by California pop group the Turtles and first released on their third album on 29 April 1967, which means (unless the Walker Brothers were given access to the song before the Turtles) it was recorded after the Sixties Walker Brothers had released their last LP and effectively split up. So, was this intended as a Scott solo track, or might it even have been recorded much later than 1967, as Scott's very country-style vocal might suggest? In any event, we can say the song was written by Alan Gordon and Gary Bonner, the team responsible for other sunshine pop hits for the Turtles including their biggest, 'Happy Together'. We can also conclude that this 'Walker Brothers' version certainly makes for an interesting cover, with the brisk happy optimism of the Turtles' original being replaced by slower more sombre reflection.

75. Don't Fight It (W. Pickett/S. Cropper)
Original release: on US-only 1966 LP *The Sun Ain't Gonna Shine Anymore*

Not currently available commercially.

A track that never received a release in the UK, 'Don't Fight It' was instead hidden away on the US-only LP *The Sun Ain't Gonna Shine Anymore* (the North American substitute for the *Portrait* album, which itself wasn't given a release in the US or Canada). It's a cover version of a minor UK hit for its co-author, Wilson Pickett, in 1965, given a John Walker lead vocal. Not an essential track, and not one that particularly rewards the difficulty of tracking it down.

76. Tell Me How Do You Feel (R. Charles)

77. Watch Your Step (C. Mighton/S. Mighton)

78. Uptight (Cosby/Moy/Wonder)

79. Dizzie Miss Lizzie (Larry Williams)

80. Twinkie Lee (Julian Bright)

81. Hold On I'm Coming (I. Hayes Jr./D. Porter)

82. Annabella (N. James/K. Duncan/G. Nash)

83. Yesterday (Lennon/McCartney)

84. Reach Out I'll Be There (Holland/Dozier/Holland)

85. Turn On Your Love Light (J. Scott/D. Malone)

86. Ooh Poo Pah Doo (J. Hill)
Original release: *The Walker Brothers in Japan* 1987 LP

In 1987, the reissue specialist record label Bam Caruso released a double live LP entitled *The Walker Brothers in Japan*. The record is a real curio for a number of reasons. Firstly, the material doesn't have a full commercial release today – it, or at least some of it, can be found on import CDs, including one confusingly titled *Everything Under the Sun*. Secondly, the record is curious as it was actually recorded in January 1968, some eight months after the group split. Scott, John and Gary were willing to temporarily reform in order to fulfil the prior contractual commitment to perform in Japan. (The performances on the record all date from concerts at the Osaka Festival Hall, 2-4 January 1968.) Thirdly, it technically contains eleven 'new' Walker Brothers songs, or versions of eleven songs not otherwise included in theirs or Scott Walker's recorded output. However exciting that prospect might sound, *In Japan* is not really very good. It's also extremely debatable as to whether the LP is very representative of a Walkers concert from the time that the group was together. For the Japanese shows they did not have the luxury of their usual accomplished backing band, the Quotations. Instead, the musicians on the *In Japan* LP seem almost at odds with each other, under-rehearsed and not at all understanding of some of the material. They trample all over 'Everything Under the Sun' and turn the versions of 'Uptight' and 'The Lady Came from Baltimore' into an unlistenable shambles. The quality of performances and recording also varies greatly from track to track, perhaps because the LP is not taken from one show but a composite of different shows. Scott is absent from a large part of the proceedings, and in fact all the LP's 'new' tracks feature either John or Gary on vocals. Notable inclusions are John's spirited rendition of Ray Charles' 'Tell Me How Do You Feel', a live rendition of John's solo single 'Annabella' (which is, as John introduces it, 'kind of a nice song'), and Gary's lead vocal spot on 'Dizzie Miss Lizzie', introduced by Scott's words, 'I'd like to present the star of our show . . . Gary Leeds.' Overall though, the 'new' tracks don't have much affinity with the Walker Brothers' released output and don't offer enough to recommend *In Japan* as anything other than a curious footnote.

---

1. Most of the lyrics to the songs discussed in this book can, of course, be found easily on the Internet these days, although care should be exercised, especially with some of Scott's own 1960s lyrics, where not all the transcriptions found on the web are always accurate.

2. John adopted the surname Walker following constant mispronunciation of his real surname, Maus – actually pronounced, 'Moss'. One can easily imagine his annoyance at forever being misaddressed as Mr. Mouse.

3. Yes, including Scott.

4. The 'hippies' in Scott's lyric should not be taken to mean anything other than hip kids. The term 'hippie' in its flower-power, long-hair, counterculture sense was first coined in 1966.

5. In simple terms, Phil Spector's trademark reverb-drenched wall of sound involved creating a pop orchestra – cramming musicians into Hollywood's Gold Star studios with multiple guitars, basses and drums, as well as instruments more traditionally associated with orchestrated scores. To Spector the pop single was all, and his self-defined goal was to create pop records that were built like Wagnerian operas but began and ended within three minutes. The most perfect realisation of his approach is 'Be My Baby' by the Ronettes – a pop record so perfect that it obsessed the Beach Boys' musical leader, Brian Wilson, to the edge of insanity in trying to better it. But if 'Be My Baby' remains the most perfect Phil Spector record, then 'You've Lost That Lovin' Feeling' deserves a special mention for its sheer over-the-top-ness, utilising every trick in the book, including masses of percussion, heavenly choirs and the point in the record where the wall of sound drops away completely, to leave just a simple bass guitar figure before resuming again.

6. No more real brothers than the Walker Brothers were real brothers, the Righteous Brothers comprised the unrelated Bill Medley and Bobby Hatfield.

7. In truth, Scott's 'Love Her' voice can be heard lurking in the shadows on 'Pretty Girls Everywhere', but is nowhere much in evidence on his pre-Walker Brothers recordings, or on 'Doin' the Jerk', or any of the songs recorded for *Shindig*.

8. UK chart statistics given here and elsewhere in the book are taken from *The Guinness Book of British Hit Singles and Albums*. It is acknowledged that in the Sixties there were a number of competing charts, but the Guinness books have become, albeit retrospectively, the definitive point of reference for chart statistics.

9. For example, George Martin was both the Beatles' record producer and the Head of A&R at Parlophone. Over time in the record industry, the two roles would become distinct occupations and the 'repertoire' part of the latter job title would lose its meaning as artists started to become more responsible for writing their own material.

10. Lesley Duncan was a recording artist with Mercury Records at the time, but none of the singles she released in the Sixties met with much success. Elton John later chose to include one of her songs on his *Tumbleweed Connection* album, and she went on to record a series of solo albums in the Seventies, as well as performing as a backing vocalist for Pink Floyd and Elton John.

11. It's telling that the Beach Boys' Brian Wilson was struck by how the Beatles' *Rubber Soul* (released, like the Walker Brothers' debut, in December 1965) was 'a whole album of only good songs', as if such an idea was totally alien to him before then. It served as his inspiration for writing and recording *Pet Sounds*.

12. The 'four tunes in a session' rule – which meant that, when musicians were employed on a three-hour session, four tracks had to be recorded – has been separately mentioned by both Scott and John Walker in interview, and is noted in *A Deep Shade of Blue* (p.40).

13. 2005 interview with John Walker by John Ellis, reproduced on John Walker's website.

14. Bob Crewe, as interviewed for the Channel 4 programme *Top Ten Heartbreakers*, broadcast February 2001.

15. John Walker, as interviewed for the programme detailed above.

16. Reg Kray, *Born Fighter* (Arrow 1991) p.97.

17. *A Deep Shade of Blue* claims that the two were 'like peas in a pod', p.63.

18. Anyone wishing to seek out Chuck Jackson's recording should be warned that he also recorded a 1965 single called 'I Need You So', which has been occasionally referred to as 'I Need You' but is not the Goffin and King song.

19. Ivor Raymonde's musical director credit on 'Where's the Girl' suggests it was recorded before 'Young Man Cried', with its musical director credit for Reg Guest.

20. Erroneously listed on the original single as Pete Autell.

21. The poll result was published in *New Musical Express*, 10 December 1966. In the same poll, the Walker Brothers came third in the world's best group category, behind the Beach Boys and the Beatles. Bizarrely, they were classed as a British act for the poll, and Scott Walker was voted third best British male singer behind Cliff Richard and Tom Jones. Given Scott's noted distaste for Mr. Jones at the time, it's unlikely he was too thrilled.

22. The Beach Boys' Brian Wilson and Mike Love disagreed over the direction the band should take; Love believed they should stick to the sun-surf-cars-girls-fun formula, and Wilson wanted to produce more abstract and sophisticated studio-created material.

23. The Beatles' run of singles from 1966 to mid-1967 comprised: 'Paperback Writer', 'Yellow Submarine'/'Eleanor Rigby', 'Penny Lane'/'Strawberry Fields Forever', 'All You Need Is Love' – all distinctively different records encompassing a wide variety of styles. The Stones' releases included the aggressive 'Nineteenth Nervous Breakdown', the sitar dominated 'Paint It, Black' and the reflective 'Ruby Tuesday'. Those by the Kinks included the neo-music hall of 'Dedicated Follower of Fashion', the social commentary of 'Dead End Street' and the reflective beauty of 'Waterloo Sunset'.

24. The original single mistakenly lists only John Stewart's name.
25. While hardly a household name, Verdelle Smith did go on to achieve much greater success. Her next single, 'Tar and Cement', reached Number One in the Australian charts and went Top 40 in the US.
26. The authors of *A Deep Shade of Blue* appear to have suffered some confusion regarding this point. Page 86 tells us, '"In My Room" is the work of the New York songwriting duo Pockriss and Vance, although Scott's credit indicates that he adapted the lyrics to stamp his own introverted personality on the track.' The credit, exactly as it appears on the record label of *Portrait*, reads: (Prieto –Eng. Lyrics Pockriss/Vance). It would appear that the authors have mistakenly read the abbreviation for English, 'Eng.', as 'Engel', and misattributed a lyrical credit to Scott. Certainly there does not appear to be any lyrical difference between the song as recorded by Verdelle Smith and the Walker Brothers, other than those associated with a change of gender: 'he made me his bride' becoming 'I made her my bride,' etc.
27. On some releases mistakenly credited as Robinson/Hill.
28. The same Jerry Butler who recorded 5 'Make It Easy on Yourself' and 16 'I Don't Want to Hear It Anymore', and co-wrote (with Curtis Mayfield) 218 'He'll Break Your Heart', as recorded by the reformed Walker Brothers in the Seventies.
29. The song has subsequently become well known in the UK, but the only time 'People Get Ready' has ever been a UK hit single is in the shape of Bob Marley's version, which charted in 1984.
30. Retrospective accusations of sexism have been made against the lyric because it tells how the girl of the song used to 'fix me my coffee' and 'butter up my toast'.
31. Although Springfield wasn't their real surname, Tom Springfield (born Dion O'Brien) and Dusty Springfield (Mary O'Brien) were really brother and sister.
32. See especially 129 'On Your Own Again' and 130 'The World's Strongest Man'.
33. The line in question, from Rudyard Kipling's 1911 poem 'The Female of the Species', is actually, 'The female of the species is *more deadly than the male*,' not 'deadlier than the male'. The latter-day group Space's 1996 composition, 'Female of the Species' (an homage to the Walker Brothers?), uses a horribly ungrammatical take on Kipling, with their song telling us that 'the female of the species is more deadlier than the male'.
34. Presumably due to Scott's objection to the track being released as a single A-side (*A Deep Shade of Blue*, p.98).
35. The next time a single was released with a writing credit for Scott on both the A-side and B-side was not until 1993 – by which time both the world and his music had changed almost beyond recognition.
36. Reg Guest, as interviewed by Brian Bell for an article subsequently reproduced on the Internet.
37. The Ronettes' version of 'Everything Under the Sun' was, according to the chronology given in Ronnie Spector's book *Be My Baby* (Macmillan 1991), recorded sometime between February and October 1965. But the track does not appear to have received a release until it was later included on a number of compilation LPs.
38. American lyricist and composer Johnny Mercer's songwriting credits or co-credits include 'Moon River', 'Hooray for Hollywood', 'Too Marvellous for Words', and 155 'When the World Was Young' and 'My Shining Hour', both of which Scott sang on his TV series.
39. Scott Walker interview from *Disc & Music Echo*, 4 March 1967, as quoted in *A Deep Shade of Blue*, p.102.

40. The sleeve notes to the *Portrait* LP famously describe Scott Walker as 'the existentialist who knows what it means and reads Jean-Paul Sartre'. Briefly put, existentialism is a philosophy that says the world cannot properly be explained either by reduction to scientific fact or by recourse to religion. Rather the concepts of freedom of choice, human consciousness and awareness of death are the essential tools of existence, not that which can be explained away. Writers that have been termed existentialists, such as Sartre, concentrate on actions, freedom and decisions.

41. The reader is at this point reminded of the dictionary definition of 'cocksure: adj. marked by excessive confidence'. Naturally no pun is intended!

42. Tennessee Williams' play *Orpheus Descending* was filmed in 1959 as *The Fugitive Kind* starring Marlon Brando. It is from this film that Scott took the song *256* 'Blanket Roll Blues'.

43. Listed on the original album as B. E. King/E. Glick. The name Elmo Glick was a pseudonym for Leiber and Stoller jointly that they occasionally used.

44. A film well worth seeing, even if one is not normally a lover of French cinema. Incidentally, the heroine of the film (played by Catherine Denueve) is called Genevieve, which may well have given Scott the inspiration for, naturally enough, *59* 'Genevieve'.

45. *The Curious Life and Work of Scott Walker*, Paul Woods (Omnibus 2013) p.347

46. Scott Walker 2017 radio interview with Jarvis Cocker for BBC 6 Music.

47. Peter Callendar wrote the lyrics for such 1960s pop hits as Vanity Fair's 'Hitchin' a Ride', Manfred Mann's 'Ragamuffin Man' and Georgie Fame's 'The Ballad of Bonnie and Clyde'.

part two

The 'God-Like Genius' Years 1967 - 1970

'I'm for permanence.' – Scott Walker, German TV Interview 1969

Following the split of the Walker Brothers in the spring of 1967, all three of the erstwhile 'brothers' planned to pursue solo projects. Scott Walker, though, was always the favourite to succeed. The owner of a singing voice described as one of the all-time greatest in popular music, had he decided to direct his career toward commercial success, there is little doubt he could have sold vast amounts of records well into the 1970s. Maybe he could even have persuaded America to fall for him. If and when record sales ever did dry up, there would have been lucrative live work. Perhaps Scott might have been, like Tom Jones, one of the highest paid vocalists in the world.

Indications that commercial success would not be the *raison d'etre* for Scott's solo career can, with hindsight, be detected back in the Walker Brothers days: the *outré* Scott Walker compositions on *Images*, the love of European culture, lack of interest in money and the trappings of the pop-star lifestyle, abhorrence of live performance and fan mania. However, what was impossible to predict from the Walker Brothers' days, even on the strength of songs like *53* 'Orpheus' or *59* 'Genevieve', was what a breathtakingly wonderful series of solo albums he would go on to record. No one else in the pop music universe has filled five LPs with such desolation and beauty as on *Scott, Scott 2, Scott 3, Scott 4* and *'Til the Band Comes In*. These are extraordinary records, made all the more so by a lyrical frame of reference that includes prostitutes, the Soviet invasion of Czechoslovakia, strippers, ageing transsexuals and sexually transmitted disease, along with the recurring themes of lost love, loss of hope, old age and mortality. The fact that these albums don't regularly appear in the top ten of those best-of-all-time lists says more about the media and the public's lack of imagination than it does about the undoubted brilliance of Scott Walker between 1967 and 1970. You *need* these albums.

Happily, although they remained out of the shops for much of the Seventies and Eighties, *Scott 1-4* have been easily available on CD since the early Nineties. *'Til the Band Comes In* was also issued on CD, drifted out of print, but was recently made available as part of the 5-CD set *Scott – The Collection 1967 - 1970*. These five LPs form the fundamental and essential parts of Scott 's 1967 - 1970 career, upon which his reputation justly resides. There were singles released between 1967 and 1970 (three in the UK[1]), but the solo Scott Walker was definitely an albums rather than a singles artist. In this, as in so many other ways, he was definitely ahead of his time.

Scott 1967 LP

87. Mathilde (Brel/Jouannest/Shuman)
Original release: *Scott* 1967 LP

Scott Walker's first solo LP, Scott – a great and courageous album.

Scott Walker's first solo LP, simply called Scott, was released in September 1967. Any record buyers expecting him to have turned on and tuned in to the psychedelic summer of love had another think coming. Not only does *Scott* have nothing in common with the prevailing fashion of its day, it was also a break with Scott Walker's own past. The black and white photograph[2] used on the album's cover, showing his head bowed in concentration and face partly obscured by scarf and dark glasses, was clearly intended to depict the serious artist rather than the pop star pin-up. And the image was backed by substance. To quote 1960s *NME* editor Keith Altham's original album sleeve notes, 'this is the album which Scott called [his] obsession and it is an LP for which you must open not only your ears but also your heart and mind.' Scott 's interpretative vocal skills and his songwriting shine like never before. And with arrangers Wally Stott and Peter Knight on board, as well as the talents of Reg Guest, the arrangements too astound like never before.

The catalyst for the brilliance of the *Scott* LP and those that followed was what Scott later described as 'the key to unlock' it all – the songs of Belgian singer Jacques Brel. Back around the time of the *Images* LP, Scott had said how he wanted to bring to public prominence the work of various European songwriters; by the time of *Scott*, there was one he wanted to champion above all others. Over the course of three LPs, Scott would record nine of Brel's songs (as well as singing a further two, 'The Desperate Ones' and 'Alone', that didn't get released). He described Jacques Brel without qualification as 'the most significant singer-songwriter in the world', and in the Belgian performer found the inspiration to take his own songwriting onwards and upwards. In those songs, Scott found a truth and honesty unknown in the standard pop fare of the day – songs about falling in or out of love – or in the phoney happiness of the flower-power/love and peace songs that were all the rage in the summer of 1967. Instead, Brel was unafraid to depict such things as army whorehouses, venereal disease, drunkenness and debauchery. However, it would be crass to celebrate Brel merely because his songs were frank enough to contain words like 'gonorrhoea'.[3] His real genius lies in his ability to capture universal concerns in song. Things like greed and hypocrisy, broken dreams, sex without love, and ambivalence in relationships are beautifully captured in the darkly romantic poetry of Brel's lyrics. Even themes that might be thought of as banal are meaningfully brought to life, such as the fact that we were all once children (*124* 'Sons of ') or are all mortal (*92* 'My Death').

Jacques Brel wrote and recorded in French. Therefore, when we speak of the Brel song 'Sons of ', we are really speaking of '*Fils de*', and when we speak of 'My Death' we are really speaking of '*La mort*', and so on. The English versions of the lyrics to all but one of the songs Scott recorded had been recently translated by lyricist Mort Shuman. Brel and Shuman met following the latter's move to Paris in the mid-Sixties, after the demise of the successful Pomus/Shuman songwriting partnership. The two men were, it seems, made for each other. In Mort Shuman, Brel had found someone he completely trusted to put his lyrics into English.[4] In Brel, Shuman had found a songwriter who meant so much to him that he ultimately turned performer to sing in a musical revue he created from Brel's songs, for which he was also the musical director. *Jacques Brel Is Alive and Well and Living in Paris* comprised more than twenty Brel songs translated into English. The show opened in an off-Broadway production in New York on 22 January 1968. Given that the *Scott* LP was released in September 1967, Scott Walker was able to record his pick of the new Shuman translations before the lyricist himself presented them to the public. How so? In the Sixties, Scott was happy to tell a story of how a girlfriend had shown him English translations of Brel lyrics, resulting in one of the happiest days of his life. The truth, as he later acknowledged in a 1995 interview for the BBC's *Late Show*, was that he had come across the Shuman translations via the less romantic route of a meeting with the Rolling Stones' manager, Andrew Loog

Oldham. Either way, both Brel and Shuman were agreeable to Scott recording his own pick of the songs first. We should be glad they made that decision, for Scott Walker's recordings of Brel's songs, aided by his arrangers, must rank as the definitive English language versions.

The *Scott* LP, then, opens in formidable style with Wally Stott's thundering orchestral arrangement of Brel's 'Mathilde'. The song, in Scott's words (from his introduction to the song as performed later on his TV show), 'deals with a sadomasochistic love affair'. To modern ears, this might lead the listener to expect a graphic tale of S&M sex, but 'Mathilde' is of course not about that. Instead it's a love-hate relationship, with the return of the eponymous Mathilde being both cause for celebration and imminent misery to the singer. It's a song about a destructive relationship, with the frank admission that there will be sex (the maid must change the sheets on the bed), rather than any hearts-and-flowers tale of a loved one returning. There's a hint of decadence to the song, with lyrical references to maids and champagne and the grandiosity of the arrangement. Scott's recording of 'Mathilde' is simply terrific, and everything the original sleeve notes say about it is true: 'a shattering piece of vocal dramatics guaranteed to stop the show'.

Whilst Scott would probably have preferred that the LP sell itself, he did embark upon some promotional activity in support of the record, including some live and TV appearances. One of these, on *The Dusty Springfield Show* from September 1967, leaves us with one of the few surviving pieces of video footage of him performing as a solo artist in the Sixties. In black and white, Scott performs 'Mathilde' against a pulsating op-art backdrop, and at the time of writing the clip can be easily found on YouTube.[5]

88. Montague Terrace (in Blue) (Engel)
Original release: *Scott* 1967 LP

Scott includes three self-penned compositions for which the word sublime might have been invented. They elevate the enterprise from what might have been an exciting first step to a truly great LP in its own right. 'Montague Terrace (in Blue)', in particular, is often singled out as one of Scott Walker's finest ever moments. The song, in his words, is about 'two very dear friends of mine – a married couple who live in a small room about the size of a shoe box . . . [but] who can still dream and this deals with their illusions of living in Montague Terrace.'[6] The Montague Terrace in question being not that one in Brooklyn, NY, or the Montagu Terrace to be found in Edinburgh, but a fictional London address with a 'blue mews cottage'. Thus the verses and their minor-chord arrangement tell of the couple's present conditions, the cold outside, the noise from the man upstairs, and the woman across the hall whose profession is presumably the world's oldest, before the chorus triumphantly erupts into major chords and tells of their hopes and dreams of a better life in Montague Terrace. In fact the words of the song are surprisingly few, but their power to evoke belies their paucity. When the couple say they are 'swallowed in the stomach room', these few words evoke a sense of being trapped, the claustrophobia of the couple's room and the intimacy between them, as well as an exercise in poetic wordplay. (Where else could one be literally swallowed to, other than a stomach?) The song tells us nothing about the better life the couple dream of, other than a statement of the title. But that is enough for the listener to be moved by their dreams. It matters not one bit that the neighbours in the song, the 'bloated belching' man upstairs and the prostitute with thighs that are 'full of tales to tell', might have stepped straight out of a Brel song, when so much else has been brought to the track. Scott's words, the melody, that voice, and a Wally Stott arrangement that is both compassionate and magnificent, all contribute to making 'Montague Terrace (in Blue)' a sublime whole that is just so beautifully romantic.

89. Angelica (Weil/Mann)
Original release: *Scott* 1967 LP

How do you follow a track like *88* 'Montague Terrace (in Blue)'? With 'Angelica', a song written by Barry Mann and Cynthia Weil who also wrote *3* 'Love Her' – the song that, as recorded by the Walker Brothers, gave the world Scott Walker's first great lead vocal. As with 'Love Her', Scott was not the first person to record 'Angelica', both Gene Pitney and folk-pop group the Sandpipers recording their respective versions in 1966. But, as he did with 'Love Her', Scott adds a new depth of feeling to the lyric and makes the song his own.

Songs don't come much sadder than 'Angelica', with its story of a lost love for which the singer holds himself entirely responsible. And, whilst on paper, lyrics about flowers bought too late for a lover who has gone, which are then watered by the tears the singer cries, might appear corny, they are transcended by Scott's performance and Reg Guest's distinctive arrangement. The result is a wonderful track that does not sound at all out of place on side one of *Scott*.

90. The Lady Came from Baltimore (Tim Hardin)
Original release: *Scott* 1967 LP

The late Tim Hardin was a singer-songwriter who never achieved the success that his talent deserved. The closest he came to mass appeal was as a writer of songs that became hits for others, including 'If I Were a Carpenter' (a hit for Bobby Darin in 1966 and the Four Tops in 1968) and 'Reason to Believe' (a hit for Rod Stewart in 1971). Hardin's song 'The Lady Came from Baltimore' was autobiographical – he fell in love with and married a Susan Morss (thinly disguised as Susan Moore in the song). Originally featured on the 1967 LP *Tim Hardin II*, it made a tasteful choice for Scott to cover. His version is more polished than Hardin's original, but it's to his credit that it succeeds in retaining the melancholic charm of such a personal song.

91. When Joanna Loved Me (Wells/Segal)
Original release: *Scott* 1967 LP

There are those who feel the *Scott* LP is marred or weakened by the inclusion of songs that might be described as middle of the road. Whilst this point is to a certain extent well taken in respect of *95* 'You're Gonna Hear from Me' and perhaps *96* 'Through a Long and Sleepless Night' on side two, 'When Joanna Loved Me' more than deserves its place. True, it was the work of Jack Segal, composer of jazz/pop standards like 'When Sunny Gets Blue' and 'Scarlet Ribbons', and was recorded in 1964 by crooner Tony Bennett. But 'When Joanna Loved Me' succeeds superbly. A beautiful song of lost love, superbly arranged by Wally Stott, with a vocal that fills the song with mournfulness, seriousness and a real sense of loss simply not found on Bennett's earlier recording. Although of course an American song, its lyrical reference to Paris fits in nicely with the very European feel of *Scott* and the albums that followed. And the song also works, by accident rather than design, as a sort of prequel to *112* 'Joanna'.

92. My Death (Brel/Shuman)
Original release: *Scott* 1967 LP

Needless to say, death – and certainly one's own death – was not a subject commonly addressed with any seriousness in the pop music of the Sixties. For sure, it could be mentioned in passing (perhaps with a promise to love you until I die), or if appropriately sanitised, and there was even a craze for teen-death songs at one time, typified by 'Leader of the Pack' (the Shangri-Las) and 'Tell Laura I Love Her' (Ricky Valence/Ray Peterson). But to write a serious song about feelings toward one's own death was surely unthinkable. There again, part of Jacques Brel's genius lay in his frankness, and his desire to tackle subjects that no other songwriter would even dream of – be it losing one's virginity in a mobile army whorehouse, or, more universally applicable, coming to terms with one's own mortality (something we all have to do in one way or another). The honesty of 'My Death' clearly appealed to Scott, and he regarded the song as so deserving of a wider audience that he performed it on TV. The producers can hardly have welcomed his choice of song. At the time of the release of *Scott*, he appeared on the popular BBC TV Saturday night variety show *Billy Cotton's Music Hall*, hosted by the jovial bandleader Billy 'Wakey Wakey' Cotton, and chose to sing 'My Death'. Scott introduced the song with these words: 'I have an album that is released tomorrow, and on it is a very, very marvellous song by a person that I idolise very much named Jacques Brel, and this song deals with death and his aspects of it [sic] – he laughs at it, drinks at it [sic] and sleeps with it. I hope you like it.' Alas, video footage of this unique piece of television does not appear to have survived. Whatever the reaction of the Saturday night TV audience, Scott was right about 'My Death' being a great song, and this must rank as its definitive English language recording. Admittedly hardly likely to set any party swinging, both Reg Guest's arrangement (its opening incorporating the theme of Hector Berlioz's foreboding 'Dies Irae') and Scott's vocal are terrific. Whilst not detracting from its existential essence, 'My Death' may even be seen as a love song of sorts (perhaps the deepest kind) as these repeated lines show: 'but whatever is behind the door [i.e. death] . . . angel or devil I don't care, for in front of that door there is you.' Either way, this track is a work of art.

93. The Big Hurt (Wayne Shanklin)
Original release: *Scott* 1967 LP

Opening side two of *Scott* is one of the greatest cover versions he ever committed to vinyl. The transformation from the original version of 'The Big Hurt', a Number Three hit in the US (and a minor hit in the UK) for Miss Toni Fisher in 1959/60, to Scott Walker's version is staggering. In Toni Fisher's hands, 'The Big Hurt' is a pop song which she sings with a voice not unlike a young Shirley Bassey. Her record also has something of a gimmick in its early use of the electronic phasing technique – which really didn't come into its own until the psychedelic era, when phasing was used to brilliant effect on the likes of the Small Faces' 'Itchycoo Park'. In Scott and Wally Stott's hands 'The Big Hurt' is transformed into an epic, its tone imparting something much more than missing a loved one, which is all a literal reading of the lyrics yields up. Sandwiched between *92* 'My Death' and *94* 'Such a Small Love', and including the line 'this is my life ticking away', the big hurt itself may be the very pain of mortal existence and all its unfulfilled desires.

94. Such a Small Love (Engel)
Original release: *Scott* 1967 LP

The second Scott Walker composition on Scott and, like *88* 'Montague Terrace (in Blue)', a sublime track. Dating from the era, soon to end, when Scott Walker was happy to explain what his lyrics were about, 'Such a Small Love' concerns a man attending the funeral of his best friend, his sense of loss, his grief, his memories, and the shallowness of the tears of a certain female mourner. The line about 'drunken madman nights ending up in jail' may, as the authors of *A Deep Shade of Blue* suggest, relate to a particular incident in Scott's life when he was arrested for being drunk and disorderly, and spent the night in a police cell.[7] The line that mentions 'Dago Red', apt to be misheard as 'dayglo red', refers to a slang term for any red wine made in the Italian style outside Italy.

It is conceivable that Scott found the inspiration and courage to write a song about a funeral from Brel, specifically *125* 'Funeral Tango', but, as with 'Montague Terrace (in Blue)', Scott's song is so much his own that the Brel influence matters not one bit. His words, the melody and Wally Stott's empathetic and magnificent arrangement make 'Such a Small Love' much more than the sum of its parts. The song says so much about all the sadness and pain that life can throw at us through loss, loneliness, uncaring people and an uncaring world, and love affairs that never were or never were what they promised to be. Arguably more moving than 'Montague Terrace (in Blue)', it would be fair to call this genius.

95. You're Gonna Hear from Me (Previn/Previn)
Original release: *Scott* 1967 LP

The least interesting track on *Scott*. 'You're Gonna Hear from Me' was written by the late Andre Previn and his then wife Dory in the days when the celebrated pianist, composer and conductor made a living composing and arranging for movies. The song featured in the 1965 film *Inside Daisy Clover*, as sung by the title character played by Natalie Wood. Middle-of-the-road fare recorded just one year earlier by Frank Sinatra, 'You're Gonna Hear from Me' sits uncomfortably on the LP due in part to its naively optimistic lyric. The narrator is a star in waiting whose world is, he assures us, going to start coming up clover. Given that any of three unreleased tracks that can now be heard unofficially (see this book's appendix) would have suited the mood better, 'You're Gonna Hear from Me' remains an incongruous inclusion.

96. Through a Long and Sleepless Night (Gordon/Newman)
Original release: *Scott* 1967 LP

'Through a Long and Sleepless Night' was written by Alfred Newman (music) and Mack Gordon (words) for the 1949 film *Come to the Stable*. Something of a standard, the song has been recorded by the likes of Dean Martin, Bobby Darin, Etta Jones and Peggy Lee. Whilst perhaps a little too middle-of-the-road for some tastes, there can be no doubting the quality of Scott's version, and the subject matter certainly does not appear out of place on *Scott*. There can be few things less enjoyable than a sleepless night, and your experience of the world never seems bleaker than it does at four o'clock in the morning. Scott's vocal captures that bleakness, making the song a worthy inclusion on the LP, though apt to be overlooked among the more grandiose company it keeps.

97. Always Coming Back to You (Engel)
Original release: *Scott* 1967 LP

The third and final Scott Walker composition on *Scott*, which singer and long-term fan Marc Almond has declared to be his personal favourite, which will always bring tears to his eyes.[8] 'Always Coming Back to You' is, like the other self-penned compositions, a beautifully touching track. Perhaps Brel inspired it, in the frank and realistic way that the song deals with a love affair and its aftermath with a sense of longing, of loss that refuses to go away. The romance of the terminated affair is tangible in Scott's words of winter parks, running for missed buses, watching the rain, and darkness kissed away, with the lovers of the song 'walking in each other's dreams'. Such romance in turn makes the sense of loss greater, as the singer tries to fool himself that he has forgotten his love and even her name,[9] only to confess to himself that, though he knows the affair is over, he can't let go. With a frankness that saves the song from collapsing into hearts-and-flowers sentimentality, the singer declares that he now sleeps with others but remains, despite himself, saddled with the destructiveness of returning, whether in his mind or in reality (the listener decides), to his earlier lover, whose eyes, he says, are now 'dead', and who no longer loves him.

98. Amsterdam (Brel/Shuman)
Original release: *Scott* 1967 LP

Scott ends with its third and final Brel interpretation. 'Amsterdam' is Brel at his most raucous – a lewd shanty concerning the sailors who meet at the Dutch port, their appetites for food, drink, drunken fights and 'the whores of Amsterdam'. The lyric, again translated by Mort Shuman, pulls no punches, and the scene described is not intended to be pretty. The sailors have potbellies, rotted teeth and eat fish heads. The whores sell their bodies for a few coins and have done so on a thousand other occasions. And the lyric suggests the scene will perpetuate itself – as one sailor dies another is born to take his place. In choosing to record this song, of which he turns in a masterful version, Scott made a brave decision – Shuman's translation of Brel's lyric contains the words 'slut', 'whore' and 'piss', which undoubtedly appalled more than a few listeners back in 1967. 'Amsterdam' makes for a great and courageous end to a great and courageous LP.

It might be supposed that Scott Walker's reward for completely ignoring 1967's 'summer of love', recording the album that he wanted to record, not releasing any singles to support it, and performing Brel's *92* 'My Death' on Saturday night television would be to sink into cult status and lose fans by the truckload. But the *Scott* LP was a commercial and critical success on its release, reaching Number Three on the UK album chart and staying on the chart for seventeen weeks. Amazingly, *Scott 2* would do even better.

99. Jackie (Brel/Jouannest/Shuman)
Original release: single A-side 1967

The opening track from *Scott 2*, 'Jackie' was released as a single in December 1967 as a taster for the LP, due in the spring, and as a further championing of the talents of Jacques Brel. On its release it met with a controversy that seems to have genuinely shocked Scott. The British public, it seems, weren't quite ready to enjoy songs that mentioned 'authentic queers and phoney virgins' over their cornflakes in the morning. Or at least that was the opinion of the BBC, who effectively banned the record from its airwaves and TV broadcasts. Starved of exposure, 'Jackie' did not achieve the success it clearly merited and stalled at Number 22 in the singles chart. The day had not yet arrived – as it would in 1969, for Jane Birkin and Serge Gainsbourg with '*Je t'aime*' (and later would for the likes of the Sex Pistols and Frankie Goes to Hollywood) – when a BBC ban would boost rather than diminish record sales. Independent television, apparently more tolerant than the BBC, did at least once allow Scott to sing 'Jackie' on the small screen.

The nation survived the experience without a notable rise in the number of opium dens or procurers of young girls being reported, and as a result the world is left with video footage of Scott Walker performing 'Jackie' on Frankie Howerd's TV show, *Howerd's Hour*. Apparently entering into the spirit of the show, Scott performed a version that might even be described as camp, accompanying his performance with hand gestures that offered as many literal interpretations of the lyrics as possible whilst holding a microphone in the other hand.

Silly controversies over the lyric aside, 'Jackie' can today be regarded as an utterly life-affirming classic. Like *87* 'Mathilde', it features an all-guns-blazing Wally Stott arrangement with a superlative vocal by Scott. Also like 'Mathilde', it can easily lay claim to be the song's definitive English language version. Not long after the release of 'Jackie', the musical *revue Jacques Brel Is Alive and Well and Living in Paris* would open in New York. The writer of the English lyrics himself, Mort Shuman, would sing 'Jackie', but his take on it lacks the drama, gravity and heart-stopping brilliance of Scott's version. And if we consider Marc Almond's 1991 version, it clearly exists in Scott Walker's shadow. The fact that it's both derivative of Scott's version and a pale imitation of it is something Almond himself would probably acknowledge.

The brilliant lyrics to 'Jackie' are sometimes said to be about Brel's childhood, but this is surely to oversimplify. Firstly, the lyrics as we hear them on Scott's record are really the work of a composite person made up of Jacques Brel and Mort Shuman. Shuman undoubtedly spiced up Brel's original French lyric a little in translation, but that is not a criticism. A less sympathetic or more literal translation would not, for example, have given us the superb line, 'cute, cute in a stupid ass way'.[10] Secondly, 'Jackie' is not just about childhood. It would be an unusual child whose dreams were to be drunk every night, the procurer of young girls, owner of an opium den and a bordello! Rather it's the narrator's daydreams (as a young man) that the song concerns, and these include the yearning for a childhood that has been lost.

100. The Plague (S. Engel)
Original release: single B-side 1967

Long hidden away on the B-side of *99* 'Jackie', but now quite well known due to its inclusion on *Boy Child* and other compilations, 'The Plague' is both classic Scott Walker and markedly different from anything that appears on *Scott* or *Scott 2*. In fact it's just about the most 'rock' song he recorded during this period – the haunting electric guitar even borders on the psychedelic. The title of the track is undoubtedly taken from Albert Camus' celebrated 1947 existentialist novel *La peste*, translated into English as *The Plague*. Unlike the later *128* 'The Seventh Seal' though, which is a fairly literal recounting of its inspiration, 'The Plague' is no direct retelling of Camus' novel.

In *The Plague*, Camus uses the concept of plague as metaphor on different levels. On one level the book is the literal story of a town whose borders are closed as its trapped residents die in great numbers from the eponymous plague. On another level, as Camus all but spells out for the reader, the plague is a metaphor for Nazi occupation – imprisonment by the Nazis represented by imprisonment by the plague. But in the book's more philosophical moments, the concept of plague is used in another way. A particular character is said to have long had the plague, not because he physically has the disease, but because, through a combination of his experiences, past actions and present feelings, he has lost his peace of mind – no longer capable of feeling at home in the world, self-torment replaces the innocence he remembers from childhood.[11] It is this third sense of 'the plague' that Scott draws upon in his lyric. The clanging bell sounds at the beginning of the track evoke the coming of a literal pestilence, but the song is about lost peace of mind, the singer recalling events, never clearly defined, that are the cause of his malaise, and at one point wishing he could be like those for whom life appears to be something they can find joy in. Unfortunately, it must be said, the track is somewhat marred by Scott's unforgivable Moon-June style rhyming of 'plague' and 'vague' at the end of the song.

Scott 2 1968 LP

101. Best of Both Worlds (M. London/D. Black)
Original release: *Scott 2* 1968 LP

Front and back cover of Scott 2 *– the only Number One hit album of the Sixties to mention gonorrhoea in its lyrics.*

Scott 2 was released in April 1968. In many ways the LP followed the pattern successfully established by *Scott*. In fact the similarities between the two albums are, on paper at least, striking. Both albums open with an all-guns-blazing Brel cover – *Scott* with *87* 'Mathilde', *Scott 2* with *99* 'Jackie'. Both albums have three Jacques Brel songs apiece, all in their English translations by Mort Shuman.

Both albums cover one Tim Hardin song each – *Scott* has *90* 'The Lady Came from Baltimore', *Scott 2* offers *102* 'Black Sheep Boy'. Both albums take a song that had previously been an unassuming pop record and turn it into something magnificent – *Scott* with *93* 'The Big Hurt', *Scott 2* with 'Best of Both Worlds'. *Scott* saw a return to songwriters Mann and Weil (composers of the Walker Brothers' second single, *3* 'Love Her') in the shape of *77* 'Angelica'; *Scott 2* sees a return to Bacharach and David (composers of the Walker Brothers' third single, *5* 'Make It Easy on Yourself') with *109* 'Windows of the World'. Both albums contain songs that originally appeared in films – *Scott* offered *95* 'You're Gonna Hear from Me' and *96* 'Through a Long and Sleepless Night'; *Scott 2* yields *107* 'Wait Until Dark' and *111* 'Come Next Spring'. And, of course, both albums offer Scott Walker compositions – *Scott* had three, *Scott 2*, reflecting his growing confidence as a songwriter, has four. But it's no simple re-run of the *Scott* formula. *Scott 2* is bigger, brasher, and in places funnier – a change of mood reflected by the image chosen for the album's cover, Scott Walker the performer caught in mid-vocal crescendo.

'Best of Both Worlds' had been recorded as a 1967 LP track by Lulu,[12] who suggested to Scott that he record the song. It was written by Don Black and Mark London, the team also responsible for 'To Sir with Love', the song that gave Lulu undoubtedly her best record and a million-selling American Number One single. And as Lulu's own version shows, 'Best of Both Worlds' is a fine song too. In Scott and Wally Stott's hands, it is turned into something very special indeed. In Lulu's version the orchestration appears almost as an afterthought, with a James Bond theme-style introduction seemingly tacked on to the beginning of the track. In contrast, Stott's majestic orchestration is the heart and soul of Scott's version, complimenting his vocal perfectly. Strings have rarely been used to such powerful effect on a pop song.

102. Black Sheep Boy (T. Hardin)
Original release: *Scott 2* 1968 LP

'Black Sheep Boy', like *90* 'The Lady Came from Baltimore' from *Scott*, originally featured on Tim Hardin's most convincing collection of songs, his 1967 LP *Tim Hardin II*. A short but wistful and evocative portrait of the family outsider, 'Black Sheep Boy' finds Scott turning in a more polished version of the song than Hardin's original, which possesses a delicate folk style and a fractured quality absent from Scott's version. Nevertheless, it remains a welcome inclusion on *Scott 2* and a worthy cover. The song's title might be considered apposite, as Scott Walker himself was pop music's 'black sheep boy' at the time – achieving commercial success, but pursuing his own artistic agenda against the mood of the times.

103. The Amorous Humphrey Plugg (S. Engel)
Original release: *Scott 2* 1968 LP

The first of four Scott Walker compositions on *Scott 2*, and an undoubted album highlight. Scott's vocals and songwriting have never sounded more assured than they do on 'The Amorous Humphrey Plugg'. The titular Plugg – a name that must have been invented for its sheer plainness and ugliness – is every man who longs to escape from a humdrum suburban existence of workaday life, kids and the telly, to leave it all behind and become the man he always wanted to be. In Scott's poetic vision, he is a giant of a man for whom the stars dance at his feet. And yet there is an ambiguity, as well as a sublime poetry, in the lyric that makes the song even more compelling. For aren't some of the lines being spoken by different characters? 'You've become a stranger, every night with the boys,' sounds like the words of a neglected wife. And isn't it Mrs. Plugg, rather than Humphrey, who is likely to have had a tiring day involving taking the kids to the park, and who has newly waxed the floor? Is the opening line, 'Hello Mr. Big Shot, say you're looking smart,' Humphrey addressing the self he fantasises himself to be, or the sarcastic words of Mrs. Plugg? And how much of Humphrey Plugg's amorous adventures are reality and how much fantasy? The questions do not need answering, for the track is evocatively sublime.

104. Next (Brel/Shuman)
Original release: *Scott 2* 1968 LP

Sixties music is not filled with songs about losing one's virginity in a mobile army whorehouse. It took Jacques Brel to consider it as suitable subject matter and the result, 'Next', is bold and brilliant. The narrator's life, and in particular his love-life, are forever blighted by the undignified manner in which he was forced to lose his innocence as a gift of the army. In choosing to cover the song, Scott, as well as giving the definitive English language performance, showed himself to be remarkably brave. As if the bordellos and phoney virgins of *99* 'Jackie' weren't enough to startle record buyers of 1968, 'Next' ups the ante by including references to 'the brothel truck', 'the queer lieutenant who slapped our asses as if we were fags', and even 'gonorrhoea'! Even more amazing then that *Scott 2* became the commercial and popular success that it did.

105. The Girls from the Streets (S. Engel)
Original release: *Scott 2* 1968 LP

In contrast to the unique 'Scott-ness' of the poetically ambiguous *103* 'The Amorous Humphrey Plugg', 'The Girls from the Streets' is the composition that wears its Brel influence most clearly on its sleeve. The characters in the song sound like they might have walked straight out of *104* 'Next' or *98* 'Amsterdam'. As such, the song has been unfairly derided. If the argument is that it lacks the authenticity of a Brel song, then this is a curious way to judge a record. The question of whether Scott actually slept with prostitutes to qualify himself to write the song is as irrelevant as whether Brel actually lost his virginity in a mobile army whorehouse. In fact, whilst it's unarguably an homage to Brel, 'The Girls from the Streets' has plenty about it that is uniquely Scott. The melody shines, as does Peter Knight's arrangement with its evocation of a merry-go-round. And who else but Scott Walker could write a song about sleeping with prostitutes and include lines as gorgeously poetic as 'snap, the waiters animate, luxuriate like planets whirling round the sun'?

This 1968 concert flyer advertises a pop-package tour with Scott as the headliner.

106. Plastic Palace People (S. Engel)
Original release: *Scott 2* 1968 LP

We may also be able to trace a Brel influence on 'Plastic Palace People '. For the Shuman-translated Brel song 'Timid Frieda', with its airy feel, has a young heroine who 'floats' through the streets, valises (as opposed to a balloon) held tightly in her hands. Another possible influence might be Tim Hardin's song 'Red Balloon', which, like the Hardin songs Scott covered, appears on the *Tim Hardin II* LP. But this is both speculative and unimportant, for Scott's six-minute epic 'Plastic Palace People ' is very much his own creation. Like *103* 'The Amorous Humphrey Plugg' the song, in part at least, concerns daydreams and the longing for escape. But this time it is from the perspective of a child who, unlike Plugg, has no desire to be a man amongst men. Instead, Billy's flight of fancy is literally that – to fly above the streets with his toy balloon. That much is clear, but the rest of the lyric is as beautiful and strange as the track itself and defies further exegesis. In a mid-Seventies radio phone-in show, a caller is heard asking Scott what 'Plastic Palace People ' was about. Having given what in later years became his stock answer to questions about his lyrics (that such an explanation would simply take too much time), Scott is then pressed by the caller with the question, 'Does it mean what I think it means?' Scott's amusingly unenlightening answer, given that the caller has not told him what she thinks it means, is, 'Yes, it does!'[13] His answer, whilst apparently flippant, does contain a grain of truth. The meaning to some of his more esoteric lyrics, like 'Plastic Palace People' and *132* 'Boy Child', is in the ear of the beholder. The song has whatever meaning the listener receives from it. And in the case of a track as beautiful and evocatively arranged as 'Plastic Palace People', we should have no complaint about this.

107. Wait Until Dark (Mancini/Livingston/Evans)
Original release: *Scott 2* 1968 LP

As with the *Scott* LP, the least interesting tracks on *Scott 2* are covers of songs originally from films. That's not to say that they're bad, just that their achievements are dwarfed by the grander company they keep. 'Wait Until Dark', with music by Henry Mancini and words by Jay Livingston and Ray Evans, is a straight-ahead romantic ballad. It originally featured in the 1967 film of the same name starring Audrey Hepburn, and the lyrics have absolutely nothing in common with the fairly dark subject matter of the film – which concerns a blind woman terrorised in her own apartment.

A signed Scott Walker fan club picture from the late Sixties.

108. The Girls and the Dogs (Brel/Shuman/Jouannest)
Original release: *Scott 2* 1968 LP

The third and final Brel song on *Scott 2*, which appeared in the musical revue *Jacques Brel Is Alive and Well and Living in Paris* (although no recording of it features on the show's soundtrack album). Brel's lyric – detailing how dogs are so much more man's best friend than women – shouldn't be taken too seriously, and Scott performs it in an almost cabaret style. The result is hugely enjoyable, the one Scott Walker track guaranteed to bring a smile to your face rather than a tear to your eye.

A note should perhaps be made of the names that sometimes appear alongside Brel's and Shuman's in the writing credits. 'Jouannest' refers to Gérard Jouannest, the pianist who co-wrote some of these songs with Brel. 'Blau', listed on some later records, refers to Eric Blau, Shuman's collaborator in the creation of the *Jacques Brel Is Alive and Well and Living in Paris* stage production.

109. Windows of the World (David/Bacharach)
Original release: *Scott 2* 1968 LP

On *Scott 2*, the singer returns to Bacharach and David, who of course wrote the Walker Brothers' third single, *5* 'Make It Easy on Yourself'. Bacharach and David's 'Windows of the World' was originally recorded by their singer of choice, Dionne Warwick. Whilst to modern ears the song might sound schmaltzy,[14] 'Windows of the World' was, at the time of its composition in 1966, an almost political statement, as its subject matter could not fail to be related to the escalating war in Vietnam. 'Everybody knows,' the lyric tells us, 'when boys grow into men they start to wonder when their country will call,' adding that, 'some have to die.' From 1964 onwards, conscription had risen dramatically in the US to provide troops for the Vietnam War, and many of these young soldiers would not return home alive.

Whilst Hal David's lyric hardly amounts to a rallying cry for burning draft cards, its plea for the 'rain' to end and appeal that 'there must be something we can do' is a gentle anti-war statement.

Whilst not matching any of the tracks on side one or the Brel or Engel compositions on side two, Scott's take on 'Windows of the World' is nevertheless a welcome inclusion on the LP.

110. The Bridge (S. Engel)
Original release: *Scott 2* 1968 LP

The final Scott Walker composition on *Scott 2*, for which the word sublime might also have been invented. 'The Bridge' is Brel-influenced, to the extent that the lyric might not otherwise have featured the word 'piss' and had a heroine called Madeleine.[15] The decadence, wine, women and sailors might also be Brel-inspired, but the universally applicable theme of the song is loss and regret. The good times and the opportunities they presented have passed. The singer is left watching from the riverbank – perhaps the ever-flowing river is also an allegory for the relentless passing of time – gazing at the scene where Madeleine once stood, whom he never treated properly. With a melody to die for, and a beautifully poetic lyric in which even 'piss' is made to sound charming, 'The Bridge' is arguably the finest and most touching composition on the album. It is also a foretaste of the direction Scott's songwriting would take on *Scott 3* – sensitively painted portraits of loss, opportunities passed, and regret.

111. Come Next Spring (Adelson/Steiner)
Original release: *Scott 2* 1968 LP

A curious choice of song on which to end *Scott 2*, more a whimper in contrast to the closing bang of *98* 'Amsterdam' on Scott. 'Come Next Spring' is not a bad track but it's one of the least exciting, although neither Scott's vocal nor Wally Stott's arrangement can be faulted. It was written for the 1956 film of the same name by Austrian composer Max Steiner, with a lyric by Lenny Adelson concerning the singer's promise to return home to his lover. The song had previously been a minor UK hit for Tony Bennett in 1956.

Although regarded as something of a cult record today, *Scott 2* was on its release a huge popular success. The unflinching, almost bawdy lyrical references notwithstanding, the album reached the Number One spot in the albums chart, and, with sales buoyed by the non-LP single *112* 'Joanna', stayed on the chart for an impressive eighteen weeks. Ever the perfectionist, Scott himself regarded *Scott 2* without satisfaction, referring to the album as 'the work of a lazy, self-indulgent man'.[16] If we must agree that the album does have a fault, then it's only that it's apt to come across as a disjointed collection of songs. The same cannot be said of the next LP, released the next spring – *Scott 3*.

112. Joanna (Hatch/Trent)
Original release: single A-side 1968

Shortly after the release of *Scott 2*, the non-LP track 'Joanna' (now, of course, available on numerous compilation albums) was released as a single with *97* 'Always Coming Back to You' as its B-side. If *99* 'Jackie' offended everyone on its release, then 'Joanna' was never likely to offend anyone. For rather than showcase Scott's more adventurous side, 'Joanna' finds him cast squarely in his romantic balladeering role, performing a mainstream song of lost love. It is true that Scott himself did not want to release a single at all at this time, but the notion that he was somehow forced to record songs like this is often overplayed. His straight-ahead ballads had been an integral part of his art since the Walker Brothers' days, and a side of himself he was happy to represent on *Scott* and *Scott 2*. It was only on his next LP that his interest in recording his own material took over. Moreover, the audio soundtrack that survives to the Scott Walker TV series hardly shows him performing romantic ballads against his will. On the contrary, Scott seems to have enjoyed singing many of the middle-of-the-road standards on his TV series, and went out of his way to praise many of the songs. The credited composers of 'Joanna', Tony Hatch and Jackie Trent, were also guests on one of the TV shows. Scott described them as 'two people who are notably musical people and very good friends of mine and so very talented.'

The multifaceted career of Tony Hatch in the Sixties included composing TV themes (*Crossroads* and *Man Alive*), working as an A&R man for Pye Records, songwriting, arranging and record production, as well as being a recording artist in his own right. His most successful songwriting credits include Petula Clark's 'Downtown' and the Searchers' 'Sugar and Spice'. In 1967 he married singer Jackie Trent, who had recently enjoyed a Number One hit with her new husband's tune 'Where Are You Now (My Love)'. The two of them became known as 'Mr and Mrs

Music',[17] a songwriting partnership with Trent supplying lyrics to Hatch's music. Whilst 'Joanna' is credited to that partnership, Scott himself apparently wrote a significant part of the lyric. In his article 'The Fugitive Kind',[18] Joe Jackson quotes him as follows: 'that whole verse about "lived in your eyes completely" is mine and I wrote the last line in the song, "you may remember me and change your mind."' Thus what is sometimes presented as a song Scott hated[19] is actually a partial composition of his. And it is his contributions – including the line about Joanna having 'made the man a child again' – that make the song as touching as it is, particularly the last line that gives the song a little bit of hope that the romance may one day be rekindled. Middle-of-the-road it may be, but 'Joanna' is a very nice record indeed. The record buying public agreed and put the disc at Number Seven in the British singles chart. Scott undertook various TV appearances to promote the single, including appearances on Dusty Springfield's show *It Must Be Dusty*, *Top of the Pops* and Simon Dee's *Dee Time*. Video footage of Scott lip-syncing a performance of Joanna, possibly recorded for European TV at the time, can now, at the time of writing, be found on YouTube.

A rare picture of Scott and his wife-to-be, Mette Teglbjaerg, taken at Heathrow Airport in late 1967.

113. The Rope and the Colt (Hossein/Shaper)
Original release: France only, single A-side 1968

Released in France towards the end of 1968, but later rescued from obscurity by its inclusion on the original version of the *Boy Child* compilation (and then also on the *Five Easy Pieces* box set), 'The Rope and the Colt' is a hugely enjoyable track. A short song of cowboy derring-do, with words by Hal Shaper and bouncy spaghetti western music by Andre Hossein, it's over all too quickly at just under two minutes long. Scott recorded his vocal to the track in Paris as a one-off contribution to the soundtrack of the film *Une corde, un colt*, released in 1969,[20] cementing his career-long association with songs for or from films. The single's B-side, '*Concerto por guitar*', is a piece of instrumental music from the film and not a Scott Walker track.

Scott 3, 1969 LP

114. It's Raining Today (S. Engel)
Original release: *Scott 3* 1969 LP

Scott's third solo album, Scott 3, *was released in April 1969 – arguably his finest collection of songs.*

After the release of *Scott 2* and *112* 'Joanna', Scott was prepared to play the popstar game to the extent of making TV and radio appearances, and even headlining a pop-package tour of the UK including 1968 chart stars the Love Affair (of 'Everlasting Love' fame) and the Casuals ('Jesamine') on the same bill. But his heart was in recording the serious work that, in his mind, *Scott 2* was not. This third solo LP was released in April 1969, and it is an undoubted masterpiece. Even the beauty of the sleeve design does not prepare the listener for the beauty of the songs. Gone are the cover versions, apart from three Brel songs – which, as the record's final three tracks, appear as an almost bolted-on bonus. Instead the record comprises ten Scott Walker compositions which had nothing in common with the pop music of the day, arguably his finest collection of songs. Unlike those on *Scott* and *Scott 2*, these compositions show no overt Brel influence. By this point Scott's biggest influence was himself, and the classical music in which he was steeping himself. Scott's arranger of choice for *Scott 3*, providing orchestral arrangements for all his own compositions (apart from *121* '30 Century Man', which clearly doesn't have one), was Wally Stott. Whilst not to belittle the obvious talents of Reg Guest or Peter Knight, both responsible for brilliant arrangements on some great tracks, Stott was clearly the right person for the job. His arrangements for *88* 'Montague Terrace (in Blue)' and *94* 'Such a Small Love', to give but two examples, demonstrated how in tune he was with Scott's art and how perfectly his arrangements could realise the songwriter's vision. Stott's career is truly remarkable. At the age of fifteen he was a professional musician, and by the age of twenty he was performing and arranging for the BBC, without, at that stage, having had the benefit of any formal training other than lessons as a schoolboy. He went on to become musical director of Philips Records at 29, and to provide scores for countless films, TV and radio shows, including the diverse likes of *Hancock's Half Hour*, *The Goon Show*, *Dallas*, *Dynasty* and (in terms of films) *The Looking Glass War*, *The Slipper and the Rose* and *Watership Down*. In 1972, Stott underwent gender reassignment surgery and became known as Angela Morley. More extraordinary than that is the fact that the late Ms Morley's website, whilst otherwise comprehensive, does not include a single mention of the sublime records that she (as Wally Stott) made with Scott Walker in the late-Sixties.[21]

Scott 3 opens with 'It's Raining Today', a song Scott saw as being about his own beatnik past – his teenage years, when he read Jack Kerouac's *On the Road* and hitchhiked across America as a result. However, it's impossible to imagine a track less teenage or beatnik-sounding than 'It's Raining Today'. It's a melancholic, sophisticated, delicately melodic performance – a sepia-tinged song of sorrow for times of romance and freedom past. A simple but effective metaphor – once there was sun, but today there is rain. A song so affecting that, as Scott sings the line, 'she smiles through the smoke of my cigarette,' smokers are likely to reach for one and non-smokers may momentarily consider taking up the habit!

115. Copenhagen (S. Engel)
Original release: *Scott 3* 1969 LP

Scott called the songs he created for *Scott 3* 'miniatures', and they are finely painted portraits in song, an idea mirrored in the oval pictures that appear inside the album's gatefold sleeve. For the representation of 'Copenhagen', the picture is of Mette Teglbjaerg, Scott Walker's then girlfriend and wife-to-be. Mette came from Denmark and Scott had met her in Copenhagen – a city he would describe as his favourite in the world. 'Copenhagen' is, as a result, a genuine love song – about being in love, as opposed to being left by your lover – and there are surprisingly few of those in Scott's recorded output. His words capture the power and the fragility of love without coming across as over-sentimental. The notion that love can make you like a child again, that Scott had used in his contribution to the lyric of *112* 'Joanna', is expanded upon here. Its fragility is reflected by the likening of the lovers to snowdrops that might melt away, and by the modest wish for 'just one more spring'. And Scott's every word is perfectly complimented by Stott's arrangement, providing an aural representation of the lyric (for example, the 'children's carousel') without ever being trite or obvious.

116. Rosemary (S. Engel)
Original release: *Scott 3* 1969 LP

Another sublime moment follows, in 'Rosemary'. From his performance of the song on his TV show, Scott introduces it with these words: 'This is from my new LP and I wrote it for a spinster named Rosemary, who's constantly haunted by the one fleeting love affair that she knew, and the frightening reality that she can never break away from her domineering mother.' All of which is fairly apparent from the lyric, but the genius of 'Rosemary' lies in the song's ability to really touch the listener via its descriptive poetry. Not a word is wasted, and so many of the lyric's phrases carry a meaning that belies their brevity. We are told that Rosemary's mother's friends 'pour antique cups of tea' and that her one-time lover 'smelt of miracles' – phrases that are literally nonsensical, but convey both a picture of the characters and Rosemary's feelings towards them. We are told that she sees a dog 'straining hard on his leash to get away', and we know she sees a metaphor for her own predicament. True, few of us will share Rosemary's particular problems, but all of us of a certain age can be touched by the track and empathise with the feeling of being trapped, of running out of opportunities, out of time, and regret for what might have been.

117. Big Louise (S. Engel)
Original release: *Scott 3* 1969 LP

Incredibly, *116* 'Rosemary' is followed by a song even more moving and poetic. Again the portrait painted is of a specific character, but the track touches the listener on a more general level. The opening bars of music, before Scott's voice is even heard, convey a sadness that is almost tangible. And then he sings, with 'that voice', of the sadness of Big Louise. Hearts might break.

In fact, the specifics of Louise's plight aren't even spelled out in the lyric. We might take it that Louise is a woman hurtfully gossiped about, for whatever reason – perhaps because she is considered too old for the 'sad young man' she has been seeing, or just because she is considered to be 'mutton dressed as lamb'. Actually, as is explained in somewhat garbled terms in Keith Altham's original sleeve notes, and in somewhat clearer terms by Scott at the time, Louise is an ageing transvestite. But the novelty of the subject matter[22] is ultimately less interesting than the sheer weight of emotion the song conveys, and its sheer poetry. To state that once time has passed it can't ever be relived is an uninteresting truism. But to listen to an expression of this fact in 'Big Louise' is to be hit by the terrible profundity of its truth. The line 'She's a haunted house and her windows are broken' says more without explanation than pages of exegesis could possibly do.

'Big Louise' remains a serious candidate for Scott Walker's finest ever track, a song beloved by latter-day fans Marc Almond, who recorded his own version of the song, and Julian Cope, who used one of its lines as the title to his Walker compilation LP, *Fire Escape in the Sky*.

118. We Came Through (S. Engel)
Original release: *Scott 3* 1969 LP

The one track on *Scott 3* whose feel belies its meaning. A cursory listen to 'We Came Through' might lead the listener to believe the song to be one of celebration – the track has a triumphant military feel, even concluding with the sound of cannon fire. Keith Altham's original, and frankly bizarre, sleeve note has this to say about the song: 'trumpet the shadows of Luther King and Che Guevara the ironic song of the Gargoyle, proud the Vietnamese girl from the *Sunday Times Supplement* but unable to smile at us.' Opaque though this comment may be, it does perhaps throw a little light on the meaning of 'We Came Through'. Though the song sounds like one of genuine celebration, the lyric is intended ironically. It is impossible to put any other interpretation on lyrics such as, 'And Guevara dies encased in his ideals / And as Luther King's predictions fade from view / We came through / We came riding through.' Scott, whose outlook was politically left of centre, can hardly have been celebrating the death of Guevara or the failure of King's dream. Rather, the 'giants' of 'We Came Through' are being ridiculed for the hollowness of their ideals in the face of the true horror of war. Not likely to beat 'Give Peace a Chance' in a competition for the most overtly stated anti-war song ever, Scott's song is still the greater work of art by many a mile.

119. Butterfly (S. Engel)
Original release: *Scott 3* 1969 LP

A perfect example of words and music in harmony. Wally Stott's arrangement captures the fluttering flight of a butterfly, while Scott's short and sweet song compares the butterfly to the girl on whose hair he temporarily settles – both are beautiful and both are free spirits. As with other tracks on *Scott 3*, this can hardly be described as pop music – it is music so unique, so delicate and beautiful, that it defies categorisation.

120. Two Ragged Soldiers (S. Engel)
Original release: *Scott 3* 1969 LP

The theme of ageing and good times past, never to be relived, surfaces again as side one of *Scott 3* draws to a close. 'Two Ragged Soldiers' was apparently inspired by a *Time* magazine article about the vagrants on New York's 'Skid Row'. And whilst the track is not quite as wonderful or touching as *116* 'Rosemary' or *117* 'Big Louise', its pathos is nevertheless exquisitely painted and genuinely poignant. The world may see two old vagrants content to drink themselves to death, and who inspire disgust from passers-by ('good mornings to faces who just turned away'), but Scott's lyric explores the sad truth that one day these vagrants must have been young, with hopes and dreams, inventing a past for them where they, as young men, 'spoke transparent phrases to looking glass women'.

121. 30 Century Man (S. Engel)
Original release: *Scott 3* 1969 LP

The second side of *Scott 3* opens with the album's shortest track, a welcome oddity. On '30 Century Man', Scott accompanies himself just by strumming a four-chord pattern on an acoustic guitar (E-D[add9]-G-A if you're interested). The stereo mix is so severe that, by listening to only the left channel, it's possible to effectively hear Scott sing the song *a cappella*, or alternatively, by listening to only the right channel, to hear just his acoustic guitar backing. The song plays with the idea that technology might one day enable a man to cryogenically freeze himself, and live centuries into his own future – an idea that remains science fiction, with even the name-checked Charles de Gaulle having to die, like the rest of us.[23] Perhaps though, the song is even more relevant today than it was a quarter of a century ago, given both that medical science is today able to 'play God' in some very real ways, and that personal health and living as long as possible have become the new religion of the mass media.[24]

(The reference to 'Saran wrap' in the song's lyric may still confuse British listeners to this day, as this plastic wrap product is almost always referred to as 'cling-film' in the UK.)

122. Winter Night (S. Engel)
Original release: *Scott 3* 1969 LP

A return to orchestral arrangement and an eight-line poem set to minor chords. As delicate and as beautiful as the snowflakes you can almost feel falling.

123. Two Weeks Since You've Been Gone (S. Engel)
Original release: *Scott 3* 1969 LP

The final self-penned song on *Scott 3* and another wonderful track. 'Two Weeks Since You've Been Gone' is a song of lost love, but cast firmly in the *Scott 3* mould of delicate sensitivity rather than grand statement. A beautiful arrangement with melancholy strings, and a hint of the 'toy piano' sound featured more prominently on the next track, *124* 'Sons of', accompanies the singer's lament for the love it will clearly take him much more than two weeks to get over. Scott's vocal is superlative, and his poignantly poetic lyric closes with a heartbreaking touch of self-delusion: 'and if I close my eyes long enough, will you happen to me again?'

124. Sons of (Jouannest/Brel/Shuman)
Original release: *Scott 3* 1969 LP

After ten uninterrupted Scott Walker compositions, *Scott 3* ends with its three Brel songs. It's telling that they're grouped together in this way, rather than mixed in as they were on *Scott* and *Scott 2*. Scott had by now travelled far beyond the Brel influence, creating music that was uniquely his own. However, we should be grateful that *Scott 3* does feature these three songs, for each one is a triumph both for Brel and for Scott. 'Sons of' begins with its 'toy piano' introduction, evoking the childhood nursery, but the song is anything but childlike. As he did in 'My Death', Brel takes a universal truth and turns it into a song in a way that wouldn't occur to anybody else. In fact, 'Sons of' draws upon several such truths: 1) that we are all somebody's child; 2) that who our parents are shapes who we are; 3) that everyone at some point was a child. And Brel makes these obvious truths not only thought-provoking, but also very entertaining – and that is genius. As with the other Shuman-translated songs that Scott recorded, it is practically impossible to imagine it performed to better effect than it is here.

125. Funeral Tango (Jouannest/Brel/Shuman)
Original release: *Scott 3* 1969 LP

A song more about greed and hypocrisy than it is about a funeral, but Brel's device of the singer watching the behaviour of his mourners is inspired. They are depicted as more concerned with what gossip they can learn about the deceased, how much the funeral is going to cost them, and what they might be left in the will, than they are with any actual grief. And Brel's words, in Mort Shuman's sympathetic translation, produce a darkly comic masterpiece. Scott too, it seems, perfectly understood the black comedy, as he turns in a vocal that fills every word with meaning, sneering and sarcastic where appropriate, without ever lapsing into hamminess. The result is truly a gem.

Contrary to popular belief, Scott did perform 'Funeral Tango' on his TV series, despite the show's producers feeling it was in poor taste. He announced, 'Did you ever have the desire to watch your own funeral? Listen to this,' before launching into the song. Alas, the reaction of the nation's TV viewers goes unrecorded.

126. If You Go Away (Brel/McKuen)
Original release: *Scott 3* 1969 LP

If the sleeve notes to the 2005 compilation CD *Classics and Collectibles* are correct, 'If You Go Away' was almost literally a bolt-on extra to *Scott 3*, having been recorded two years earlier, in 1967. If so, the reason it did not receive an earlier release may have been the fact that John Walker also chose to record the song, and released it as the title track to his debut solo LP in 1967. But either way, neither of the erstwhile Walker Brothers made a particularly unique decision. Almost from the moment American poet and singer Rod McKuen came up with the song's

English lyric, 'If You Go Away' became an instant standard. The song began life as *'Ne me quitte pas'* (literally, 'Do Not Leave Me') as written by Jacques Brel in 1959. In 1966 McKuen translated/adapted the original French lyric into English, giving us 'If You Go Away' as we know it, recording his own version that same year. And the world, it seems, followed suit. There are easily over a hundred different recordings of the song by different artists, including Tom Jones, Jack Jones, Jackie Trent, Terry Jacks, Frank Sinatra, Brenda Lee, Glen Campbell and Neil Diamond. American singer Damita Jo appears to have been the first to record the song after McKuen, releasing her version in 1966. In 1967 alone, versions of the song were released by Dusty Springfield (on her LP *Where Am I Going*), the Seekers (on their LP *Seen in Green*) and Shirley Bassey (on her LP *And We Were Lovers*). At some point a consensus was quickly arrived at regarding one particular line of McKuen's English lyric, which comes across as clumsy in translation. McKuen's version has the line, 'I'd have been the shadow of your dog,' which for most other versions, including both John and Scott Walker's, has become the more palatable, 'I'd have been the shadow of your shadow.'

Whilst there can be no doubting that Scott's version of 'If You Go Away' is wonderful, it remains perhaps the least interesting track on the album. True, this is a bit like saying it's the poorest millionaire, but one or two points are still worth making. Firstly, 'If You Go Away' is the least Brel-like of all the Brel songs Scott recorded – which is to say that Rod McKuen's approach to translating Brel was very different to Mort Shuman's, and involved dropping much of the content of Brel's original lyric in favour of his own input. Secondly, as noted above, many other versions have been recorded, with many beating Scott to a release date. And in particular there is Dusty Springfield's sublime version, recorded like Scott's at Philips' studios, which she sings with the voice of an angel and scores bonus points by singing part of the French lyric. Scott's version is not the definitive one.

As a whole, *Scott 3* was an artistic triumph. Not only is it one of those rare LPs that does not have a bad track on it, but it also contains some of the most poignant and beautiful recordings made in the popular music of the past century. Were the record-buying public prepared to follow Scott into a unique new world that existed somewhere between pop and classical music? It seems they were. *Scott 3* reached Number Three in the British album chart. For the time being, Scott Walker was still a huge popular success.

127. The Lights of Cincinnati (Macaulay/Stephens)
Original release: single A-side 1969

The non-LP single 'The Lights of Cincinnati' was released shortly after *Scott 3*, with *123* 'Two Weeks Since You've Been Gone' as its B-side. Not a Scott Walker or Brel composition, it was the work of Tony Macaulay and Geoff Stephens, who had built up a considerable songwriting pedigree in the Sixties British pop scene. Macaulay was a writer and producer at Pye Records, responsible for co-writing 'Let the Heartaches Begin' (a 1967 Number One for Long John Baldry) and 'Build

Me Up Buttercup' (a 1968 Number One for the Foundations). Stephens, who had been around for a little longer than Macaulay, had written or co-written 'Tell Me When' (a 1964 hit for the AppleJacks), the haunting 'The Crying Game' (a hit for Dave Berry, and much later used in the film of the same name) and 'Semi-Detached Suburban Mr James' (a 1966 hit for Manfred Mann). As a partnership, Macaulay and Stephens were responsible for the 1969 hits 'Sorry Suzanne' (a Top Ten hit for the Hollies) and 'Smile a Little Smile for Me' (a Top Ten US hit for the Flying Machine). As they were a British songwriting partnership, it's to be wondered whether 'The Lights of Cincinnati' was actually inspired by the American city at all. Perhaps the title phrase just scanned better than 'The Lights of Wolverhampton'! The song was also recorded in 1969 by Long John Baldry and included on his LP *Wait for Me*.

As had been his stance at the time of *112* 'Joanna', Scott wasn't keen on releasing a single at all, disliking the need to play the pop star and feeling that the LP format was where his art truly lay. But whereas he had some regard for 'Joanna', a song he was prepared to promote through TV and radio appearances, his attitude toward 'The Lights of Cincinnati' was decidedly cooler. He appears to have undertaken little in the way of promotion, and is recorded as describing the song as 'boring'. Scott's attitude would appear to remain cool after all these years, as the song is conspicuous by its absence from the *Five Easy Pieces* box set compilation.[25] But, as with *Scott 2* and many of his other records, his opinion is unfairly harsh. True, Scott was understandably now more interested in his own compositions than in interpreting the work of established pop writers. But the delicate miniatures of *Scott 3* were just never meant to be pop singles. And despite the fact that 'The Lights of Cincinnati' is more a belated follow-up to 'Joanna' than it is representative of Scott's art at the time, it is a great record, a gorgeous ballad, a much stronger song than 'Joanna', beautifully arranged and sung superbly. The only minor complaint is that the line about the 'same old rocking chair' might have been a little odd for someone of Scott's years to sing – he was 26 at the time. Otherwise, those unmoved by the record should probably get themselves medically examined, just to check that they do in fact have a heart. With minimal promotion, the single reached Number Thirteen in the British charts in the summer of 1969.

Scott 4 1969 LP

128. The Seventh Seal (S. Engel)

Original release: *Scott 4* 1969 LP

The follow up to *Scott 3* proper was released late in 1969. Between *Scott 3* and *Scott 4* another album, *Scott Walker Sings Songs from His TV Series*, had also been in the shops. As its title suggests, it compiled songs Scott performed on his BBC TV series during the months of March and April 1969. But because the *TV Series* LP fits better in 'Part Three: The Singer Not the Song' than it does here, chronology is being temporarily eschewed and it will be dealt with in this book's next section.

Scott 4 – *the only LP released under the singer's real name of Scott Engel, and the one many regard as his masterpiece.*

Scott 4 is often regarded as both Scott Walker's masterpiece and the album with which he went too far for the public to follow him. But whilst there is some truth underlying these ideas, some of them are misconceived. *Scott 3* is also a serious candidate for his best LP, as are, to those of more iconoclastic tastes, *Tilt*, *The Drift* or *Bish Bosch*. True, he wrote all of *Scott 4*'s ten tracks, but there are ten self-penned compositions of comparable distinction to be found on *Scott 3*. *Scott 4* is sometimes presented as lyrically and musically more obscure than *Scott 3*, a situation encouraged by his own description of the LP as an attempt to 'link lyrics by Sartre, Camus and Yevtushenko to Bartok modal lines, but nobody noticed'.[26] But in fact a number of its lyrics could not be much more straightforward; the record's melody lines are often tighter than those on *Scott 3*, and whilst *Scott 4* isn't exactly pop music, it does make use of drums, bass guitar and electric guitar – instruments conspicuous by their absence from *Scott 3*. The commercial failure of *Scott 4* was, as we will discover (see *137* below), more the result of non-musical factors than of Scott taking his music to a new level of obscurity.

Having said that, the track that opens *Scott 4* is not the usual stuff of pop music. In 1957, Swedish filmmaker Ingmar Bergman, made what many regard as his best film, *Det sjunde inseglet* (to give it its English title: *The Seventh Seal*). Filmed in black and white, *The Seventh Seal* is set in the Middle Ages and concerns a knight returning to his homeland to find his country beset by plague and religious zealots, whose hobbies include burning suspected witches at the stake. He also meets Death personified, waiting to take his life. In a bid to prolong his existence, the knight challenges Death to a game of chess for his life. Inescapably bleak, the film tackles head-on the philosophical subjects of death and godlessness. Scott chose to set this little lot to music for the eponymous opening track, 'The Seventh Seal'. Opening with some flamenco guitar and the lonely sound of a trumpet, the track builds into a glorious opus, moving along in an almost funky manner and throwing what sounds like the chanting of a mass choir of monks into the mix. Scott's lyric is a near literal retelling of the film, brilliantly executed; the arrangement by Peter Knight is masterful; the vocal is sublime and the whole is gloomy yet magnificent.

129. On Your Own Again (S. Engel)
Original release: *Scott 4* 1969 LP

But if the subject matter of *128* 'The Seventh Seal' is esoteric, that of 'On Your Own Again' is nothing of the sort. Its theme is nothing more obscure than lost love, but this short song is one of the most beautiful things that Scott Walker ever recorded. He sings a handful of lines of reminiscence against a gentle acoustic guitar, before, at the mention of the word 'love', the drums and swirling strings enter as Scott sings the song's title. The brief lyric includes enough to truly touch your heart, from the self-delusion of 'You're on your own again and you're your best again, that's what you tell yourself,' to the tender realisation of how much has really been lost, in the lines, 'except when it began, I was so happy I didn't feel like me.'

130. The World's Strongest Man (S. Engel)
Original release: *Scott 4* 1969 LP

Opening with an introduction that sounds like it was inspired by Glen Campbell's 'Wichita Lineman' – no bad thing – comes another song whose subject matter is far from esoteric. 'The World's Strongest Man' is really nothing more than a song of lost love. But it's truly great. For sure, there is the phrase 'towers of my naked shine like a dime', the meaning of which is evocative rather than literal, but other than that the meaning of the lyric is as clear as day, including wonderfully poetic touches ('longing for belongings here again' and 'I came back here to replace your place in my life') and an irresistible portrayal of love, loss and humility. It would be a cold-hearted lover who didn't take Scott back again after hearing this.

131. Angels of Ashes (S. Engel)
Original release: *Scott 4* 1969 LP

After two superb tracks that find Scott at his most straightforward, musically and lyrically, are a pair that find him at his esoteric best. Musically, both 'Angels of Ashes' and *132* 'Boy Child' take the classical influence present on *Scott 3* a stage further, to the extent that they have been described as baroque. Lyrically, 'Angels of Ashes' is not straightforward either, being more poetry than narrative. The message is clearly one of hope delivered at the point of despair, but, in marked contrast to the secular salvation of Leonard Cohen's 'Sisters of Mercy' (which

'Angels of Ashes' may have been inspired by) or Robbie Williams' 'Angels' (which may conceivably have been inspired by 'Angels of Ashes'[27]), Scott's song appears to offer a salvation that borders on the religious. The angels of the title are recommended to the listener, along with an exhortation to confess and a promise of life 'above' as a reward for humility. Saint Francis of Assisi is mentioned, and even the ashes of the song's title carry a strong religious connotation – signifying mourning or contrition (as in 'sackcloth and ashes'), as well as the literal part of the Catholic Church's Ash Wednesday service, where churchgoers are marked on the forehead with a cross of ashes. 'Angels of Ashes' is also filled with other imagery, and is evocative rather than literal to the extent that its meaning is whatever it imparts to the listener. But the religious imagery is definitely there, and exists in curious contrast to the atheistic vision of *128* 'The Seventh Seal'.

132. Boy Child (S. Engel)
Original release: *Scott 4* 1969 LP

The stronger of the two 'baroque' pieces on *Scott 4*, 'Boy Child' is often singled out for high praise. And whilst there are arguably other songs more deserving of the title of Scott Walker's best,[28] there is no denying the haunting beauty of its melody and arrangement or the poetry of Scott's lyric. In a foretaste of his post-1978 world, the lyric is stripped to its essence, no longer the stuff of literal narrative. Once again, the meaning of the song is whatever the listener gets from it, but various images and ideas are evoked. There is the notion that love can make the man a child again, as in *115* 'Copenhagen' and *112* 'Joanna'; the inner child in us all, that needs to be somehow kept alive in order for us not to lose our way in the world; the past as something that is perhaps best passed ('mirrors dark and blessed with cracks') and at the same time made romantic with its 'forgotten courtyards'; the ties of blood that bind a child to its parent or the ties of love that bind lovers; the vision of the ideal woman, perhaps forever unattainable, 'on the edge of dawn', who will give to one's life and make it whole. But everything is abstract and ambiguous. To take but one line as an example: 'if you stay one, you'll stay free.' Does this mean that if two lovers stay as one then they can be free? Or does it mean that the man and his inner child can be as one, if he can balance the adult and child in himself? Curiously, the last thing we needed was for Scott to break his customary silence and tell us – if indeed he could have. The ambiguity of 'Boy Child' is what makes the song compelling, and its genius lies in its ability to evoke so much, all of the above notions and more.

133. Hero of the War (S. Engel)
Original release: *Scott 4* 1969 LP

It is almost too easy today to look back on the 1960s through rose-tinted glasses, and overlook the truly horrible global politics of the time. In the stand-off played with the stakes of global destruction that was the Cold War, America convinced herself it was a good idea to kill the population of South East Asia in ever increasing numbers, whilst sending her own young men off to die in Vietnam. Russia, meanwhile, convinced herself it was a good idea to answer a new political liberalism in Czechoslovakia by sending in the tanks. In his own idiosyncratic way, and with the two most overtly political songs he ever recorded,[29] Scott addresses both sides of the Cold War on 'Hero of the War' and *134* 'The Old Man's Back Again'. The former does not mention Vietnam, but it must have been in Scott's mind, and in the mind of anybody listening even half-attentively to *Scott 4* when it was released. The hero of the song is no real hero at all – his heroism is empty and driven by a meaningless cause, as the last verse attests. But 'Hero of the War' is not mere sloganeering. Instead, it's a portrait of the ruined lives of the 'hero' and his mother, and of the fact that it's easier on the public conscience for their war heroes to come home either dead or able-bodied rather than disabled and unable to care for themselves.[30] With an up-tempo song whose cheery almost pop feel is as ironic as the song's title, Scott's lyric tells of the girl next door who has no interest in a crippled hero ('once you couldn't keep that whore from hanging round'), and of how pathetic medals and glory seem in the face of the true horror of war.

134. The Old Man's Back Again (S. Engel)
Original release: *Scott 4* 1969 LP

Driven along by a superb, almost funky bass-line comes the brilliant 'The Old Man's Back Again', Scott's comment on the 1968 Soviet invasion of Czechoslovakia. Given the subtitle ('Dedicated to the Neo-Stalinist Regime'), it is clear that the old man of the song's title is Joseph Stalin, the Russian dictator with a penchant for mass murder to rival Adolf Hitler's – who may have died in 1953, but whose policies of oppression returned with a vengeance in 1968. The so-called Prague Spring of '68 found the then Communist Czechoslovakia in the process of reform. With popular support, the Czech government relaxed censorship and made moves towards democracy and greater political freedom. Ultimately, the response of the Soviet Union was to send in troops *en masse*, with an estimated 5,000 tanks to occupy Czechoslovakia. The vision, the dream was 'crushed . . . to the ground, just like a beast', and Stalinism was back again. However, as with *133* 'Hero of the War', Scott's political comment is not sloganeering but humanitarian. The Russian poet Voznesensky (the 'Andrei V.' in the lyric) is said to be crying. And in the song's final verse is the human face of the invaders: the Russian soldier, who is pained by the role he is forced to play, and as much a victim of history and insane global politics as the people he is forced to oppress.

135. Duchess (S. Engel)
Original release: *Scott 4* 1969 LP

A song incomprehensibly passed over for inclusion on the two attempts to compile the essential Scott Walker collection. 'Duchess' is not featured on either the *Boy Child* compilation or the *Five Easy Pieces* box set (although its lyric is included in the book of selected lyrics *Sundog*). A track arguably as stunning as any Scott has recorded, it's perhaps only prejudice that keeps it from getting the recognition it deserves. Is 'Duchess' too country, too pop, too straightforward to be considered among Scott Walker's best work? As if it mattered anyway. The track opens with a mournful piece of slide guitar, but that's about all it has in common with country music. Unlike some of Scott's more delicate miniatures, the track has drums, but this hardly makes it an ordinary pop song. On the face of it, it's a love song to a presumably older woman who still has a 'look of lost' and 'a young girl's face'. But it's an oddly uncomplimentary love song. Is there a woman alive who wants to be told she has 'Rembrandt swells'[31] and an 'old girl's grace'? Does the duchess of the song really exist, or is she the unattainable ideal who, like the lady of *132* 'Boy Child', gives but does not take away? This 'Duchess' lights candles for and puts all the love back in the singer, so much so that he feels like a thief. Scott ends the lyric with, 'I'm lying, she's crying.' So is it she who needs comfort from the singer? And isn't that the way a real relationship needs to work, with each giving to each other? Is the duchess in some sense many women, or even all women? She is painted as both young and old in the lyric, saying yes and saying no,[32] and with different names that she sheds 'with the seasons'. As with 'Boy Child', the meaning of the song is whatever the listener takes from it. Its ambiguity is, along with its beauty, what makes the track so compelling. If it makes sense to talk of highlights on *Scott 4*, then 'Duchess' is one of them.

136. Get Behind Me (S. Engel)
Original release: *Scott 4* 1969 LP

In contrast to the consistently classical feel of *Scott 3*, *Scott 4* does pay more than a passing nod to contemporary music. On *Scott 3*, Scott had used Wally Stott as the arranger of choice. On *Scott 4* only two tracks are arranged by Stott (*129* and *132*); four are arranged by Peter Knight (*128*, *131*, *133* and *134*), and the remaining four are arranged by a man who had not previously received an arrangement credit on a Scott Walker record, Keith Roberts.[33] The contemporary influences are never more present than they are on the Roberts-arranged tracks. Whilst they don't turn the songs in question into anything that might be called country music, both *135* 'Duchess' and *137* 'Rhymes of Goodbye' make use of steel guitars. The country sound was big news in 1969, with Gram Parsons, the Byrds and, with his *Nashville Skyline* LP, Bob Dylan spearheading a genre that was soon labelled 'country rock'. Even Britishers the Rolling Stones did country music pastiches.[34] 'Get Behind Me', however, goes further in its concession to contemporary sounds. After a lovely acoustic guitar figure introduces the first verse, we meet distorted electric guitar and a mass of female backing singers on the chorus. The ubiquity of the lead guitar in late Sixties pop/rock music hardly needs pointing out, but it's worth mentioning that the big female backing singer sound was very much 'in' in 1968/69, having been used to memorable effect on Joe Cocker's hit version of 'With a Little Help from My Friends' and the Rolling Stones' 'Salt of the

Earth'. Scott's song has a strong chorus which makes literal sense, even if it's not spelled out what exactly the singer is putting behind him. The verses are fairly impenetrable, but there are hints that maybe the singer is addressing the darkest thoughts in his mind, or possibly the vision of a woman, maybe even the ideal woman? Some words even hint at a straightforwardly religious answer, evoking the biblical quotation, 'Get thee behind me Satan.' Scott was hardly alone in 1969 in writing poetic rather than literal lyrics. True, 'Sugar Sugar' by the Archies, which was a huge hit, was pretty literal, but 'Windmills of Your Mind'[35] or the Beatles' 'Come Together' made little or no literal sense at all. In a parallel universe not too different to ours, 'Get Behind Me' could have been a hit single. As it is, it remains a unique and rather wonderful track on *Scott 4*.

137. Rhymes of Goodbye (S. Engel)
Original release: *Scott 4* 1969 LP

Scott 4 ends fittingly on a goodbye note, with the gorgeously country-tinged 'Rhymes of Goodbye'. The pedal steel guitar at the start hints at a melancholy closedown, but it's so much more than that. An uncomplicated song, its lyric is poetic but far from inaccessible. The notion of the 'night children' who fly is particularly evocative, evoking both a dreamlike Peter Pan world of innocence and the world of young socialites flitting through the city's nightlife, from one hedonistic distraction to another. However, amongst the imagery can be found a clear declaration of personal freedom, hope and passion, delivered not with arrogance but with humility. (The singer builds his figurative 'empire' from 'nakedness' and 'makeshift designs'.) But what makes it ultimately so touching is that it is a love song, as well as a declaration of the singer's belief in himself. The song's most poignant moment is the declaration of love in the lines, 'I'm seeking a star . . . I turn and it's gone, you smile and it's born.' 'Rhymes of Goodbye' makes for a wonderful end to an LP that, like *Scott 3*, truly does not have one bad track on it.

Arguably the artistic equal of *Scott 3*, and many would say its superior, *Scott 4* did not sell well and failed to chart at all. With its release, Scott Walker, who had had two Top Ten hit albums, one hit single and his own BBC TV series during 1969, effectively disappeared from the public consciousness. Why? To say that it was due to the album's content, which is anyway more musically accessible than *Scott 3*, is not very convincing. In truth, the commercial failure of *Scott 4* was undoubtedly a combination of the following factors. Firstly, there was Scott's frankly silly decision to release *Scott 4* under his real name of (Noel) Scott Engel, rather than Scott Walker[36] – having an audience for these songs was a hundred times more important than the name on the record. Secondly, there was the fact that *Scott 4* was the third album of new Scott Walker material to be released in the same year – even the Beatles, who by anybody's standards were prolific, never released more than two new LPs during one year. Thirdly, by the time of *Scott 4*'s release Scott found himself without a manager, having dispensed with the services of the commercially-minded Maurice King earlier in the year. Fourthly, the record company didn't back the record very strongly. Fifthly, Scott was by now widely perceived as behind the times – fashion mattered in the Sixties, in a way that it doesn't today (at least not in the same unified manner). Whilst Scott had managed to ride out the flower-power of 1967 and the back-to-basics rock of 1968, he couldn't continue to let fashion pass him by and retain his popularity in the face of late 1969's post-Woodstock hairy hippieness. To use a further Beatles comparison, Scott's image hardly changed at all between 1967 and 1969 (compare his hairstyle on the front of *Images* with the *Scott 4* cover and it's virtually the same), whereas the Beatles clearly had a different image for each year (compare their 1967 'shortish hair with optional moustache ' look to 1969's 'very long hair with optional full beard' look). Finally, Scott's recorded output had long had a split personality – on the one hand, there was the singer (one hesitates to say crooner) of middle-of-the-road ballads that could offend nobody, and on the other hand, there was the Jacques Brel-loving existentialist-artist who sang about whores and bordellos. Thus one could say we have the Scott of *112* 'Joanna' versus the Scott of *99* 'Jackie', or the Scott of *Scott 3* versus the Scott of *Scott Walker Sings Songs from His TV Series*. To the Walker fan today, the diversity of his records doesn't matter a bit – we can enjoy both *127* 'The Lights of Cincinnati' and *128* 'The Seventh Seal' without feeling the slightest bit schizophrenic. But let's say you're a potential buyer in 1969, you're an older fan who prefers the nice songs and

Rare promo pic of 'Scott Engel' of the Walker Brothers. When Scott reverted to his real name for Scott 4, it may have undermined sales.

enjoyed Scott's TV series. Do you go out of your way to buy *Scott 4*? (It's badly marketed, don't forget.) Well you probably don't, because you've only just bought the *TV Series* LP. Then let's say you're a younger fan who is interested in what's happening at the cutting edge of music. Do you go out of your way to buy *Scott 4*? You probably don't, because Scott Walker's got unfashionably short hair and he's somebody your mum and dad like watching on the telly, so you go out and buy something by Iron Butterfly or Jethro Tull instead. Doubtless we are painting caricatures here, but something like it happened to seal the tragic commercial fate of *Scott 4*.

'Til the Band Comes In 1970 LP

138. Prologue (Scott Walker/Ady Semel)
Original release: *'Til the Band Comes In* 1970 LP

'Til the Band Comes *In – an
album it wouldn't be unfitting to
think of as* Scott 5.

Scott had one more artistic shot left to fire before his premature retirement from songwriting – *'Til the Band Comes In*, released in December 1970. Like *Scott 3* and *Scott 4*, it contains ten Scott Walker compositions of high quality, yet for some reason it seems to be regarded as a much poorer cousin to *Scott 1- 4*. That view is unfair, and it wouldn't be unfitting to think of *'Til the Band Comes In* as *Scott 5*. Like the *Scott* LPs, it is produced by Johnny Franz and features arrangements by Wally Stott and Peter Knight, and, also like the *Scott* LPs, it is an essential item for the collection of any Scott Walker fan today (even if it's been harder to obtain at times than *Scott 1-4*[37]).

Scott's compositions on *'Til the Band Comes In* all feature a co-writing credit for his new manager, Ady Semel. It's unclear exactly what Semel's contributions to the songs were, but the sleeve notes to the BGO Records CD of the album tell us Scott had already written the tunes and most of the lyrics before working on them with Semel, and that part of the latter's contribution was to strike out words likely to 'offend old ladies'.[38] There were no lyrics at all on the opening track – instead, 'Prologue' has the distinction of being the only instrumental Scott Walker track from this era, and it brilliantly sets the scene for the cycle of songs to follow. It opens with the sound of a dripping tap and then a mournful cello,[39] and as the orchestration builds, more sounds are heard – doors closing, children's voices. Are these the sounds of everyday life or something more sinister? An adult voice can also be heard in there, shouting, 'No.'

139. Little Things (That Keep Us Together) (Scott Walker/Ady Semel)
Original release: *'Til the Band Comes In* 1970 LP

Without waiting for *138* 'Prologue' to end, 'Little Things (That Keep Us Together)' comes in with an all-guns-blazing Wally Stott arrangement, as Scott details a seemingly endless list of the horrendous things that human beings (by accident or design) are capable of doing to themselves and each other – road accident fatalities, the Vietnam war, starving children, suicide and plane crashes. And how do these little things keep us together? That is left for the listener to decide, but perhaps the song is telling us a truth that we probably don't want to hear – that we all take a morbid interest in the tragedies of others, and derive some sort of comfort from the fact that it has not happened to us. All this is hardly the stuff of hit records, but this track is truly brilliant, curiously life affirming, and well deserving of the inclusion it was given on the *Boy Child* and *Five Easy Pieces* compilations.

140. Joe (Scott Walker/Ady Semel)
Original release: *'Til the Band Comes In* 1970 LP

According to the sleeve notes to the BGO CD release of *'Til the Band Comes In*, Scott envisaged a song cycle on the album about the lives of 'an assortment of characters dwelling in a noisy seedy apartment block'. The first of these specific characters is old age pensioner Joe, who, the lyric makes clear, has already died ('a postcard from Sun City was found lying by your side . . . they say towards the end you hardly left your shabby room'). The last days of Joe's life are miserable: noise from the neighbours, abandonment by friends and acquaintances living and dead, loneliness and squalor. There is some comfort in the lyric perhaps, in that it implies Joe achieved some understanding before dying, but not much comfort. Despite the song's loungey, piano-led arrangement, this is bleak stuff.

141. Thanks for Chicago Mr. James (Scott Walker/Ady Semel)
Original release: *'Til the Band Comes In* 1970 LP

One of those Scott Walker tracks that is so wonderfully stirring, it can fill the listener with emotion even before he starts singing with 'that voice'. According to Ady Semel's original sleeve note to *'Til the Band Comes In*, the central character of 'Thanks for Chicago Mr. James' is a 'a kept cowboy', who is presumably composing his thank you and farewell note to his keeper. Given that he's thanking Mister, rather than Miss or Mrs. James, the subject of the song, as with *117* 'Big Louise', is homosexuality.[40] But whereas Big Louise's 'secret' could not be detected from the lyric sheet alone, because the natural assumption would be that she is a woman (and this is not contradicted by the lyric), Mr. James and the kept cowboy's relationship is more apparent.[41] As with 'Big Louise', the portrait painted is neither judgmental nor clichéd, but human. The homosexual relationship is treated as a simple matter of fact. More important are the singer's

97

reflections on what Mr. James has given him and why, at the same time, he feels he must leave him. The song is simply wonderful, and its glorious arrangement is the aural equivalent of the sun breaking through the clouds (especially following *140* 'Joe'). Another track that could have been a hit single, in a parallel universe not too different from ours at all.

142. Long About Now (Sung by Esther Ofarim) (Scott Walker / Ady Semel)
Original release: *'Til the Band Comes In* 1970 LP

The next character, according to Ady Semel's original sleeve note, is 'a resigned girl lover'. Surprisingly, there is a girl singing the song, one Esther Ofarim. Before becoming Scott's new manager, Semel's most famous clients had been the Israeli husband and wife singing duo Esther and Abi Ofarim, best remembered for their 1968 UK Number One hit 'Cinderella Rockefella' (a novelty number which those members of the British public who remember it probably still haven't forgiven them for). In 1970, Esther and Abi divorced and Esther continued singing as a solo artist under Semel's management. And it must be said, her take on Scott's 'Long About Now' is very nice indeed, in a Barbra Streisand-type way. The song is a lovely ballad, its theme of waiting for one's lover to return home reminiscent of Scott's much earlier song, *42* 'Archangel'. Musically the song has echoes of both *119* 'Butterfly' and *129* 'On Your Own Again', and enough 'Scott-isms'[42] for the listener to be in no doubt about who wrote it.

143. Time Operator (Scott Walker / Ady Semel)
Original release: *'Til the Band Comes In* 1970 LP

This track is notable on several counts. The jazzily laid-back arrangement and the languid, almost gravelly vocal are hardly typical Scott Walker fare. The use of a sound effect – the voice of the British speaking clock – to bookend the track is similarly atypical. But what is most remarkable about it is how (here and on the following track, *144* 'Jean the Machine') Scott actually injects a little humour into the proceedings. The apartment block character of 'Time Operator' is 'a telephone crank' who, having had his water and his electricity, but not his telephone, cut off, attempts to chat up the time operator in the middle of the night with possibly the worst (and most hilarious) line of all time: 'And I wouldn't care if you're ugly, 'cos here with the lights out I couldn't see, you just picture Paul Newman and girl, he looks a lot like me.'

144. Jean the Machine (Scott Walker / Ady Semel)
Original release: *'Til the Band Comes In* 1970 LP

This is the tale of a Hungarian singer who couldn't make it, and so turned to being a stripper: 'she made her way from Hungary, a refugee with a voice like Callas, but somehow she couldn't get on, so she took it all off at the local palace.' Unfortunately, as the song's narrator relates, Jean's paranoid landlady has evicted her because she's convinced the girl's a communist spy, and has the absurd idea that Jean's act is a ruse to pass on secret codes. 'Jean come back,' repeats the song's chorus, and adds a final reminder to 'bring the microfilm'! The music, arranged, as with all the Walker/Semel tracks, by Wally Stott,[43] is terrifically striptease-like. And the burlesque feel is completed by applause and a spoken 'thank you' at the end of the song. An oddly amusing track.

145. Cowbells Shakin' (Scott Walker/Ady Semel)
Original release: *'Til the Band Comes In* 1970 LP

The last in the list of specific apartment block characters is the 'immigrant waiter' of 'Cowbells Shakin'', a migrant from an unspecified village who, try as he might, can't make it in the city. *Scott 3* and *Scott 4* both featured some short songs, but with 'Cowbells Shakin'' brevity is taken to an extreme, the song being over in an all-too-quick one minute and six seconds. In a style that might be seen as a sequel to *121* '30 Century Man', this time with a more down-to-earth subject, Scott is accompanied by just a strummed acoustic guitar playing three chords (A, E and D, if you're interested). A welcome if slight track that ends side one of the original vinyl edition of *'Til the Band Comes In*.

146. 'Til the Band Comes In (Scott Walker/Ady Semel)
Original release: *'Til the Band Comes In* 1970 LP

After the cast of specific characters, it's back to classic Scott Walker in the shape of the album's title track. Taken at face value, the song's lyric is simply about the singer leaving his lover with a promise to return one better day. But in Scott and Wally Stott's hands this becomes absolutely magnificent stuff. As earlier songs such as *42* 'Archangel' or *130* 'The World's Strongest Man' prove, Scott did not need particularly profound subject matter in order to deliver the poetic or musical goods. Lines like 'Keep your friends with their windows so high. / Keep your city with children that shine through its eye,' are so evocative you can almost feel the city that the singer is leaving. The melodies to both the verses and the song's middle eight ('the times we sat and sang of all the hidden things we knew . . .') are absolutely sublime, and the chorus is stirring stuff indeed. It is also perhaps possible to detect an autobiographical element. With the commercial flop of *Scott 4* a recent memory, Scott sings that he's 'here on the outskirts of life' and, somewhat self-deprecatingly, 'still alive with my subhuman sound to the ground.'

147. The War Is Over (Epilogue)[44] (Scott Walker/Ady Semel)
Original release: *'Til the Band Comes In* 1970 LP

The final song in the Walker/Semel song cycle is, by way of contrast, a subdued closedown – a gentle epilogue unlike the stirring prologue that began the album. What this specific war is, is left for the listener to decide – it is not the Vietnam War, which continued well into the 1970s. Perhaps the war is just the drama of daily life in the apartment block and the stream of bad news coming from outside, via radio and TV. In which case, the war being 'over' is just a respite at the end of the day, when, for a short time, everything is still and silent 'as after the rain'. (British TV and radio used to close down by midnight in 1970.[45]) Or maybe the end of the war is just a memory of the old lady in the song, who remembers the street celebrations at the end of the Second World War and their promise of a better life that hasn't come true. It's possible to speculate for ages, but the genius of 'The War Is Over' is that, with so few specific narrative details, the song manages to make you feel an empathy with its characters every time. It is a truly great and beautiful track. But with this song, apart from one B-side released the following year, Scott Walker's career as a songwriter was over until four songs appeared on *Nite Flights* in 1978. The tragedy of this hardly needs pointing out. Scott's songs on *'Til the Band Comes In* aren't perhaps as consistently outstanding as those on *Scott 3* or *Scott 4*, but the highpoints – *138/9* 'Prologue/Little Things (That Keep Us Together)', *141* 'Thanks for Chicago Mr. James', *146* ''Til the Band Comes In' and 'The War Is Over' – are a match for almost anything on the *Scott* LPs. *'Til the Band Comes In* shows that Scott was in no way losing his muse. In fact, his songwriting was moving in some interesting directions that, as fate would have it, would remain further unexplored. When Scott Walker the songwriter returned in 1978, it was with an entirely different agenda.

148. Stormy (Buie/Cobb)
Original release: *'Til the Band Comes In* 1970 LP

The remaining five tracks on *'Til the Band Comes In* are covers. It is undoubtedly their inclusion that makes some people think of it as a much poorer relation to the *Scott* LPs, but that view is unfair. There is nothing substandard about either Scott's singing or Peter Knight's arrangements on these tracks. Whilst Wally Stott can be rightly considered the most significant of Scott's arrangers, this shouldn't be at the expense of Knight (or Reg Guest or Keith Roberts). It is to be remembered that Knight was responsible for the arrangements on such classic moments as *105* 'The Girls from the Streets', *128* 'The Seventh Seal' and *134* 'The Old Man's Back Again'. Also, lest countless lazy-minded reviewers of the album be believed, the five songs covered on *'Til the Band Comes In* were fresh, not 'old standards' in 1970. *149* 'The Hills of Yesterday', *150* 'Reuben James' and *151* 'What Are You Doing the Rest of Your Life?' are all songs whose composition dates from 1969. 'Stormy' dates from late 1968. The LP's detractors may think better of *'Til the Band Comes In* as a short ten-song LP[46] composed by Scott Walker, with five bonus tracks added. But, with perhaps one exception, there's no reason to be disappointed with the five tracks that appear at the end.

'Stormy' was a million-selling American hit for the Classics IV in 1968/1969, but did absolutely nothing in the UK charts. Scott's version is, frankly, a vast improvement on the original. Wisely dispensing with the original's weedy saxophone solo, and with Scott's baritone adding a darker edge to the song, Knight turns in an arrangement that is flintier and funkier. The result is a Scott Walker track it's possible to dance to. The reader might like to try it.

149. The Hills of Yesterday (Webster/Mancini)
Original release: *'Til the Band Comes In* 1970 LP

Like *107* 'Wait Until Dark' from *Scott 2*, 'The Hills of Yesterday' is a Henry Mancini film song – this time with words by Hollywood lyricist Paul Francis Webster, from a 1970 film starring Sean Connery and Richard Harris, *The Molly Maguires*. It's a fine ballad, much more poignant than 'Wait Until Dark', lovingly arranged by Peter Knight and faultlessly sung by Scott.

150. Reuben James (Etris/Harvey)
Original release: *'Til the Band Comes In* 1970 LP

The least convincing moment on *'Til the Band Comes In*, perhaps chosen because, like *148* 'Stormy', it had been a US hit without troubling the UK charts at all. 'Reuben James' was written in 1969 by Alex Harvey and Barry Etris, who apparently pitched their song to Kenny Rogers by performing it outside his dressing room door for days until the country music star finally took an interest. It became a Top Thirty US hit for Kenny Rogers and the First Edition later that same year. Unfortunately, whilst the song may have suited Rogers' unashamedly cornball mainstream country style, it does not suit Scott Walker at all. It's not the strongest song in the world, and, despite the social conscience of its friendship-in-the-face-of-racism lyric, its straight-ahead country jollity hardly fits in with the rest of the album – a problem exacerbated by a particularly bad piece of sequencing that sees 'Reuben James' bookended by two orchestrally arranged ballads.

151. What Are You Doing the Rest of Your Life?
(Bergman/Bergman/Legrand)
Original release: *'Til the Band Comes In* 1970 LP

'What Are You Doing the Rest of Your Life?' was written by French songwriter Michel Legrand, with his collaborators Alan and Marilyn Bergman, for the 1969 film The Happy Ending. And whilst the title might sound like a corny chat-up line, the song is really quite superb. It must have sounded like a timeless standard from the moment it was written. It's been recorded over the years by all the usual suspects, such as Frank Sinatra, Jack Jones, Barbra Streisand and Shirley Bassey. Scott's version of this deeply romantic ballad must rank as one of the song's finest recordings.

152. It's Over (Rodgers)
Original release: *'Til the Band Comes In* 1970 LP

The most wonderful of the non-original tracks on *'Til the Band Comes In*, which some lazy or ill-informed reviewers have described as a cover of the Roy Orbison song.[47] It is not. The Orbison song of the same name is entirely different, its authorship credited to Orbison and Dees. This 'It's Over' was written by

American pop-folk singer Jimmie Rodgers, who recorded and had a minor Top 40 US hit with the song in the summer of 1966. What makes Scott's version so successful is that it takes Rodgers' sweet little song and turns it into a glorious epic. The original is performed with just an acoustic guitar backing and a vocal that is whimsical in comparison to Scott's. Peter Knight's arrangement takes Rodgers' original acoustic guitar figure as its opening, but builds on it to an orchestral crescendo as Scott adds the celebrated voice of heartbreak with dignity. Elvis Presley later recorded the song in 1973, but Scott's version is easily the more convincing.

So, are the five songs that end *'Til the Band Comes In* really the disappointing embarrassment that Messrs. Cocker and Walker would have one believe?[48] It's hard to see them that way, given that they contain two covers that transcend the originals (*148* 'Stormy' and 'It's Over') and two ballads that are stronger than some of the middle-of-the-road tracks on *Scott* and *Scott 2*. Only Scott's take on Kenny Rogers fails to convince. That track aside, *'Til the Band Comes In* is a record of obvious quality, including tracks which could have been hit singles (*141* 'Thanks for Chicago Mr. James' or 'It's Over') if Philips had bothered to release any singles from the album. Unfortunately, it joined *Scott 4* in selling hardly any copies and failing to chart at all. And with that Scott Walker retired from his songwriting career, and the 'God-like genius' era was over.

---

1. The three UK singles were *99* 'Jackie', released in 1967, *112* 'Joanna', 1968, and *127* 'The Lights of Cincinnati', 1969. *113* 'The Rope and the Colt' was a French only release.

2. For the CD reissue the album cover has been reproduced in sepia, for reasons best known to the designers.

3. As Mort Shuman translated Brel's use of the French word 'vérole'. Alternative translations might be 'pox' or 'syphilis sore', but the point remains the same.

4. See sleeve notes by Richard Jay-Alexander to the CD reissue of the *Jacques Brel Is Alive and Well and Living in Paris* soundtrack album. More recent comments have been made to the effect that Shuman abused that trust by changing the meaning of Brel's words too much. But this seems both revisionist and unfair. It is true that Shuman rewrote Brel's *'Les Flamandes'* ('The Flemish Women') with a completely different meaning as 'Marathon', but in general his translations, and in particular those that Scott recorded, are both sympathetic and brilliant. They are certainly no whitewash, in the way that all the cynicism, black humour and frankness of Brel's *'Le moribond'* ('The Dying Man') was written out of it when it was translated by Rod McKuen into 'Seasons in the Sun'.

5. On the same edition of *The Dusty Springfield Show* Scott also performed *91* 'When Joanna Loved Me', footage of which also survives and can, at the time of writing, be found on YouTube.

6. Scott's introduction to the song when performed on his TV show, broadcast 30 December 1968.
7. *A Deep Shade of Blue*, pp.49-50.
8. Marc Almond, 1990 sleeve note to the *Boy Child* compilation CD.
9. Another possibly Brel-influenced aspect, as the Shuman-translated Brel song 'I Loved' ends with the line, 'You see, I've forgotten your name,' which of course the singer doesn't really mean.
10. Brel's original French lyric has '*Beau, beau, beau et con a la fois*,' a literal translation of which would be 'Beautiful, beautiful, beautiful and an idiot at the same time.'
11. The character in question is Tarrou, whose description of having 'the plague' in this metaphorical sense can be found in Part Four, Chapter Six of Albert Camus' *The Plague*.
12. 'Best of Both Worlds' was later released as a 1968 American single by Lulu, after it originally appeared on her 1967 British LP *Love Loves to Love Lulu* (and, incidentally, after the release of *Scott 2*).
13. The radio phone-in clip can be heard in the 1995 BBC2 *Late Show* segment on Scott Walker.
14. In particular the line, 'Everybody knows whenever rain appears, it's really angels' tears.'
15. The Brel song 'Madeleine' was translated by Mort Shuman and included in *Jacques Brel Is Alive and Well and Living in Paris*.
16. Scott Walker, as quoted by Jonathan King in his original sleeve note to *Scott 2*.
17. *Mr and Mrs Music* was also the title of a Tony Hatch and Jackie Trent LP, as well as a TV special broadcast in 1969 on which Scott Walker appeared.
18. The article 'The Fugitive Kind' was written by Joe Jackson ostensibly to be included with the *Five Easy Pieces* box set. It was not used, but the article was subsequently published on the Internet.
19. This is pretty much the presentation of 'Joanna' in *A Deep Shade of Blue* passim.
20. The film, a French spaghetti western (if that's not a contradiction in terms), is also known by the alternative titles *The Rope and the Colt* and *Cemetery without Crosses*.
21. Angela Morley's website can be found at www.angelamorley.com
22. And for 1969, the subject matter certainly was novel. The Kinks' famous and considerably less serious song about a transvestite, 'Lola', wasn't released until 1970.
23. The French military leader and statesman lived to be almost 80, but died on 9 November 1970.
24. Not of course necessarily a bad thing, but the way in which advertisers use the notion of 'health' to sell everything from breakfast cereal to potato crisps has become tiresome.
25. Whilst the track listing for the *Five Easy Pieces* box set is credited to 'Cally at Antar', it's believed that the man himself had both an influence on and approval of the selection.
26. Scott Walker quoted from 1976, *A Deep Shade of Blue* p.140.
27. Okay, it's unlikely, but although he has been less obvious about his appreciation than other famous Scott fans (Messrs. Hannon, Cope, Almond and Cocker, for example), Robbie Williams has mentioned Scott Walker as an influence on many occasions.
28. Perhaps *88* 'Montague Terrace (in Blue)', *94* 'Such a Small Love', *106* 'Plastic Palace People', *110* 'The Bridge', *114* 'It's Raining Today', *117* 'Big Louise' or the overlooked *135* 'Duchess' – or even *130* 'The World's Strongest Man' or the later 141 'Thanks for Chicago Mr James'.

29. There are of course songs that could be called 'political' that occur later in Scott's career, but the esoteric lyrics of, say, *235* 'The Electrician' or *265* 'Patriot' do not make for very overt political statements.

30. Cf. Oliver Stone's Oscar-winning film, *Born on the Fourth of July*.

31. Cf. the Rembrandt nudes *Danae* (1636) and *Bathsheba with King David's Letter* (1654).

32. Curiously, although they are both very 'Scott' songs, a lingering trace of Brel's influence can be found in both 'Boy Child' and 'Duchess'. 'Boy Child' has its 'city's thighs', reminiscent of Scott's Brel-inspired lyrics on *Scott 2*. 'Duchess' has 'it says no, it says yes', a phrase which is almost a direct lift from Mort Shuman's translation of Brel's 'Old Folks' (*'Les vieux'*), which has 'it says yes, it says no'.

33. A freelance arranger and composer, Keith Roberts' first hit as an arranger had been 'Race with the Devil' in 1968 by one-hit wonders Gun.

34. 'Dear Doctor' on the Stones' 1968 LP *Beggar's Banquet*, 'Country Honk' on their 1969 LP *Let It Bleed*.

35. A hit in the UK for Noel Harrison and in the US for Dusty Springfield, both in 1969.

36. The credit on the record label of *Scott 4* is to Scott Engel. However, a prominent credit on the LP's sleeve announces, 'All songs by Noel Scott Engel.' The word 'Walker' is conspicuous by its absence.

37. Quite possibly as a result of Scott's own insistence. The July 2000 issue of *MOJO* magazine cited him as having blocked a CD reissue of an augmented version of *'Til the Band Comes In*, along with reissues of *Scott Walker Sings Songs from His TV Series*, *The Moviegoer* and *Any Day Now*.

38. Unfortunately, publicising the fact that Ady Semel had removed anything offensive from his lyrics somewhat backfired on Scott, when the *NME* satirically headlined an article, 'Scott Walker: New Version Guaranteed Harmless to Old Ladies'!

39. What the cello actually plays is a slowed-down version of the melody to the chorus of *141* 'Thanks for Chicago Mr. James'.

40. Whether the cowboy and Mr. James have a consummated relationship is not specified, but it is clear that Mr. James wants more in return from the cowboy than 'the smile he wore'.

41. Obviously none of this should be taken to be suggest that Louise is a homosexual because he/she is a transvestite. Clearly Louise could be one without being the other. But that she is both is implied by the reference to the 'sad young man' who has gone away.

42. For example, 'ashes', 'rain', 'butterflies', and the idiosyncratic use of the words 'design' and 'steel'.

43. So says the record sleeve, but clearly the next track, *145* 'Cowbells Shakin'', is an exception, as it does not have an orchestral arrangement.

44. Curiously, 'The War Is Over' has two subtitles. It is listed as 'The War Is Over (Epilogue)' on the record label, but 'The War Is Over (Sleepers)' on the record sleeve.

45. Listeners to *'Til the Band Comes In* may wonder where the apartment block in which its characters live might be situated. The answer would seem to be somewhere in America. Where else would one find Cadillacs, sheriffs and cowboys? But the telephone crank of *143* 'Time Operator' listens to the British speaking clock. The obvious answer is that, as the apartment block is a fictitious concept, it doesn't have to exist anywhere.

46. To be precise, 26 minutes and six seconds long. But then *Scott 4* is only 32 and a half minutes long.

47. Reviews of *'Til the Band Comes In* that make this mistake can be found on the Internet.

48. The Pulp song 'Bad Cover Version' – written by Jarvis Cocker and the band and produced by Scott Walker – includes a list of disappointing letdowns. Among them we find the second side of *'Til the Band Comes In*. It's a little unkind really, probably reflecting Scott's own harsh opinion, especially since the other items in the list (including own-brand corn flakes and the *Planet of the Apes* TV series) are seriously bad. 'Bad Cover Version' can be found on Pulp's 2001 album *We Love Life*, which was produced by Scott.

part three

The Singer
Not the Song
1969 - 1974

Imagine for a minute that you have recorded an LP as good as *Scott 4*. And then you recorded another LP, as good as *'Til the Band Comes In*. Then you watched them both sell next to no copies and be derided by the critics, whilst at the same time records like Rolf Harris's 'Two Little Boys' climbed to the top of the UK charts (as it did at Christmas 1969). Do you carry on casting your pearls before swine? Put this way, Scott's decision to retire from songwriting at the beginning of the Seventies is quite understandable, regardless of how much it was down to personal choice and how much was bowing to record company pressure. But this does not mean that there are no good Scott Walker records from the 1970s. The Walkers reunion is a slightly different matter, but all of Scott's lost albums from the period between the Walker Brothers' split and their reformation have been unfairly maligned and are actually worth seeking out. Scott's talent was never just about being a singer of his own compositions – if he had never written a single song, then he still would still have been an astounding interpreter of other people's work. As Marc Almond put it in his sleeve notes to the 1990 *Boy Child* compilation: 'that powerful soaring voice, making delivery seem supremely effortless, and delivery is all – Scott Walker could sing "Three Blind Mice" and make it sound like the only song in the world.' If you love Scott Walker's voice, then you owe it to yourself to hear his lost albums: 1969's *Scott Walker Sings Songs from His TV Series*, 1972's *The Moviegoer*, *Any Day Now* and *Stretch* (both from 1973), and, with some reservations, 1974's *We Had It All*. No one in their right mind would claim these records to be the match of the *Scott* LPs, but that is simply too high a standard by which to judge whether a record is good or bad.

Unfortunately it is not possible to buy all the lost LPs on CD. *Stretch* and *We Had It All* have long been available on a single CD comprising both albums, but *Scott Walker Sings Songs from His TV Series*, *The Moviegoer* and *Any Day Now* have never been issued on CD, reissues having been blocked by the man himself. However, some tracks from these LPs do appear on various compilations (in particular the 2005 two-disc *Classics and Collectibles*). Notes on the current availability of the tracks on these three lost albums are included below. For those seeking the complete picture, vinyl copies of the original albums regularly come up for sale on Ebay, and it would be foolish to pretend that unofficial CD copies don't exist, or that the missing songs are not easily available to listen to on, or download from, the Internet (albeit unofficially).

Scott Walker Sings Songs from His TV Series 1969 LP

153. Will You Still Be Mine (Dennis/Adair)

Original release: *Scott Walker Sings Songs from His TV Series* 1969 LP
Not currently available commercially.

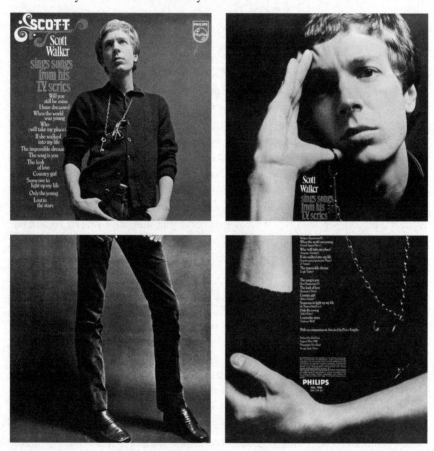

Scott Walker Sings Songs from His TV Series *was released in the summer of 1969, housed in a handsome gatefold sleeve.*

Scott Walker Sings Songs from His TV Series was released between *Scott 3* and *Scott 4*, but is dealt with here because it contains no Walker originals and is a lost LP to the extent that it's never been available on CD. Strange as it may sound today, in 1969 Scott did have his own BBC1 series. Back in 1968, the BBC had invited him to record a television special. Mindful of his reputation for disliking publicity and live performance and generally being 'difficult', they actually recorded enough material for two half-hour shows, supposing that they could make one composite show out of the recorded material.[1] As it happened, Scott exceeded their expectations and both shows were broadcast, the first on 16 August and the second on 30 December 1968. Satisfied, the BBC commissioned a series of six 25-minute programmes simply billed as *Scott Walker*, broadcast at 9.55pm on six consecutive Tuesday nights between 11 March and 15 April 1969.

The bad news for anybody who might like to see them is that no video copies are known to survive. The BBC simply didn't keep the original shows and no one had a video cassette recorder in their home in 1969.[2] All that is known to survive of the TV series is its audio soundtrack which, through homemade recordings by fans, can be heard in its entirety.[3]

The six TV shows that comprised Scott's TV series proper each followed a fairly set formula. After an instrumental burst of 'Joanna' as the show's theme tune and the announcer's words, 'Ladies and gentlemen, this is Scott Walker,' the show would typically run like this: an up-tempo opening number sung by Scott; another song by Scott; another by Scott, this time with the regular feature of an accompaniment by Johnny Franz at the piano; a performance from the show's first guest; another song from Scott; a song from the second guest; then a big number from Scott to finish. That's it – no jokes, no sketches, no big money prizes, no phone-in competitions, just (very nice) songs and one or two words of introduction between them. It's impossible to imagine any TV company commissioning a show like that today, but it would undoubtedly be fascinating to be able to see it.

The first thing to note about the album is that whilst it does indeed contain songs that Scott sang on his TV series, it isn't at all representative of the series as a whole. In addition to the kind of songs that fill the LP, Scott used his TV series to perform his own songs and to further spread the gospel of Jacques Brel. Over the six shows he performed a total of seven of his own songs (all from *Scott 3*) and a total of five Brel songs. Notable among the latter is the Shuman-translated 'Alone', which, despite Scott declaring it to be 'probably my most favourite song to sing,' has never been released on record. Had it been included on *Scott Walker Sings Songs from His TV Series* it would have changed the whole tone of the album.

As it was, no Brel or Scott Walker songs were included on the LP. Record companies back then weren't perhaps quite the big cynical marketing machines they are today who are more than happy to sell people the same thing twice, and so the *TV Series* LP offered all and only 'new' songs. The first of these is the song that Scott actually used to open the final TV show in the series, 'Will You Still Be Mine'. As an opening number, it's up-tempo and very enjoyable in a *108* 'The Girls and the Dogs'-type way.

Given that the song contains a lyrical reference to actress Julie Christie, then a sex symbol of the day, it's perhaps surprising that the song actually dates from

1940, before Ms. Christie was even born. So whilst the fantastic line, 'when moonlight on the Hudson's not romancy, and spring no longer turns a young man's fancy,' is part of the original lyric, the equally amusing, 'when Julie Christie doesn't make me tingle, and I can't sing in tune or make a single,' is a more recent addition. It's not known who added that line, but, being a 'list song', it has an interesting history of additions. Buddy Greco, performing the song in the Fifties, added lines like, 'when Orphan Annie drops her youth', 'when *Confidential* tells the truth', 'when my *paisans* don't sing "*O sole mio*"' and 'when Macy knows what Gimble buys'!

154. I Have Dreamed (Rodgers/Hammerstein II)
Original release: *Scott Walker Sings Songs from His TV Series* 1969 LP
Currently available: on *Classics and Collectibles* compilation

A truly lovely song from the 1951 Rodgers and Hammerstein musical *The King and I*, and it's a delight to hear Scott singing it. The song in the musical is performed as a duet, but Scott doesn't even need to sing the whole of Oscar Hammerstein's lyric for this track to be supremely romantic.

155. When the World Was Young (Gerard/Vannier/Mercer)
Original release: *Scott Walker Sings Songs from His TV Series* 1969 LP
Currently available: on *Classics and Collectibles* compilation

The production of *Scott Walker Sings Songs from His TV Series* is credited to Johnny Franz, who appeared on the show each week at the piano to accompany Scott singing a standard. One such performance was 'When the World Was Young', which Scott introduced with the words, 'Our song this evening was written by Johnny Mercer and Gerard Phillipe,[4] it's one of those songs that we wish we would have written.' In its original form it was called '*Le chevalier de Paris*' and was recorded by Edith Piaf in 1950. Scott performs the song with Mercer's English lyric. It's a beautiful song, its theme of the melancholy side to an apparently hedonistic man-about-town suiting him perfectly.

156. Who (Will Take My Place) (Aznavour/Kretzmer)
Original release: *Scott Walker Sings Songs from His TV Series* 1969 LP
Currently available: on *Classics and Collectibles* compilation

The French theme continues with Scott's take on Charles Aznavour's very nice but distinctly odd 'Who (Will Take My Place)'. Originally written and recorded by Aznavour in French as '*Qui?*', the song was given its English translation by South African lyricist Herbert Kretzmer – best known for writing the lyrics to the hugely successful musical *Les miserables*. 'Who (Will Take My Place)' concerns the singer's worries that when he dies, someone else will take his lover. There can't be many songs with that subject matter. Also recorded by Dusty Springfield at around the same time for her *Dusty Definitely* album, it's another of a number of songs recorded by both singers.

157. If She Walked into My Life (J. Herman)
Original release: *Scott Walker Sings Songs from His TV Series* 1969 LP
Currently available: on *Classics and Collectibles* compilation

Arguably the highlight of the *TV Series* LP, another song performed with Johnny Franz at the piano. It's from the 1966 Broadway musical *Mame*, where it's called 'If He Walked into My Life' and is performed as a duet between the lead character, Auntie Mame, and her nephew Patrick. Scott sings only the male half of the lyric, and, stripped of its setting in a musical and any of the mawkish sentimentality associated with that format, the song is allowed to shine, with Scott turning in a convincing vocal. Incidentally, the original LP sleeve and label credits this song to J. Norman – this should read J. Herman, as in Jerry Herman, the musical's composer.

158. The Impossible Dream (Leigh/Darion)
Original release: *Scott Walker Sings Songs from His TV Series* 1969 LP
Currently available: on *Classics and Collectibles* compilation

Scott introduced this song on his TV series with these words: 'This next song is from the show *Man of La Mancha*, it's sung by an insane idealist, Don Quixote, Cervantes' ageing knight who pursues the impossible dream that finally leads him to his death.' Ever the idealist himself (albeit not one insanely tilting at windmills), Scott's delivery of the song is magnificent. *Man of La Mancha* had opened on Broadway in 1965 and was still running there at the time of the *TV Series* LP's release. But perhaps more a source of inspiration to Scott was a French version of the show, *L'homme de la Mancha*, which had at the time recently opened in Paris – with French lyrics written by a certain Jacques Brel, who also starred in the show playing the role of Don Quixote.

159. The Song Is You (Kern/Hammerstein II)
Original release: *Scott Walker Sings Songs from His TV Series* 1969 LP
Not currently available commercially.

Side two of the LP once again opens with a song that Scott used as a show opener. In this case it's an up-tempo big band treatment of 'The Song Is You', from the 1934 Jerome Kern and Oscar Hammerstein II musical *Music in the Air*. Like other tracks on *Scott Walker Sings Songs from His TV Series*, it is a song that Frank Sinatra had previously recorded.[5]

160. The Look of Love (Bacharach/David)
Original release: *Scott Walker Sings Songs from His TV Series* 1969 LP
Currently available: *The Collection* compilation

Much as Scott Walker and Bacharach and David is usually a winning combination, this just pales in comparison to Dusty Springfield's version. Dusty recorded the definitive version of this song in 1967, and nobody among the countless artists who have covered it since, even Scott, really stands a chance.

161. Country Girl (Robert Farnon)

Original release: *Scott Walker Sings Songs from His TV Series* 1969 LP
Currently available: on *Classics and Collectibles* compilation

Those expecting to hear a cover of Neil Young's song of the same title might be disappointed by this, written by easy listening legend Robert Farnon. But Scott's version is really quite lovely, provided you find yourself in the right easy listening mood. A song previously recorded by Tony Bennett with some success.

162. Someone to Light up My Life (de Moraes/Jobim/Lees)

Original release: *Scott Walker Sings Songs from His TV Series* 1969 LP
Currently available: on *Classics and Collectibles* compilation

A tune by the Brazilian pioneer of bossa nova, Antonio Carlos Jobim, that was originally the Portuguese language song '*Se todos fossem iguais a você*', with lyrics by Vinicius de Moraes, before its English version by Canadian lyricist Gene Lees. It's a pleasure to hear Scott sing this song of lost love with such touching lines as, 'like a smile that I know will keep haunting me endlessly, sometimes in stars or the swift flight of sea birds, I catch a moment of you.'

163. Only the Young (Ahlert/Fisher)

Original release: *Scott Walker Sings Songs from His TV Series* 1969 LP
Not currently available commercially.

Another song performed with Johnny Franz at the piano, that today sounds as charmingly old-fashioned as its reference to the brass ring on the merry-go-round – on older merry-go-rounds, if you grabbed the just-out-of-reach brass ring you won a free ride. A song previously recorded by jazz singer Nancy Wilson,[6] and also by Tony Bennett.

164. Lost in the Stars (Anderson/Weill)

Original release: *Scott Walker Sings Songs from His TV Series* 1969 LP
Currently available: on *Classics and Collectibles* compilation

The *TV Series* LP ends with Kurt Weill and Maxwell Anderson's 'Lost in the Stars', from their 1949 musical of the same name. Whilst coming across as perhaps the corniest thing on the LP (Scott sings 'little stars' and there's a little musical tinkle from the orchestra), Anderson's lyric, with its God who has gone away and/or no longer cares for the world, has a surprising affinity with the theme of *128* 'The Seventh Seal'.[7]

Ultimately, how much you take the *TV Series* LP to your heart depends on your personal taste for the songs it contains, but there can be no doubting the quality of Scott's performances throughout. The notion that he was somehow forced into performing these songs against his will just doesn't ring true. When, for example, he says of *155* 'When the World Was Young', 'it's one of those songs that we wish we would have written,' he's either being a very good liar or he means it – money could safely be put on the latter. Never mind that it's not a terribly *outré* record, *Scott Walker Sings Songs from His TV Series* is far from being worthless. Within its genre it deserves to be considered as a great LP, with a number of tracks that are all too easy to love. Released by Philips in the summer of 1969, in a gatefold sleeve depicting a casually dressed Scott with a key and a pair of sunglasses[8] dangling around his neck, it rose to Number Seven in the British album chart. It would be the last charting Scott Walker LP until *Climate of Hunter* made it into the much lower reaches, some fifteen years later.

1971

165. I Still See You (Shaper/Legrand)
Original release: single A-side 1971
Currently available: on *Classics and Collectibles* compilation

Scott Walker's solitary record release of 1971 was the non-LP single 'I Still See You'. And a quite wonderful record it is. With music by Michel Legrand and words by Hal Shaper,[9] it was written to be the theme tune to the British film *The Go-Between*, starring Julie Christie and the late Alan Bates. Legend has it that Scott was uncooperative and extremely drunk on the day he recorded the song, but none of this shows in the finished record. The authors of *A Deep Shade of Blue*, in an account based on a telephone interview with the late Hal Shaper, who was present at the session, describe how Scott arrived drunk and then proceeded to drink two bottles of vodka.[10] Unless the bottles in question were miniatures, it suggests he consumed much more than a lethal dose of alcohol in one session. What seems more likely is that Scott, perhaps a little worse for drink, changed one line of Shaper's lyric and Shaper wasn't particularly happy about it. The line as Shaper wrote it ran: 'I see the fields so green and fair, the silent ghosts are everywhere'; and as Scott re-wrote it: 'I see the fields in still green air, the silent ghosts to dance their hair.' Shaper felt this change was 'psychedelically stupid', and it apparently embittered him until his dying day. But it really doesn't mar the record at all. The general listener probably wouldn't notice anything odd about the line, and to fans in the know it adds an interesting bit of additional 'Scott-ness' to the record. The song, arrangement and vocal are all superb, with Scott striking exactly the right note of wistful sadness. If the vocal really was recorded following the ingestion of a superhuman quantity of alcohol, we ought to be doubly impressed!

Alas the single was not a hit, but this says more about the vagaries of fashion in 1971 than it does about its obvious quality. As the Seventies got underway, glam rock replaced psychedelia as the style of the day in British pop culture. And whilst glam was a genre that would produce some great records as well as some not so great,[11] it was not a genre that Scott Walker could have any more affinity with than he did psychedelic hippiedom.

166. My Way Home (Engel/Semel)
Original release: single B-side released 1971
Most recently available: on *Five Easy Pieces* box set

The final Scott Walker composition released before his premature retirement from songwriting at the age of 28. 'My Way Home' is a hidden gem, a lovely, wistful song in which Scott and Ady Semel play it fairly straight with the lyrics, but still manage to evoke so much – sadness, hope, homecoming and reunion. The song's American setting undoubtedly helps ('watching Greyhounds roll through the giant dawn') – it's never a good idea to write a travelling song set in the UK, as the country just isn't big enough.

The Moviegoer 1972 LP

167. This Way Mary (Barry/Black)
Original release: *The Moviegoer* 1972 LP
Currently available: on *Classics and Collectibles* compilation

Front and back covers of the original Philips release of The Moviegoer. *The album was later reissued on a budget record label with a different sleeve design.*

If you read summaries of Scott Walker's career, you sometimes come across statements like 'he released a series of limp albums in the early Seventies'. There seems to be a received opinion that Scott's lost albums (*Scott Walker Sings Songs from His TV Series*, *The Moviegoer*, *Any Day Now*, *Stretch* and *We Had It All*) are pure rubbish. This is unfair in the extreme. Taking *The Moviegoer* as a case in point, for sure there are no original Walker compositions and the songs are all safe material, middle-of-the-road if you like. But there is nothing substandard about the arrangements or Scott's vocals, which are generally superb. If this is the sound of him not really trying (which it probably isn't), then it's still well worth hearing. So where does the conventional wisdom come from? Some speculation: reviews of *The Moviegoer* et al from the time of release seem to be so lost in the mists of time that, good or bad, their influence can be discounted. By the late Seventies and 1980s, critical appraisal of Scott's career was non-existent. Take for example a couple of reference books from that time. The *NME Book of Rock*, published in 1977, doesn't include an entry for Scott Walker[12] – clearly he wasn't thought important enough to merit one. The *Faber Companion to 20th Century Popular Music*, from 1990, only mentions him as a member of the Walker Brothers, and goes on to get the release dates of his solo albums wrong without proffering any critical opinion of them.[13] Critical appraisal of Scott Walker's career really only began in the early Nineties, with the re-release of the *Scott* LPs on CD. There was Stuart Maconie's terrific 'Great Scott' piece for *NME* in 1992, but that doesn't mention the lost albums, concentrating solely on the *Scott* LPs alone. So where does the damning opinion come from? Three factors present themselves: 1) Scott himself didn't rate them, calling them 'useless'.[14] But hey, let's not confuse 'God-like genius' with 'God'; the fact that Scott Walker himself didn't like them doesn't mean they're bad – he was always his own fiercest critic.[15] 2) The related fact that the lost albums are not available on CD encourages the notion that they are not worth hearing, preventing listeners from making up their own minds. 3) The authors of *A Deep Shade of Blue*'s comments on the lost albums are particularly dismissive. It's almost as if they decided it would make a better story if Scott had 'lost the plot' and released some terrible records, then listened to the records having already decided they must be bad. The book contains a series of particularly unkind remarks about just about everything Scott released from and including side two of *'Til the Band Comes In* up until *Nite Flights*.[16] For example, they say of *The Moviegoer*, 'The sleeve showed a Stetson-clad Scott looking suitably disinterested next to a large cinema ticket marked "rear stalls". In all honesty most people would not have wanted to be much closer to the action contained within,' going on to add that it is full of 'forgettable moments' with 'little to commend it'.[17] And that's mild in comparison to the scathing comments they make about *Any Day Now*. The notion that Scott Walker's lost LPs are worthless appears to born out of laziness or prejudice on the part of writers. The records deserve a fair hearing, despite the fact that *The Moviegoer*, *Any Day Now*, *Stretch* and *We Had It All* were all commercial failures on their release.

The Moviegoer comprises Scott's versions of songs taken from films. Most of the selections are from then very contemporary films (nine of the twelve selections from between 1970 and 1972). It's not all Hollywood either, with a number reflecting Scott's fondness for European films. The LP opens with 'This Way Mary', a John Barry composition from the 1971 British film Mary, Queen of Scots, with a lyric by Don Black – the co-writer of *101* 'Best of Both Worlds' and a number of James Bond theme songs. The authors of *A Deep Shade of Blue* described this track as 'awful'.[18] Presumably they were listening to a different record, as this is a lovely ballad arranged and sung beautifully.

168. Speak Softly Love (Rota/Kusik)[19]
Original release: *The Moviegoer* 1972 LP
Currently available: on *Classics and Collectibles* compilation

Probably the best known tune on *The Moviegoer* and the love theme from Francis Ford Coppola's 1972 gangster epic, *The Godfather*, a film rightly acknowledged as one of the greatest of all time. 'Speak Softly Love' appears only in instrumental form in the film, without Larry Kusik's lyric, and accompanies the scenes set in Sicily where Don-in-waiting Michael Corleone courts his young bride before, shortly after their marriage, she is killed by enemies of his family. With its lyric, 'Speak Softly Love' was also recorded in 1972 by Al Martino, who had appeared in the film, and by Andy Williams, who had an American Top 40 hit with the song. Effortlessly superior to that version, Scott's take on 'Speak Softly Love' is a gorgeously romantic highlight on the LP.

169. Glory Road (Diamond)
Original release: *The Moviegoer* 1972 LP
Most recently available: on *Five Easy Pieces* box set

A Neil Diamond song that featured on the soundtrack of the 1970 film *WUSA*, starring Paul Newman as an announcer at the eponymous radio station. A very good song, the narrator travels across America with all his 'worldlies' in a sack looking for the glory road he'll probably never find.

170. That Night (Schifrin/Gimbel)
Original release: *The Moviegoer* 1972 LP
Currently available: on *Classics and Collectibles* compilation

More traditional soundtrack fare than *169* 'Glory Road', the haunting ballad 'That Night' was composed by Lalo Schifrin – the Argentinean composer who wrote music for countless films, including classics like *Bullitt*, *Dirty Harry* and *Enter the Dragon* – with lyrics by Norman Gimbel, the man responsible for the English lyric to *56* 'I Will Wait for You'. It's from the somewhat daring (for its time) 1967 film *The Fox*, an adaptation of D. H. Lawrence's short novel of the same name concerning the plight of two female lovers. Another fine vocal by Scott on a track that isn't as immediate as others on the album, but one that the listener may find well worth revisiting.

171. The Summer Knows (Legrand/A. & M. Bergman)
Original release: *The Moviegoer* 1972 LP
Most recently available: on *Five Easy Pieces* box set

The first of two Legrand numbers on *The Moviegoer*. Scott was, of course, no stranger to the compositions of French songwriter Michel Legrand, having recorded *50* 'Once upon a Summertime', *56* 'I Will Wait for You', *151* 'What Are You Doing the Rest of Your Life?' and, just the previous year, *165* 'I Still See

You'. The song is from the 1971 film *Summer of '42*, and was deemed worthy of inclusion on the *Five Easy Pieces* box set compilation in 2003.

172. The Ballad of Sacco and Vanzetti (Baez/Morricone)
Original release: *The Moviegoer* 1972 LP
Most recently available: on *Five Easy Pieces* box set

Generally regarded as the best track on the album, 'The Ballad of Sacco and Vanzetti' is wonderful. The song was written by Ennio Morricone and Joan Baez for the 1971 Italian/French film *Sacco e Vanzetti*, about two anarchists sentenced to death more for their political beliefs than any proven crimes. 'Blessed are the persecuted,' sings Scott in a powerful performance, against an arrangement recalling the cinematic feel of *128* 'The Seventh Seal'. Comparisons with Baez's original version are not helpful, because the song as Scott sings it is a mere three-and-a-half-minute distillation of the seventeen-minute original. Spread over three parts, Baez's is a quite extraordinary piece of work, only the more accessible parts of which are recognisable on *The Moviegoer*'s version. Baez's version has a remarkable affinity with the much later Scott Walker/Ute Lemper track, *282* 'Lullaby (By-By-By)', in terms of its extraordinary length, its sectional approach with less melodic spoken-word passages, its discordant sounds, and a female vocal delivery more time-honoured than contemporary.

173. A Face in the Crowd (Bergman/Legrand)
Original release: *The Moviegoer* 1972 LP
Currently available: on *Classics and Collectibles* compilation

Side two of *The Moviegoer* opens with another Michel Legrand tune. 'A Face in the Crowd' is from the 1971 film *Le Mans*, starring Steve McQueen – the sound effect of a racing car can be heard at the start and end of the track. This is probably the least interesting of all the Legrand numbers recorded by Scott Walker or the Walker Brothers, but it's still of the highest quality.

174. Joe Hill (Grossman)
Original release: *The Moviegoer* 1972 LP
Not currently available commercially.

An extremely likeable song, 'Joe Hill' is a cheery little country-ish number about a ghost – 'says I but Joe you're ten years dead, I never died said he . . . the copper bosses killed you Joe, they shot you Joe says I, takes more than guns to kill a man says Joe, I did not die.' Like *172* 'The Ballad of Sacco and Vanzetti', this is also from a film about an execution carried out on political rather than criminal grounds, in this case that of Swedish-born early US union leader Joe Hill, as depicted in the obscure 1971 Swedish/American film *The Ballad of Joe Hill*. In another link with 'The Ballad of Sacco and Vanzetti', Joan Baez performed the song 'Joe Hill' at Woodstock.

175. Loss of Love (Mancini/Merrill)
Original release: *The Moviegoer* 1972 LP
Currently available: on *Classics and Collectibles* compilation

Henry Mancini was another film-music giant whose songs Scott had recorded before. *107* 'Wait Until Dark' from *Scott 2* and *149* 'The Hills of Yesterday' from *'Til the Band Comes In* were Mancini film compositions, and 'Loss of Love' carries on that fine tradition. The song is from the 1970 Italian language film *I girasoli*, its English title being *Sunflower*.

176. All His Children (Henry Mancini/A. & M. Bergman)
Original release: *The Moviegoer* 1972 LP
Not currently available commercially.

Another Mancini tune follows directly, from the 1971 American film based on Ken Kesey's novel of the same name, *Sometimes a Great Notion*, released in the UK under the title *Never Give an Inch*. And if *'Til the Band Comes In* had its 'cornball schlock' moment with *150* 'Reuben James', then *The Moviegoer* has its own in 'All His Children'. Despite being an Oscar-nominated song, particularly beloved of the Australians for some reason,[20] Marilyn and Alan Bergman's lyric is corny in the extreme. The notion of mankind being one big happy family hardly accounts for our penchant for killing each other through war and preventable starvation. Arranged on *The Moviegoer* in a polite country style, with a vocal in which Scott puts on a thoroughly unconvincing country accent, 'All His Children' is very much the album's weakest track. If all of *The Moviegoer* were of a quality with this track, then the received poor opinion of the LP would be justified.

Scott at the end of the Walker Brothers' glory days. His public profile would peak with his early solo career and TV show. By the 1970s, he was fading into the horizon.

177. Come Saturday Morning (Karlin/Previn)

Original release: *The Moviegoer* 1972 LP
Currently available: on *Classics and Collectibles* compilation

Scott returns to form with a faultless vocal on 'Come Saturday Morning'. An Oscar-nominated song with music by Fred Carlin and words by Andre Previn's ex-wife Dory, from the 1969 film *The Sterile Cuckoo* starring Liza Minnelli, released in the UK under the title *Pookie*. And a very nice song it is too.

178. Easy Come Easy Go (Green/Heyman)

Original release: *The Moviegoer* 1972 LP
Currently available: on *Classics and Collectibles* compilation

The Moviegoer ends in a laid-back fashion with 'Easy Come Easy Go', a song from (albeit not written for) the 1969 film *They Shoot Horses Don't They?* Starring Jane Fonda, the film is set in the 1930s Depression era and centred around a gruelling dance marathon which the contestants endure in the hope of winning some sorely needed cash. The song dates from 1934, when bandleader Johnny Green wrote it with lyricist Ed Heyman. On *The Moviegoer*, Scott performs it against a piano accompaniment. 'Darling, au revoir,' he sings as the record draws to a close. *The Moviegoer* is not a bad record at all – it contains one duff track, and no startling new agenda, but has plenty in common with Scott's previous work (Johnny Franz production, film songs in general, Mancini and Legrand songs in particular), some definite highlights, and, with but one exception, his voice is in fine form throughout.

Any Day Now 1973 LP

179. Any Day Now (Hillard/Bacharach)

Original release: *Any Day Now* 1973 LP
Currently available: on *The Collection* compilation

Front and back cover of Any Day Now – *Scott's final Philips LP.*

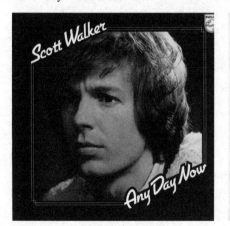

Scott's next LP, *Any Day Now*, was released in 1973. It's the most accessible, likeable and easy to enjoy of his lost albums, and is in fact the closest thing to a pop album he ever recorded, with its eclectic and at times curious choice of songs. The introduction might lead you to believe you're heading for a cheese festival, but 'Any Day Now' is a great song that will get under your skin. (You might have to stop yourself from calling your loved one 'my wild beautiful bird'.) The song was written by Burt Bacharach with Bob Hilliard, rather than his more celebrated lyricist partner Hal David, and originally recorded by Chuck Jackson in 1962. Elvis Presley also recorded the song in 1969, and both these earlier versions are also well worth a listen.

180. All My Love's Laughter (Webb)
Original release: *Any Day Now* 1973 LP
Currently available: on *Classics and Collectibles* compilation

Jimmy Webb is another of those great songwriters, like Randy Newman and Tim Hardin, whose songs are much better known as hits for other artists than for their author's original versions. Amongst them are 'Wichita Lineman' (a truly great song if ever there was one), 'By the Time I Get to Phoenix', 'Up, Up and Away' and 'MacArthur Park'. This is the first of two Webb songs on *Any Day Now*, and the first of four that Scott recorded in total. 'All My Love's Laughter' is an intriguingly beautiful love song. Scott's version, it must be said, surpasses Jimmy Webb's original by a mile.

181. Do I Love You? (Pelay/le Govic/Dessca/Piolot/Anka)
Original release: *Any Day Now* 1973 LP
Currently available: on *Classics and Collectibles* compilation

By the time of *Any Day Now*, Scott himself no longer held the upper hand in deciding what material he would record. Back in the days of the Walker Brothers, and the early solo LPs, the choice of cover versions appears to have been a friendly collaboration between Scott and producer Johnny Franz. But by *Any Day Now*, at least in his retrospective view, he had handed complete say over to Franz and Philips and would record whatever 'crap' they wanted him to.[21] And on paper, covering a Paul Anka song[22] that had recently flopped doesn't sound like a great artistic idea. But Scott, perhaps despite himself, pulls it off. 'Do I Love You?' is a straight love song, but no less touching or pleasant for that, with a convincingly impassioned performance by Scott. In no way ought it to be considered an embarrassment to anyone concerned.[23] Unfortunately the same cannot be said of the next track.

182. Maria Bethania (Veloso)
Original release: *Any Day Now* 1973 LP
Not currently available commercially.

Three songs into *Any Day Now* and all seems well, and then . . . oh dear! Along comes 'Maria Bethania', unintentionally hilarious and, without qualification, the worst track that Scott Walker ever recorded. Okay, so it's a Calypso-style number, but what ruins it is Scott's decision to sing it in a ludicrous attempt at a Jamaican accent. What can he have been thinking!!?? It's just dreadful. As if to make things more painful it's the longest track on the album, clocking in at a full five minutes worth of torture. This track is quite possibly the reason why *Any Day Now* will never achieve the official re-release it otherwise deserves.

183. Cowboy (Newman)
Original release: *Any Day Now* 1973 LP
Currently available: on *Classics and Collectibles* compilation

From the ridiculous to the sublime. Scott's version of Randy Newman's 'Cowboy' is a true highlight of *Any Day Now*. Melancholy resignation never sounded better, and if this track catches you in the right (or wrong) mood it will reduce you to tears. Superb.

184. When You Get Right Down to It (**Mann**)
Original release: *Any Day Now* 1973 LP
Currently available: on *Classics and Collectibles* compilation

The composer of this song is Barry Mann, of Mann and Weil/Brill Building/'Love Her' fame. Perhaps not a song that suits Scott particularly well, but still an enjoyable track. It had been a minor UK hit for Ronnie Dyson in 1971.

185. If (Gates)
Original release: *Any Day Now* 1973 LP
Not currently available commercially.

Lest anyone were to suppose that Scott recorded this after *Kojak* star Telly Savalas had had a UK Number One hit with the same song, Savalas's version was in 1975 – two years after *Any Day Now*. Ironically, if Scott had had a Number One hit with the arguably touching but borderline corny 'If' in 1973, his credibility might not be all that it is today. The original version was by David Gates and Bread, and Scott's version clearly has a close affinity with it. It goes without saying that he sings the song twenty zillion times better than Telly Savalas later spoke it.

186. Ain't No Sunshine (Withers)
Original release: *Any Day Now* 1973 LP
Not currently available commercially.

Although Bill Withers' original version of 'Ain't No Sunshine' is well known today, it was a young Michael Jackson who had the only ever big UK hit with this song. Jackson's version reached Number Eight in the UK singles charts in 1972. (Try for a second to imagine two singers more different than Scott and a thirteen-year-old Michael Jackson.) Thankfully, Scott did not try to replicate the 'talking bit' from Jackson's version, and his take on it is no embarrassment. The long instrumental passage at the end of the song is a surprising inclusion, its spacey guitars sounding reminiscent of Pink Floyd from about the same period.

187. The Me I Never Knew (Black/Barry)
Original release: *Any Day Now* 1973 LP
Currently available: on *Classics and Collectibles* compilation

The movie-going theme of Scott's previous album is not left behind completely on *Any Day Now*. This distinctive John Barry film composition was, like *167* 'This Way Mary', written with lyricist Don Black. It's from the 1972 film *Alice's Adventures in Wonderland*, in which it was sung by Fiona Fullerton as Lewis Carroll's young heroine Alice. But, stripped of that context, there's no sense of the song being about growing up from childhood. Rather it's a song sung by an adult who's surprised even himself by falling in love. The result is really quite touching, and a true highlight of the album.

188. If Ships Were Made to Sail (Webb)
Original release: *Any Day Now* 1973 LP
Not currently available commercially.

A beautiful piano introduction begins the second Jimmy Webb composition on *Any Day Now*. Like *180* 'All My Love's Laughter', this is from Webb's 1971 LP *And So On*. There have been plenty of songs written about longing to escape, but he takes things further than anyone with the suggestion that he would sail to Alpha Centauri (the closest star to Earth, but still four light years from the sun). But the song is no novelty number, Webb's songwriting and Scott's performance making it into a poignant ballad with an otherworldly feel.

189. We Could Be Flying (Colombier/Williams)
Original release: *Any Day Now* 1973 LP
Currently available: on *Classics and Collectibles* compilation

Any Day Now ends with another fine and unusual track. Some eerie orchestral sounds lead us in to Scott's voice singing *a cappella* for a couple of lines, before he is accompanied by an arrangement that is by turns jazzy, brassy, funky, breezy and spooky. The song is from a now fairly obscure album called *Wings*, released by French composer Michel Colombier in 1971. *Wings* was something of a grand concept album by all accounts, with Columbier enlisting almost a cast of thousands to record it – including Paul Williams, who wrote the optimistic lyric for 'We Could Be Flying' ('love is rising like a summer sun, caught in the silence of hello, rolling the words across the sky') and Lani Hall (Mrs. Herb Alpert) who provided the vocal for the original version.

Unfortunately, the optimism of 'We Could Be Flying' did not translate into record sales, and the LP joined *The Moviegoer* on a fast track to the bargain bins. And with that Scott Walker's nine-year career as a recording artist for Philips Records was over.

Stretch 1973 LP

190. Sunshine (M. Newbury)
Original release: *Stretch* 1973 LP

Front and back cover of Stretch – *the first of two albums Scott recorded for CBS in the Seventies.*

Scott's move to his new record label, CBS, in 1973 signalled an end to his long relationship with producer Johnny Franz, and a marked change in style with a move in the direction of country music. *Stretch* is not exactly 'Scott in Nashville' though – it was recorded no further south than London, though the steel guitar is to the fore on one or two tracks and the album also has Southern soul leanings – even having two songs in common with Dusty Springfield's *Dusty in Memphis* LP. But nothing on the album is as corny as *150* 'Reuben James' – as the CD reissue sleeve notes for *Stretch* put it, 'what's to dislike about it?'

    Stretch opens with one of its most country-style tracks, Mickey Newbury's 'Sunshine'. The late Texan songwriter Newbury is probably best remembered for writing (or rather compiling from existing songs) 'American Trilogy', which became such an epic in the hands of Elvis Presley. But his own songs were many, including hits for Joan Baez and Willie Nelson. 'Sunshine', a song recorded by Gene Pitney and Ray Charles amongst others, is not the tale of happiness its title might suggest, as the lyric begs the sunshine to leave its singer alone with his friend the darkness. It makes for a strong, poignant start to the LP.

191. Just One Smile (R. Newman)
Original release: *Stretch* 1973 LP

Randy Newman's songs were not new to Scott. *16* 'I Don't Want to Hear It Anymore', from way back on the Walker Brothers' first LP, had been written by Newman. 'Just One Smile' dates from his working songwriter days, before he also became a recording artist himself, and must rank as one of his very best songs from that era. Before appearing on *Stretch*, the song had been recorded by Gene

Pitney, Blood, Sweat and Tears, and Dusty Springfield, amongst others. Scott's version can be counted as a success, but it must be acknowledged that Dusty's version, on her 1969 *Dusty in Memphis* album, is the definitive reading of the song. Perhaps it just works better from the female perspective. Dusty's sublime vocal is filled with a yearning and a vulnerability, where Scott comes across as wearily resigned in comparison.

192. A Woman Left Lonely (Oldham/Penn)
Original release: *Stretch* 1973 LP

Another song that some will be more used to hearing from the female perspective, as it was recorded by Janis Joplin for her *Pearl* album. Written by songwriters Dan Penn and Spooner Oldham (who, amongst many credits, wrote the wonderful 'Do Right Woman, Do Right Man' for Aretha Franklin), 'A Woman Left Lonely' is a soulful classic. The version on *Stretch* is markedly different to Joplin's version; gone are the musical rawness and hysterical vocals, to be replaced by a very polished sound and Scott's typically clear diction. Whilst it isn't obviously superior to Joplin's, it really does work, coming over all melancholy before its heavenly choir of backing singers and a big guitar solo come into the picture. It's a true *Stretch* highlight.

193. No Easy Way Down (Goffin/King)
Original release: *Stretch* 1973 LP

The other song on *Stretch* that can also be found on Dusty Springfield's *Dusty in Memphis* album, Gerry Goffin and Carole King's 'No Easy Way Down'. And Scott's version does appear to be derivative of Dusty's, with its soulful treatment and female backing singers on the title line. As with *191* 'Just One Smile', it must be said that Dusty, who got there first and had the Memphis Horns behind her, recorded the finer version of the song.

194. That's How I Got to Memphis (T. T. Hall)
Original release: *Stretch* 1973 LP

Side one of *Stretch* ends with an unashamedly country number, the very nice 'That's How I Got to Memphis', which Scott handles sincerely without a hint of pastiche. The song was written and originally recorded by country singer-songwriter Tom T. Hall, who's nicknamed 'the Storyteller' and whose most famous song is probably 'Harper Valley PTA' (a hit for Jeannie C. Riley).

195. Use Me (B. Withers)
Original release: *Stretch* 1973 LP

Presumably pleased with his version of *186* 'Ain't No Sunshine' on *Any Day Now*, Scott opens side two of *Stretch* by tackling Bill Withers' US hit single 'Use Me'. And whilst, artistically speaking, it's the equivalent of high-class karaoke, it's really not bad at all. Definitely the funkiest thing Scott Walker ever recorded.

196. Frisco Depot (M. Newbury)
Original release: *Stretch* 1973 LP

The second Mickey Newbury song on *Stretch*, possibly the most morose lyric Scott ever sang (and there's some strong competition for that accolade). The singer is penniless, homeless, cold and alone, and there is not one single ray of hope in the lyric: 'When you're alone, you ain't got much reason for livin', but while you're alive well you just gotta live with your pain, unless you've been alone for so long, there's no love left for giving.'

197. Someone Who Cared (D. Newman)
Original release: *Stretch* 1973 LP

This song was written by Del Newman, the producer and arranger for Scott's two CBS LPs. Newman had previously worked as arranger and producer for Cat Stevens on his hugely successful early Seventies albums, and would go on to work with such stars as Elton John, George Harrison – and Uri Geller. The only brand new song on the LP, 'Someone Who Cared' is so understated it might be overlooked on the first few listens to *Stretch*, but it is a definite album highlight. It even sounds like the missing link between the *Scott* LPs and *Climate of Hunter*, or even *Tilt*. Perhaps Scott did write this, or had a hand in writing it and did not want to be given a writing credit, to avoid any hype about a return from his songwriting exile. The fact that there are not many Del Newman songwriting credits in existence, outside of the songs he co-authored with celebrated spoon-bender Geller,[24] adds weight to this suggestion – as does the fact that 'Someone Who Cared' is the only song from the whole *Any Day Now / Stretch / We Had It All* period to be included on the *Five Easy Pieces* box set.

198. Where Does Brown Begin (J. Webb)
Original release: *Stretch* 1973 LP

Many otherwise good albums have at least one bad track on them. *Stretch* has its weakest moment with this Jimmy Webb composition, much as it's all too easy to love the other Webb songs that Scott recorded. Webb says he wrote the song instantly on a napkin at the dinner table, after Sammy Davis Jr. had challenged him to write a song with that title.[25] Unfortunately, the song sounds like it was written instantly to order. It is incredibly hard to put a general plea for racial harmony into song without the result being trite and clichéd. Stevie Wonder and Paul McCartney tried and failed with their woefully corny 'Ebony and Ivory', and Webb's song, with its crass metaphors of salt and pepper and night and day, succeeds little better. Scott fails to redeem the song either, turning in a performance that is uncharacteristically schmaltzy.

199. Where Love Has Died (J. Owen)
Original release: *Stretch* 1973 LP

Definitely a country song, if not performed in an overtly country style, 'Where Love Has Died' is one of those sad songs that country music does so well. The singer relates how he would leave his loveless marriage if 'my years were less,' or 'I could dream as I once could.' Very sad and very touching – and not a million miles away from the sentiments of *116* 'Rosemary' from *Scott 3*, who feels the nails pounding into the 'coffin of her youth', and who would escape if her feet would only fly, whilst she, like the singer of 'Where Love Has Died', knows they won't.

200. I'll Be Home (R. Newman)
Original release: *Stretch* 1973 LP

Stretch ends with a very atypical vocal on Randy Newman's 'I'll Be Home'. Accompanied only by piano for most of the track, Scott's delivery is exceptionally understated throughout. The listener might keep expecting the big Scott Walker voice to boom out, but it never does. The result is really quite poignant.

Alas, once again the public passed the LP by and sales were poor. Perhaps the artwork didn't help. To those only familiar with the CD reissue, the little pictures of the LP sleeve that you see doesn't prepare you for the horror of the real thing. Two extremely unflattering pictures of Scott grace the front and back, with the front cover presenting a very orange-looking Scott presumably having a stretch(!), and the words 'Scott Walker' written in a weird, illegible Coca Cola-style typeface. *Stretch* seems to have been cursed with bad packaging, as the BGO reissue has possibly the most amateurish cover design in the history of CDs. The LP deserves better.

We Had It All 1974 LP

201. Low Down Freedom (B. J. Shaver)
Original release: *We Had It All* 1974 LP

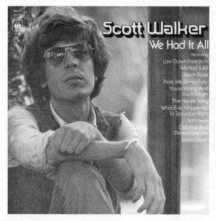 

Different album, same outfit – the CBS budget for We Had It All *apparently didn't extend to a new photo session.*

Scott's second and final CBS album, *We Had It All*, was released in August 1974. It's not quite *Stretch Part Two* (despite Scott apparently wearing exactly the same outfit on both LP sleeves), being much more country orientated and the song selection much less eclectic. Just how un-eclectic it is can be spelt out as follows. Here is the track listing for Waylon Jennings' classic album *Honky Tonk Heroes*, released in July 1973:

Honky Tonk Heroes, Old Five and Dimers like Me (B. J. Shaver), Willy the Wandering Gypsy and Me, Low Down Freedom (B. J. Shaver), Omaha, Ask Me To, Ride Me Down Easy (B. J. Shaver), Ain't No God in Mexico, Black Rose (B. J. Shaver), We Had It All (D. Fritts/T. Seals).

And here is the track listing to Scott Walker's *We Had It All*, released in August 1974:

Low Down Freedom (B. J. Shaver), We Had It All (D. Fritts/T. Seals), Black Rose (B. J. Shaver), Ride Me Down Easy (B. J. Shaver), You're Young and You'll Forget, The House Song, Whatever Happened to Saturday Night?, Sundown, Old Five and Dimers like Me (B. J. Shaver), Delta Dawn.

Coincidence? It is hard to see it that way. Songwriter Billy Joe Shaver was apparently pretty much an unknown before he hooked up with Waylon Jennings, who agreed to record almost a whole album's worth of his songs on *Honky Tonk Heroes*. Therefore it seems extremely unlikely that whoever chose the songs for *We Had It All* heard them anywhere else. Add the song 'We Had It All' and half the songs on Scott's LP come from *Honky Tonk Heroes*. There seems to be no other interpretation but that 50 percent of Scott Walker's *We Had It All* is a rerecording of Waylon Jennings' *Honky Tonk Heroes*.[26] And that is surely unprecedented, particularly so soon after the first album's release. Add to this the fact that Waylon Jennings' record is the 'real deal', one of the records that actually defined a sub-genre of country music, 'the outlaw movement',[27] whereas Scott's record was recorded with London session musicians, and *We Had It All* looks more like a curious footnote than an artistic statement. And perhaps that really is the best way to view it, as a curio in Scott's career. But is it enjoyable? Ironically, if you're a person who really knows and loves country music (or a big Waylon Jennings fan), it probably isn't. But if you're not seriously into country it probably is, given that (A) you love Scott's voice, and (B) the sound of a steel guitar doesn't immediately send you running for the skip button.

We Had It All's opening track is one of those Billy Joe Shaver songs taken from *Honky Tonk Heroes*, so all the above applies. 'Low Down Freedom' is the tale of a man who is about to leave his lover, not because he must or even really wants too, but because that's the kind of guy he is – a kind of 'Wherever I Lay My Hat' song for the outlaw country. If you're thinking this doesn't really sound like Scott, you'd be right. If you like the song and want to hear how it should sound, invest in a listen to *Honky Tonk Heroes*, which is available on music streaming services or easy to obtain on CD.

202. We Had It All (D. Fritts/T. Seals)
Original release: *We Had It All* 1974 LP

Scott is much more convincing on this ballad and, despite the song coming from *Honky Tonk Heroes*, the backing musicians are at their least countrified here. And because, when Scott Walker sings a great ballad, he truly sings a great ballad greatly, this is a standout track – even though Waylon Jennings' recording of the same song is actually more touching.

203. Black Rose (B. J. Shaver)
Original release: *We Had It All* 1974 LP

Another Billy Joe Shaver/Waylon Jennings song, it simply doesn't suit Scott at all. This time it's a tale of drink and fornication among the sugar canes, with the eponymous devil woman Rose.

204. Ride Me Down Easy (B. J. Shaver)
Original release: *We Had It All* 1974 LP

And another Billy Joe Shaver/Waylon Jennings song from *Honky Tonk Heroes*. This one is slightly more successfully covered, and maybe even enjoyable – if you can suspend disbelief for a few minutes and see Scott as the hard-living, hard-loving, hard-drinking 'rodeo bum' of the song. Or maybe not. Incidentally, the authors of *A Deep Shade of Blue* declare the B. J. Shaver covers to be the best thing about the album, and suggest they were a positive artistic move.[28] Sadly, whilst Scott Walker was many things to many people, a honky tonk hero he definitely was not.

205. You're Young and You'll Forget (J. Reed)
Original release: *We Had It All* 1974 LP

More country pop than outlaw country, 'You're Young and You'll Forget' is extremely enjoyable. The truth, which Scott may never have wished to acknowledge, is that he could sing pop songs very well and that when he did the results were well worth hearing. The song was written and first recorded in 1967 by Jerry Reed (AKA Jerry Reed Hubbard), the man who wrote the well-known Elvis Presley hits 'Guitar Man' and 'US Male'. Thematically similar to *201* 'Low Down Freedom', the singer prepares to leave his lover because his nature doesn't allow him to settle down with her. But perhaps part of what makes this song suit Scott in a way that 'Low Down Freedom' doesn't are the romantically altruistic touches in the lyric. Sentiments such as, 'I know time will help you find the perfect man to really love you . . . who's worthy of you' are almost reminiscent of the gorgeous *3* 'Love Her' way back when.

206. The House Song (Bannard/Stookey)
Original release: *We Had It All* 1974 LP

An intriguing song with a strange pedigree, 'The House Song' was written by Noel Paul Stookey with Robert H. Bannard. Stookey is none other than the 'Paul' from perennially unhip folk group Peter, Paul and Mary, of 'Blowin' in the Wind' and 'Puff the Magic Dragon' fame, who first recorded 'The House Song' on their 1967 LP Album *1700*. (Goldie Hawn also recorded the song in 1972 on her *Goldie* album.) What makes the song intriguing, however, are the questions the lyric raises and doesn't answer. Why is the house being taken on and off the market? Has the singer lost his wife and children somehow, or is he just recalling the past? Why is the room where the lady slept the hardest one to pass? And isn't the song really about the man rather than the house? Whatever the answers, Scott's version really adds something to the original. In his hands the song is much darker and, by choosing not to sing the original final verse (some garbled wordplay concerning the attic[29]), he ends it on its most poignant and intriguing note.

207. Whatever Happened to Saturday Night?
(R. Meisner/D. Henley/G. Frey/B. Leadon)[30]
Original release: *We Had It All* 1974 LP

A song originally called just 'Saturday Night' when it was written by the Eagles and included on their second album, *Desperado*, just the previous year, 1973. The Eagles may have dressed up as Wild West outlaws for the cover of *Desparado*, but their sound was always a very Californian take on country. 'Saturday Night' is a charming rock ballad, slowed down and lushly arranged, and Scott's version is very nice indeed.

208. Sundown (Gordon Lightfoot)
Original release: *We Had It All* 1974 LP

Canadian singer/songwriter Gordon Lightfoot's *Sundown* album was released at the end of 1973, making this another very recent song covered on *We Had It All*. Like *206* 'The House Song', it's a number that actually benefits from Scott's treatment. His version is less chirpy, more dramatic and moody than the original, and all the better for it.

209. Old Five and Dimers Like Me (B .J. Shaver)
Original release: *We Had It All* 1974 LP

The final B. J. Shaver/Waylon Jennings cover on *We Had It All* and, like the others, another unconvincing moment. Whereas Scott can sing about life's losers in the third person and be utterly engaging, this first-person portrayal of the 'old five and dimer' who's spent his whole life trying and failing and is now resigned to his lot ('fenced yards ain't hole cards, and like as not, never will be') is another

129

song that just does not suit him at all. Again, if you want to hear how the song should sound, invest in a listen to *Honky Tonk Heroes*.

210. Delta Dawn (Alex Harvey)
Original release: *We Had It All* 1974 LP

Lest there be any misunderstanding, the Alex Harvey who wrote this song is not the Scottish Alex Harvey of Sensational Alex Harvey Band fame, but the Tennessee-born country singer who co-wrote *150* 'Reuben James'. 'Delta Dawn' has an obvious affinity with 'Reuben James' – both songs have sing-along choruses beginning with the eponymous character's names – but it's the better song. It had been a US Top Ten country hit for the then thirteen-year-old Tanya Tucker in 1972, and Scott's version was chosen to be the one single taken from *We Had It All*. Needless to say, it flopped. The problem with 'Delta Dawn', as a song for Scott Walker, is that it lacks any depth. Potentially we might feel some empathy with the song's title character, who has lost her looks and possibly her mind, but all you get is the sing-along chorus which sounds like it's mocking the poor woman.

With the final track from *We Had It All*, we reach the end of Scott's lost albums period. And although it's a lesser album than *Stretch*, all of Scott's lost albums are worthy of attention despite the bad press. Where they do fail it is only in places, and through an ill-considered choice of cover versions – with the only really terrible choices being *182* 'Maria Bethania', and the unimaginative decision to cover 50 per cent of Waylon Jennings' *Honky Tonk Heroes* on *We Had It All*. On these tracks, Scott is pretentious in the literal sense of the word, by pretending to be, respectively, a Jamaican or a Texan/modern cowboy, and the results are unconvincing. But still, the lost albums contain a variety of riches, and to dismiss them as simply middle-of-the-road rubbish would be wrong. When Scott did middle of the road, he did it arguably better than anybody else. On the whole, the lost albums deserve to be found.

---

1. Sourced from Scott Walker interview with Keith Altham recorded circa late 1968/ early 1969 (audio recording, original source unknown).
2. The home VCR does not appear to have been introduced until 1972, and even then remained beyond most pockets until the late Seventies. Videotape machines existed in 1969, but only in the hands of TV companies or perhaps the very wealthy.
3. These recordings aren't of pristine release quality, but the best of them, made via a lead from the TV output (rather than the practice of standing a microphone in front of the TV's speaker), at least give a listenable version of the soundtrack. And, most importantly, these recordings give us fifteen performances by Scott Walker not otherwise available. For further details see this book's appendix.

4. A mistake perhaps due to nerves, he should have said Phillipe Gerard.

5. Frank Sinatra recorded earlier versions of the following songs from the TV Series album: *154* 'I Have Dreamed', *155* 'When the World Was Young', *158* 'The Impossible Dream', *159* 'The Song Is You' and *164* 'Lost in the Stars'. *162* 'Someone to Light up My Life' was also recorded by Sinatra, but was not released until 1971. This makes it a total of at least 50 per cent of the songs on the *TV Series* LP that Frank Sinatra also recorded.

6. On her 1967 LP *Lush Life*, an album that also includes *155* 'When the World Was Young' and 'Free Again', both of them recorded by Scott Walker though the latter remains unreleased. Quite possibly Scott was familiar with her album.

7. The song 'Lost in the Stars' has been recorded by countless artists over the years, including, most bizarrely, Leonard Nimoy. His version can be found on *Leonard Nimoy Presents Mr Spock's Music from Outer Space*!

8. One of the strange-but-true stories about Scott Walker in the Sixties is that he temporarily joined a monastery, at the height of the Walker Brothers' fame. The key seen around his neck on the cover of the *TV Series* LP was apparently given to him by the Quarr Monastery on the Isle of Wight, as a symbol that he was welcome to return at any time he wished.

9. The Ivor Novello Award-winning songwriter also responsible for the lyrics to 'The Rope and the Colt', who died in January 2004.

10. This and other information in this paragraph taken from *A Deep Shade of Blue*, pp.160-162.

11. Some great 'glam' records would include David Bowie's *The Rise and Fall of Ziggy Stardust and the Spiders from Mars* (1972), Roxy Music's first three albums (1972-3) and numerous singles by T.Rex and Slade.

12. *The NME Book of Rock 2* (Star paperback 1977).

13. *The Faber Companion to 20th Century Popular Music* (Faber 1990).

14. Scott Walker interview, published in *MOJO* magazine, July 2000.

15. Famously, Scott said that he chose not to listen to his old records, and therefore the opinions he gave of *The Moviegoer et al* may have been based on 30-something-year-old memories of a time which, for personal reasons, he did not wish to remember. He described the early Seventies with clear distaste as 'years of drinking, for a number of reasons' (as interviewed by Joe Jackson in his article 'The Fugitive Kind'. See footnote 18 to *112* 'Joanna').

16. Curiously, the authors of *A Deep Shade of Blue* dismiss side two of *'Til the Band Comes In* in its entirety – including the Scott Walker/Ady Semel compositions *146* 'Til the Band Comes In' (a 'weak chorus' in their view p.158) and *147* 'The War Is Over' (which they said fails to deliver a melody to match its intentions – also p.158).

17. *A Deep Shade of Blue*, pp.169-70.

18. Ibid., p.170.

19. Mistakenly credited on the original LP to Rota only.

20. Apparently there were three competing versions of the song in the Australian charts in 1972, none of them Scott Walker's version.

21. Scott Walker interview by Joe Jackson in 'The Fugitive Kind'. See footnote 18 to *112* 'Joanna'.

22. Based on an original French song, hence the writing credit includes the French songwriters.

23. Joe Jackson, in 'The Fugitive Kind', seems to dismiss 'Do I Love You?' on the grounds that an existentialist shouldn't sing a song that, in Jackson's words, 'compare[s] love to a "bible full of prayers"'. But this dismissal is too simplistic. The lyric doesn't say anything quite so crass, rather that the singer's love is as sacred as a bible full of prayers – which doesn't make the song particularly religious or corny. One could easily quote phrases or lines out of context from Scott Walker's own lyrics (especially from *131* 'Angels of Ashes') and make them sound extremely religious!

24. Uri Geller became a television personality in the Seventies due to his apparent psychic ability to bend metal objects, like spoons, without applying any physical force. Believing his talents extended to music as well, he recorded an LP for Columbia Records in 1975, on which Del Newman provided all the arrangements and co-wrote many of the tracks.

25. Jimmy Webb's own liner notes to his 1993 *Archive* compilation CD.

26. The only thing that casts any doubt on this at all is a quote attributed to Scott in *A Deep Shade of Blue* (p.175), that says, 'I had it all when it was new.' It's unclear however exactly what is being referred to, and the statement may just mean comparatively new or new to the UK. The notion of Scott having the B. J. Shaver material before Waylon Jennings recorded it just doesn't stack up with the dates. *Honky Tonk Heroes* was recorded and released before *Stretch*, in November 1973 – let alone the release of *We Had It All*, which followed the best part of a year later. Besides which, some of the songs had been already been recorded and released in America (by Shaver himself or by Bobby Bare) as early as March 1973, at a time when Scott was still under contract to Philips and yet to release *Any Day Now*.

27. The outlaw country movement was a breakaway from the dominant and formulaic Nashville sound of the day. Waylon Jennings recorded B. J. Shaver's 'modern cowboy songs' with his own band and without a sterile Nashville production. So – oh the irony! – what does Scott Walker do on *We Had It All*, but record very polished versions of these very same songs!

28. *A Deep Shade of Blue*, p.176.

29. The final verse that Scott doesn't sing is as follows: 'How much will you pay to live in the attic? / the shavings off your mind are the only rent, / I left some "would" there if you thought you couldn't, / or if the shouldn't that you've bought has been spent.'

30. Curiously credited to 'writer unknown' on the original LP.

part four

The Walker Brothers' Seventies Reunion 1975 - 1978

With the poor sales of all Scott Walker's records from *Scott 4* to *We Had It All*, it is fair to say that, commercially, his career was in the doldrums by 1975. But Scott's solo career had been flourishing in comparison to those of the other erstwhile Walker Brothers, John and Gary. Since the Walkers split, John had achieved one solitary solo UK hit single with 'Annabella', way back in 1967, then a hit in the Dutch charts with 'If I Promise' later that same year. Then nothing. Gary meanwhile, whilst he achieved some success in Japan with his new group Gary Walker and the Rain, had not managed to achieve any post-split UK hits.[1] By the mid-Seventies John was even performing on the UK cabaret circuit with a group he called the New Walker Brothers, complete with a faux-Scott in the shape of singer Jimmy Wilson. Commercially, and by all accounts personally, all three ex-Walker Brothers were at a low ebb, so, at the instigation of John, the decision was made to reform the group that had first made them a success. The history of groups reforming is not filled with notable examples of artistic merit: Did the Beatles really add anything to their towering legacy by adding overdubs to a couple of John Lennon demos in the mid-Nineties, or did they diminish it? Did the Sex Pistols achieve anything (other than making money) by reforming to play their angry-young-man songs as middle-aged men? Happily, the Walker Brothers' Seventies reunion is one of pop music's more successful reformations. They did not pretend to be the same group they were in the Sixties either in terms of image, style or choice of songs. The image presented on the cover of the *No Regrets* LP, with its bare chests, denim, Newcastle Brown Ale and smiles, would have been unthinkable for the Sixties Walker Brothers. Their sound was no recreation of the Sixties either. Gone was the Spector-esque melodrama, in came the contemporary country-tinged rock sound, before it turned into something entirely different on the *Nite Flights* LP. Although the Walker Brothers reunion can hardly be classed a 100 per cent artistic success – none of the three LPs they released are consistently good – there is enough brilliance in the songs *222* 'Lines', *226* 'We're All Alone', *234* 'Nite Flights' and *235* 'The Electrician' to make it something to celebrate.

No Regrets 1975 LP

211. No Regrets (Rush)
Original release: *No Regrets* 1975 LP[2]

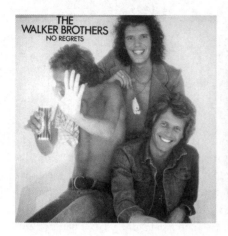

The No Regrets *LP – bare chests, denim, Newcastle Brown Ale and smiles.*

The track chosen to be the Walker Brothers' comeback single, and the biggest commercial success of their Seventies reunion. 'No Regrets' was an inspired choice of song, because it allowed the group to present just the right balance of the new and the familiar. In common with their celebrated hits of the Sixties, the track boasts a huge, confident lead vocal by Scott, a 'big' sound (albeit more contemporary to its own period) and a tale of a relationship breaking up. 'No Regrets' is a more adult acknowledgement that a relationship is over. Part of the appeal of the song lies in the unanswered question – does the singer genuinely have no regrets, or is he trying to convince himself that the ending of the relationship is a good thing? There is definite melancholy in lines like, 'I woke last night and spoke to you, not thinking you were gone, and it felt so strange to lie awake alone.' Credit for the song must of course go to its author, Tom Rush, who recorded not one but two original versions: the first a more acoustic take in 1968, and the second closer to the Walkers version in 1974. But the Walker Brothers' recording of 'No Regrets' eclipses both original versions with its epic proportions, shining guitar solo and, most of all, 'that voice'. An obviously strong single, 'No Regrets' met with a shaky start but eventually took off, climbing to Number Seven in the UK singles chart at the beginning of 1976. It gave the Walker Brothers their only Top Ten hit since 1966, and saw Scott back in the Top Ten for the only time since 1968's *112* 'Joanna'. Plenty of colour television footage of the Walkers performing the song survives, most of which finds all three band members looking uncharacteristically cheerful.

212. Remember Me (A. Dayam)
Original release: single B-Side released 1975

The 'No Regrets' single was accompanied by a non-LP B-side, 'Remember Me'. The writing credit A. Dayam is a pseudonym – the song's author was one John Walker, who takes the lead vocal on the song. Not earth-shatteringly essential, but a good B-side.

213. Hold an Old Friend's Hand (Weiss)
Original release: *No Regrets* 1975 LP

Had the Walker Brothers been able to record a whole LP with the strength of the *211* 'No Regrets' single, or even just score another hit single from the LP, there might have been no stopping them. Unfortunately it wasn't to be. Produced by Scott and the other brothers with engineer Geoff Calver,[3] the *No Regrets* LP has its moments but the standout track always will be 'No Regrets' itself. No other single was even released from the LP.

The Seventies Walker Brothers was from the outset always going to be a more democratic affair. And on *No Regrets*, Scott and John take it in turns to take a lead vocal on alternating tracks. The arrangement wasn't quite as democratic as it could have been, since each side of the LP starts with Scott's lead vocal – thus, over five tracks per side, giving Scott six lead vocals to John's four. So since *No Regrets* opens with the title track and Scott's lead vocal, the LP's second track features John's vocal. 'Hold an Old Friend's Hand', like most of the selections, was a fairly new song back in 1975. First recorded in 1974 by Tracy Nelson, former lead singer of West Coast hippie group Mother Earth, it mourns the passing of time and suggests that ex-lovers can still be friends.

214. Boulder to Birmingham (Harris/Danoff)
Original release: *No Regrets* 1975 LP

The 'Harris' in the songwriting credit is acclaimed country singer Emmylou Harris, and, though the song may sound like a timeless classic, at the time of *No Regrets* it was very new indeed. It comes from Emmylou's first major label solo album, *Pieces of Sky*, released earlier that same year, and was inspired by a very specific event – the untimely death of Gram Parsons in September 1973. Parsons was one of the founding fathers – if not the founding father - of country rock, a member of and guiding force in the Byrds at the time of their *Sweetheart of the Rodeo* LP, a founder member of the Flying Burrito Brothers, and a solo artist with his own very un-Nashville take on country music. Emmylou Harris was co-vocalist with Parsons on the two solo LPs he recorded before his death. Ever one to live the rock and roll lifestyle to the full, he died in the Californian desert of alcohol and drug-related causes at the age of 26. 'Boulder to Birmingham' is a beautiful tribute, but also addresses loss in a more universal and wide-reaching way. Ms. Harris has performed this classic song in a variety of different musical settings over the years, right up to this day. Many artists have also covered it. Scott's take is gentle and country-ish for the song's verses, building to an almost gospel interpretation of the chorus. One of the better tracks on *No Regrets*.

215. Walkin' in the Sun (Barry)
Original release: *No Regrets* 1975 LP

A John Walker lead vocal follows, on Jeff Barry's 'Walkin' in the Sun'. Barry, an almost ubiquitous name in Sixties pop music (with or without songwriting partner and former wife Ellie Greenwich), was inspired to write the song by his own blind father – the lyric tells how even a blind man knows when he's walking in the sun.

216. Lover's Lullaby (Ian)
Original release: *No Regrets* 1975 LP

Janis Ian will always be best remembered for her teenage angst classic 'At Seventeen'. 'Lover's Lullaby' comes from the same album, 1975's *Between the Lines*, making this another very contemporary choice of song to cover. 'Lover's Lullaby' perhaps isn't a match for 'At Seventeen', but it is a very nice song. Unfortunately something of its charm is lost in Scott's version. Ms. Ian's original version, weighing in at over five minutes, is an epic closing song to her album, with its gentle build-up to a big chorus, before the song ends with a very lullaby-like section which is entirely missing from the Walker Brothers' cover. One can understand Scott's reluctance to sing lines like, 'the moon was made of old green cheese to keep the night away' from the original's lullaby ending, but perhaps overall their version may have benefited in places from a less assertive, more gentle vocal, such as was heard on *200* 'I'll Be Home'.

217. I've Got to Have You (Kris Kristofferson)
Original release: *No Regrets* 1975 LP

Side two of *No Regrets* opens with one of its best tracks. Perhaps Kris Kristofferson's lyric is a little trite, or even a little bit crass, but in Scott's hands the song is utterly charming. A wonderful country-tinged love song, Carly Simon previously recorded it on her 1971 LP *Anticipation*.

218. He'll Break Your Heart (Mayfield/Butler)
Original release: *No Regrets* 1975 LP

A John Walker lead vocal, and definitely the low point of *No Regrets*. It's not known what Curtis Mayfield and Jerry Butler's very nice little soul song (a US Top Ten hit for Butler in 1960) did to deserve such awful cod-reggae treatment. Opens with a pointless in-joke – 'Did you hear that Scott? I said flattery will get you anywhere.'

The reformed Walker Brothers pictured circa 1976. Left to right: Scott, Gary and John.

219. Everything that Touches You (Kamen)

Original release: *No Regrets* 1975 LP

Not the song that was a US hit for the Association, but an obscurity of the same name written and originally recorded by Michael Kamen. The name may not be instantly recognisable, but the late Kamen achieved more in his lifetime than most of us can dream of. Amongst his list of disparate achievements are musical direction for Bowie's *Diamond Dogs* tour; scoring blockbuster films such as *Lethal Weapon* and *Die Hard*; writing the melody of the monster 1991 Bryan Adams hit, 'Everything I Do', and conducting orchestras for Metallica. Compared to that, writing 'Everything that Touches You' doesn't really register on the scale. It's a fairly unremarkable song, which even the Scott Walker treatment fails to ignite.

220. Lovers (Mickey Newbury)

Original release: *No Regrets* 1975 LP

Scott had covered Mickey Newbury's songs on *Stretch*, and here John takes on Newbury's 'Lovers'. It's another sad song – the lovers of the title don't even speak to each other anymore, as the female half has found somebody else and the male half drinks himself legless each night. Easily John's best track on the album.

221. Burn Our Bridges (J.Ragovoy/L.Laurie)

Original release: *No Regrets* 1975 LP

'We'll Burn Our Bridges Behind Us', as the song was originally known, was cowritten by Jerry Ragovoy (whose great songwriting credits include 'Time Is on

My Side', 'Piece of My Heart' and, as covered by the Walker Brothers, *47* 'Stay with Me Baby') and appeared on Dionne Warwick's 1975 LP *Then Came You*. The song has potential hit written all over it, and it's very surprising that neither Ms. Warwick's nor the Walkers' version was ever released as a single. With the latter's very mid-Seventies sound and memorable chorus, it would have sounded great on the radio. Instead, no second single was even released from the *No Regrets* album.

Taken as a whole, the LP is not a great record, but it does contain some very good tracks – in particular, the title track of course, and *214* 'Boulder to Birmingham', *220* 'Lovers' and 'Burn Our Bridges'.

Lines 1976 LP

222. Lines (Jerry Fuller)
Original release: *Lines* 1976 LP

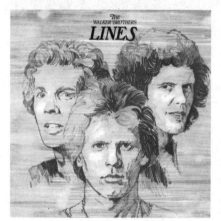

The Lines *LP cover, and the photograph used to create the line drawing.*

The second Seventies Walker Brothers LP, *Lines*, followed the next year, 1976. Like *No Regrets*, it was produced by Scott Walker and Geoff Calver and comprises ten songs, mainly cover versions of contemporary material handled in the same style as the previous LP. Once again, the lead vocals are alternated between Scott and John, with Scott being 'more equal than others'.

Side one opens with 'Lines'. Whenever this song is discussed, for example in the sleeve notes to the Walker Brothers CD compilation *If You Could Hear Me Now*, the claim is made that it's about cocaine addiction. This is hard to see. The only drug mentioned or implied in the lyric is cheap wine. True, only songwriter Jerry Fuller (who wrote Gary Puckett's 'Young Girl' and Ricky Nelson's 'Travelling Man', amongst many other non-drug related tunes) can give the definitive answer, but it's very doubtful. It doesn't need cocaine's dubious glamour. 'Lines' is an excellent track. A haunting piano introduction leads us into a superlative vocal by Scott, with a powerful, lushly orchestrated chorus. Fuller's word play on the word 'lines' (bus line, centreline, dotted line, breadline, between the lines) is never corny, and it's a touching song of loneliness and loss. A fine record that, although released as a single, alas received next to no media interest and failed to sell.

223. Taking It All in Stride (Tom Snow)
Original release: *Lines* 1976 LP

A fine track sung by Scott is followed by a fine track sung by John. 'Taking It All in Stride' was the title track to a now obscure LP released by Tom Snow in 1975. It's simply a lovely country/pop song, with a theme of melancholy and loss mixed with encouraging optimism.

224. Inside of You (Tom Jans)
Original release: *Lines* 1976 LP

If the *Lines* LP had retained the quality of its first two tracks throughout, then it might well have been a classic. Alas, with this track and the next, things go downhill rapidly. Inexplicably included on compilations, 'Inside of You' may have its fans somewhere, but will otherwise have listeners reaching for the skip button. Depending on your point of view, the most annoying thing about it is that (A) it's ungrammatical, due to its superfluous use of the word 'of' in the title phrase; (B) it's a little too much information, thank you (do we want to hear the singer recounting being 'inside of' his lover?); (C) it's unintentionally hilarious; (D) it's a morose dirge, or (E) the pomposity of the lyric, especially the final verse, is beyond belief.

The authorship of 'Inside of You' is mis-credited on the original LP to both 'Tom Jarvis' on the sleeve and 'Tom Janis' on the record label. The person actually guilty of writing the song was singer-songwriter Tom Jans, in 1975.

225. Have You Seen My Baby (Randy Newman)
Original release: *Lines* 1976 LP

A John Walker lead vocal. Hardly the greatest of Randy Newman songs in the first place, it's given an absolutely dreadful treatment here. Everything about it is uninspired, from the bouncy sub-Bay City Rollers backing track to the cheesy sax break to the groaning noises that, for some inexplicable reason, end the track itself.

226. We're All Alone (Boz Scaggs)
Original release: *Lines* 1976 LP

After two fairly dreadful tracks, *Lines* recovers to finish side one on a high point. 'We're All Alone' will probably be more familiar from its Top Ten hit version by Rita Coolidge, but the Walker Brothers' arguably superior version was recorded first and released as the *Lines* LP's second single. In retrospect, it can only have been bad marketing and media prejudice that prevented them achieving a chart success to follow *211* 'No Regrets'. Boz Scaggs' instant blue-eyed soul classic,

'We're All Alone', first featured on his 1976 *Silk Degrees* LP, released at a time when he had yet to achieve a commercial breakthrough and was still best known as a former member of the Steve Miller Band.

Two rarely seen GTO publicity photos circa Lines. Above, left to right: John, Gary and Scott. Below: Scott with guitar.

227. Many Rivers to Cross (Jimmy Cliff)
Original release: *Lines* 1976 LP

Side two of *Lines* opens with Jimmy Cliff's 1970 song 'Many Rivers to Cross'. Cliff's original is such a classic that it might be thought best not to attempt it, but the Walker Brothers' everything-but-the-kitchen-sink approach actually works quite well: a gentle piano introduction, a fine Scott Walker vocal, a big Walkers sound, heavenly choirs and a shining guitar solo make the track a definite *Lines* highlight.

228. First Day (A. Dayam)
Original release: *Lines* 1976 LP

Only the second Walker Brothers original to feature so far in their 1970s career. John's authorship of 'First Day' is again hidden behind the pseudonym 'A. Dayam'. Unfortunately it's an uninspiring exercise in songwriting by numbers.

229. Brand New Tennessee Waltz (Jesse Winchester)
Original release: *Lines* 1976 LP

The remainder of the LP plays out without either reaching the peak of *222* 'Lines' or plumbing the depths of *224* 'Inside of You'. 'Brand New Tennessee Waltz' first appeared on composer Jesse Winchester's self-titled 1970 LP. The song is a kind of sequel to the standard 'Tennessee Waltz', made famous by Patti Page and later adopted as an official state song of Tennessee. And despite the 'Brand New' epithet, Winchester's song isn't too different in style to the original. Both are simple country tunes with a sad tale to tell, and it would be impossible to imagine either being performed without some country fiddle playing far away. (Years later, Patti Page even recorded a version of Winchester's song.) The Walker Brothers' version retains the country feel of the original and passes the time pleasantly enough – if you can stop yourself from puzzling over how one literally waltzes on air.

230. Hard to Be Friends (Larry Murray)
Original release: *Lines* 1976 LP

A good track sung by John, 'Hard to Be Friends' had been previously recorded by then husband and wife team Kris Kristofferson and Rita Coolidge, on their 1973 LP *Full Moon*. (The unreleased *242* 'Loving Arms' also features on the same Kristofferson and Coolidge LP.)

231. Dreaming as One (David Palmer/William Smith)[4]
Original release: *Lines* 1976 LP

The *Lines* LP closes with Scott and John duetting in veritable Everly Brothers style on 'Dreaming as One'. Perhaps they could have picked a more appropriate lyric (something less obviously intended for conjugal lovers), but the result is pleasant enough. The original version of the song was recorded by Richie Havens on his 1976 LP, *The End of the Beginning*, on which the song's co-writer, William Smith, was keyboard player. The song was later covered by Blood, Sweat and Tears in 1977 and the Pointer Sisters in 1979.

Like the *No Regrets* LP, *Lines* is a hit and miss affair – although the misses, when they happen, are wider of the mark. With *Lines*, the Walker Brothers had in effect recorded *No Regrets Part Two*, following the same formula and style. It also followed the *No Regrets* LP's lack of commercial success. In the case of *Lines*, sales cannot have been helped by the curious yellow artwork the LP was given.[5]

Nite Flights 1978 LP

232. Shutout (S. Engel)
Original release: *Nite Flights* 1978 LP

The Nite Flights *LP – by far the darkest Walker Brothers product.*

The Walker Brothers' third and final Seventies LP, released in 1978, was anything but a continuation of the *No Regrets-Lines* formula. *Nite Flights* tore the rulebook to shreds. Comprised entirely of the Walkers' own compositions, it is a much darker record than anything else they ever recorded.

The years 1976 to 1978 saw great change in popular music. Punk and disco had both happened in a big way, with the result being that the musical landscape of 1978 was very different to that of 1975. A third album of cover versions of songs written by men with beards (which pretty accurately describes *No Regrets* and *Lines*[6]) would have sounded hopelessly behind the times. Thankfully though, the Walker Brothers' idea of moving on did not involve a total embracing of either new wave, which would have been risible, or disco. (Can you imagine Scott singing falsetto a la the Bee Gees?) Instead they rose to the challenge of the times in a different way. If *Nite Flights* has any affinity with contemporary music, it is with David Bowie's mid-Seventies 'European' albums, *Station to Station* (1976), *Low* (1977) and *'Heroes'* (1977). What brought about this change in musical style? Well, apart from changing times, there was also the collapse of the Walker Brothers' Seventies record label, GTO, which meant that they already knew this was going to be their final LP before they recorded it. The decision was made to make the record they wanted to make without compromise. Scott, once again the album's co-producer, was the guiding force both in this decision and the mood of *Nite Flights*. In a 1984 radio interview, he put it as follows: 'I said to the other guys, this is going to be the last album so everybody just get as self-indulgent as you want.'[7] Like the Beatles' 'White Album', *Nite Flights* is at the same time a group album and a collection of solo tracks, identifiable by the singer and the writing credit. On *Nite Flights* the first four tracks are Scott's, the next two are Gary's and the final four are John's. The respective writing credits are given under their real names: Engel, Leeds and Maus.

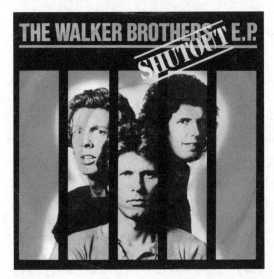

Would Nite Flights *have made a great EP? Actually it did – all four of Scott's tracks were also released by GTO as the* Shutout *EP.*

The most important tracks on *Nite Flights* are without a shadow of a doubt those by Scott. They marked his return to songwriting, his first writing credit since 1971's B-Side *166* 'My Way Home'. And all four tracks are magnificent, in effect setting the agenda for the rest of Scott's solo career. The Scott Walker of *Nite Flights* was a very different songwriter to that of *'Til the Band Comes In*. Most importantly, the notion of compromise was gone. In 1970, Scott seemed to welcome Ady Semel's moderating influence in the hope that it would make his songs more accessible. Since 1978, his songwriting almost redefined the word 'uncompromising' – so clearly has it been the case that he made the works that he wanted to create irrespective of generating sales. The new Scott Walker was not the romantic of old. Nothing in the *Nite Flights* universe (or that of *Climate of Hunter* or his modern albums) is pretty or sentimental. Also absent are any literal or obvious meanings to Scott's lyrics. In the case of songs like *106* 'Plastic Palace People' and *132* 'Boy Child', they at least possess a form that gives them the superficial appearance of narrative. The same cannot be said of Scott's material from 1978 onwards. This in itself is not a problem; a great song does not require a literal or obvious lyric in order to be great. If a song evokes some feeling or meaning for its listener, then it has done its job. Moreover, ambiguity can also add interest and intrigue. Taking the *Nite Flights* opening track, 'Shutout', as a case in point, one does not have to know exactly what the 'Shutout' is or exactly who 'the great doll' in the lyric is to get the following from the song: a declaration of intent that things are going to be different, somehow more genuine from now on, in the song's opening line, 'throw off those gimmicks to the boys'; a sense that someone, or some group of people, is being persecuted; the evocative wordplay of 'ratmosphere', etc. To some ears, 'Shutout' might even be conceived as a futurist sci-fi nightmare vision a la Bowie's *Diamond Dogs*, when one takes into account lyrics such as 'something attacked the earth last night'. Either way, there is no denying its power. Against an almost disco backing, guitars wail into frenzied feedback and Scott intones his dark lyric with all the conviction in the world. A strange and brilliant track that no one could have predicted from listening to *No Regrets* or *Lines*.

233. Fat Mama Kick (S. Engel)
Original release: *Nite Flights* 1978 LP

On some releases, 'Fat Mama Kick' is credited as 'dedicated to Bertrand-Henri Levy', an unfortunate typographical error and presumably the result of someone confusing their philosophers – the British Bertrand Russell with the French Bernard-Henri Levy. The dedication must be taken to be to the Frenchman. As much intellectual celebrity as philosopher, Levy had, at the time of *Nite Flights'* release, recently published his book *La barbarie à visage humain* (*Barbarism with a Human Face*), in which he attacked Communism as being inescapably bound to state terror. The book title alone suggests an inspiration for 'Fat Mama Kick' – the human face of 'Mama' and the barbarism of the kick. And if the song does indeed draw its inspiration from Levy's book, then it might even be seen as a sequel to *134* 'The Old Man's Back Again' – a story of state terror and betrayal of ideals in a godless universe. Whether or not this is the case, Scott's lyrics are the stuff of nightmares and the instrumental backing is equally strange, with disturbing electronic noises and the tenor sax sounding as if it were being strangled on the solo. A great track, but perhaps not quite as great as Scott's other three contributions to *Nite Flights*.

234. Nite Flights (S. Engel)
Original release: *Nite Flights* 1978 LP

The nightmare landscape continues on 'Nite Flights'. There is the 'cold', the 'dark', 'the raw meat fist', and the 'broken necks' of Scott's lyric, but with the song's soaring hook-line there is also the promise of love and of hope – 'be my love, we will be gods on nite flights.' If *232* 'Shutout' is Scott's equivalent to Bowie's *Diamond Dogs*, then 'Nite Flights' is his take on Bowie's glorious song 'Heroes'. Both 'Nite Flights' and 'Heroes' are powerful records with a driving electronic backing, superlative vocals by their respective composers, and a message of love and hope where it seems there should be none. And 'Nite Flights', of course, later came to be recorded by David Bowie himself, and is included on his 1993 *Black Tie, White Noise* album.

235. The Electrician (S. Engel)
Original release: *Nite Flights* 1978 LP

In general, the 'new Scott Walker' post-*Nite Flights* was extremely reluctant to discuss the meaning of his lyrics, but 'The Electrician' is one song with which he did acquiesce. In the above-mentioned 1984 radio interview, Scott described it as follows: 'a political song . . . having to do with . . . the Americans sending in these people, trained torturers in South America . . . I imagined these lovers in a conversation . . . if you listen the words of "The Electrician" it really explains itself after I've started.' So what meaning does one get from 'The Electrician'? The answers are not pleasant, nor are they intended to be: The eponymous electrician is a professional torturer. He uses electricity to break and to kill his subjects ('if I jerk the handle you'll die'). He drills into their souls, and possibly literally drills into their bodies. The line, 'he's drilling through the Spiritus Sanctus tonight' is one of the most horrific in the song, carrying a number of possible connotations. 'Spiritus Sanctus' literally means holy spirit, thus the line could mean the electrician is breaking the spirit of the person he is torturing. But it has also been used as a name for God, so the line might be taken to mean that the electrician is defiling God with his activities. We are left in no doubt that the electrician enjoys his work ('you'll thrill me, and thrill me, and thrill me'). From Scott's comments, the electrician is not to be taken as a fantasy figure but a real person, the like of whom genuinely exists because the government of the United States (supposedly 'the land of the free') sponsors his activities. The electrician is also a human being who, like any other, has a lover, though it seems his sadism has overtaken him to the point where it dominates his relationships. Perhaps the most disturbingly brilliant thing about 'The Electrician' is that, just after the repeated 'thrill me' line, the otherwise morose backing breaks into one of the most beautiful passages of music to grace any of Scott Walker's records – all swirling strings and Spanish guitar, the aural equivalent of the sun breaking through the clouds. Scott would not record another track this disturbing or this brilliant for another seventeen years.

236. Death of Romance (G. Leeds)
237. Den Haague (G. Leeds)
238. Rhythms of Vision (J. J. Maus)
239. Disciples of Death (J. J. Maus)
240. Fury and the Fire (J. J. Maus)
241. Child of Flames (J. J. Maus)
Original release: *Nite Flights* 1978 LP

The four Scott Walker tracks that open *Nite Flights* were always going to be hard for Gary and John to follow. And ironically, the kindest thing that can be said about their contributions overall – that they try to fit in with the mood of the album, as dictated by Scott – is also the reason why they fail so badly. Scott's *Nite Flights* vision was so uniquely his own that, when Gary and John tried to follow in his footsteps, the results ended up as mere pastiches. Perhaps surprisingly, given that Gary's vocal and compositional abilities were hitherto conspicuous by their absence from Walker Brothers records, Gary's tracks are much better than John's. Both 'Death of Romance' and 'Den Haague' are at least entertaining, the latter amusingly featuring the Walkers' frankest ever lyric as Gary warns us to 'look out for the muff king with a big black whopper in a two-way mirror mood'. In contrast, John's tracks find him so clearly writing against his own style that the results are a leaden, derivative mess. Sadly, none of his *Nite Flights* contributions sparkle in any way and, next to what has gone before, they sound uninspired and cliché ridden. John Walker had undoubtedly shown a strong talent for songwriting with his superb compositions for the Sixties Walker Brothers, *40* 'Saddest Night in the World' and *58* 'I Can't Let It Happen to You'. And the unreleased *247* 'The Ballad', recorded at the time of *Nite Flights*, proves that he still had that talent. But by trying to emulate Scott's vision, with which he clearly had no artistic empathy, John ended up recording obviously inferior and uninspired tracks. 'Rhythms of Vision', for example, is a plodding rocker with a cheesy organ solo and bad poetry for a lyric. And 'Fury and the Fire' wants to sound like Bowie's *Station to Station* LP. But had David Bowie come up with a track this dull he would probably have left it on the train!

It is hard to think of another non-compilation LP in the history of popular music that is quite like *Nite Flights* – a record totally dominated by its first side and let down by its second.[8] There might be any number of vinyl copies of *Nite Flights* out there with side one almost worn out and side two in pristine condition.

Despite the quality of Scott's tracks (all four of which were also released as an EP by the record company) and clearly superior cover artwork,[9] *Nite Flights* did not find an audience at the time of its release and the LP joined *Lines* in being a commercial flop. The Walker Brothers' reunion was over.

Extras

Seven previously unheard Seventies Walker Brothers tracks received an official release in 2001 on the CD compilation *If You Could Hear Me Now*. All seven of these tracks are now also included on the *Everything Under the Sun* box set.

242. Loving Arms (Tom Jans)
Original release: not applicable, outtake from *No Regrets*

The most remarkable thing about the previously unreleased tracks is that a number of them are much better than some of those that did make it to release. 'Loving Arms' is a case in point. Tom Jans may have written the ghastly *224* 'Inside of You', but this is a much better song that a number of artists have covered. Here it receives a wistful John Walker lead vocal that really suits the song, a much better track than, say, *218* 'He'll Break Your Heart', which did make it on to the *No Regrets* LP.

Scott pictured at a recording of The Vera Lynn Show in November 1975, the first TV show on which the Walker Brothers performed 'No Regrets'.

243. I Never Dreamed You'd Leave in Summer (Stevie Wonder)
Original release: not applicable, outtake from *No Regrets*

Also recorded for, but not released on, the *No Regrets* LP, this is Scott's take on the Stevie Wonder song originally featured on his 1971 LP, *Where I'm Coming From*.

244. The Moon's a Harsh Mistress (Jimmy Webb)
Original release: not applicable, outtake from *No Regrets*

Scott had recorded Jimmy Webb songs for *Any Day Now* and *Stretch*, so it's not too much of a surprise to find he recorded another one during the Walker Brothers' reunion. 'The Moon's a Harsh Mistress' is a beautiful song which, despite the title being taken from Robert A. Heinlein's science fiction novel *The Moon Is a Harsh Mistress*, is no otherworldly tale of space travel like *188* 'If Ships Were Made to Sail'. Instead, the appeal of 'The Moon's a Harsh Mistress' lies in its theme of unattainability – we have all wanted something or someone that we can't have. In Jimmy Webb's words, it's the song that 'became a standard without ever becoming a hit'.[10] Scott Walker is a clearly worthwhile addition to the long list of artists who have sung the song.[11]

245. Marie (Randy Newman)
Original release: not applicable, outtake from *No Regrets*

Randy Newman's song 'Marie', sung by John Walker. Again, it's better than most of his tracks that did make it onto the released LPs. Newman's original version featured on his 1974 LP *Good Old Boys*.

246. 'Til I Gain Control Again (Rodney Crowell)
Original release: not applicable, outtake from *Lines*

Less material, it seems, was recorded for the *Lines* LP than its immediate predecessor, and this is the only outtake from that album included on the *If You Could Hear Me Now* and *Everything Under the Sun* anthologies. A perfectly good Scott Walker vocal graces this compelling ballad, which would have made a better addition to *Lines* than *224* 'Inside of You', *229* 'Brand New Tennessee Waltz' or *231* 'Dreaming as One', all of which were included on the record. ''Til I Gain Control Again' was written by Rodney Crowell who, at the time, was a member of Emmylou Harris's touring band. The song features on Emmylou's 1975 LP *Elite Hotel*.

247. The Ballad (AKA The Ballad of Ty and Jerome) (John Walker)
Original release: not applicable, outtake from *Nite Flights*

Obviously not a track that would have fitted in with the style of *Nite Flights*, but, ironically, John's 'The Ballad' is far superior to any of his offerings on that LP. It's an absolutely great song, a lovely, contemplative ballad that doesn't hurry to get where it's going and remains genuinely touching.

The song's correct title is incidentally 'The Ballad' and not 'The Ballad of Ty and Jerome'. That longer title, and a Douglas John co-writing credit that were given on the *If You Could Hear Me Now* CD, resulted from a mistake made by Sony when they printed the CD. ('The Ballad of Ty and Jerome' is a completely different song on their catalogue that has nothing to do with the Walker Brothers.)

248. Tokyo Rimshot (Scott Walker)
Original release: not applicable, outtake from *Nite Flights*

A more typical *Nite Flights* outtake is 'Tokyo Rimshot', an instrumental track with a vaguely Japanese electronic sound (hence presumably the 'Tokyo' of the title). It is not known whether Scott penned or intended to write any lyrics for the track. It sounds like it might be a working title rather than pertaining to a lyric ('rimshot' is a drumming term). But it's a little too 'up', and even a little too disco, to have added anything to the creative statement made by Scott on his four released *Nite Flights* songs. It remains an interesting curio and an indication of the musical direction Scott's thoughts were capable of taking him in.

---

1. Gary Walker's two UK chart singles, 'You Don't Love Me' and 'Twinkie Lee', both date from 1966 when the Walker Brothers were still together. Coincidentally, both Gary's hits reached a peak of Number 26 in the charts.
2. The single and the LP versions of 'No Regrets' do actually differ. The single features a John Walker harmony vocal not present on the album, and the album version features female backing singers absent from the single.
3. The recording/production credit on the *No Regrets* album sleeve goes to the Walker Brothers and Geoff Calver. But that appears to be just an indication of the group's new democracy, rather than any particular involvement by John or Gary on the production side. By the time of *Lines*, the production credit read 'Scott Walker and Geoff Calver'.
4. Oddly listed as 'unknown' on the original LP record.
5. The original album also contained a print of the photograph used to create the cover's line drawing. The photograph is even worse. The lack of background, and the way the black and white image joins the three Walkers together, makes them look like a three-headed Walker monster!
6. With apologies to Emmylou Harris, Donna Weiss and Janis Ian!
7. This interview with Alan Bangs, one of the longest Scott Walker interviews of the post-1978 era, was broadcast on the BBC's BFBS (British Forces Broadcasting Service) in Germany in 1984. Bangs' radio programme was, coincidentally or otherwise, called *Night Flight*.
8. Perhaps only the Plastic Ono Band's *Live Peace in Toronto* comes close: side one – pretty good rock'n'roll by John Lennon, side two – far too much of Yoko's wailing.
9. The *Nite Flights* artwork was created by Hipgnosis, the company also responsible for numerous famous Pink Floyd designs and other Seventies album covers that political correctness would rather the world forgot. The artwork includes two rare pictures of Scott Walker smoking; one of them can be seen on the inside back cover of the *Lines* CD booklet; the other, it seems, went AWOL for the CD reissue.
10. Jimmy Webb's own liner notes to his 1993 *Archive* compilation CD.
11. Apart from the Walker Brothers' unreleased cover, the song has been recorded by Joe Cocker (1974, *I Can Stand a Little Rain*), Glen Campbell (1974, *Reunion*), Judy Collins (1975, *Judith*), Jimmy Webb himself (1977, *El Mirage*), Linda Ronstadt (1982, *Get Closer*), Joan Baez (1987, *Recently*) and Pat Metheny (1997, *Beyond the Missouri Sky*). There are many other versions as well.

part five
A Road Less Travelled
1984 - 2018

'I'm not a get up and sing a song singer.' –
Scott Walker, *The Tube*, Channel 4 TV Interview, 1984

If Scott Walker's four *Nite Flights* tracks were hardly a runaway commercial success, they were at least a critical success in some quarters. On the strength of these alone, Virgin Records signed Scott to record a series of solo LPs for them. For a brief moment post-*Nite Flights*, it must have looked as though his solo career was set to return from the wilderness. The record company wanted Scott the vocalist and composer, not just Scott the singer. At that time, no one could have predicted the way in which his solo career would unfold. It did of course become a recording career without parallel, but one which was also defined by the infrequency of his output. After *Nite Flights* and up to 2006 (some film soundtrack work and other bits and pieces aside) there had been just three Scott Walker albums in 28 years – 1984's *Climate of Hunter*, 1995's *Tilt* and 2006's *The Drift*. Prior to 1978, a new Scott Walker or Walker Brothers album had been in the shops every year but two, from 1965-77.

None of Scott Walker's albums from *Climate of Hunter* onwards are what one might call 'immediate' records and they're certainly not easy listening. (In fact one could invent a category of music called 'uneasy listening' if one were determined to pigeonhole the loose trilogy of *Tilt*, *The Drift* and *Bish Bosch*.) As stated in Part Four of this book, the agenda (almost the manifesto) for Scott's subsequent career was set in place on those *Nite Flights* tracks. Past glories were not going to be revisited and commercial compromises were not going to be made. The resulting records are brave, at times beautiful, at times disturbing, moving, deep, dark works of art. That is not necessarily to say that they surpass the younger Scott's greatest records (although some consider that they do), or that they are perfect. In particular, both *Climate of Hunter* and *Tilt* are at best, and for different reasons, flawed masterpieces. Scott himself considered *The Drift* and *Bish Bosch* to be their superiors. But in making these records – and with *Bish Bosch* in particular meeting with almost universal critical acclaim on its release – Scott's reputation was assured, and we can and should celebrate the fact that Scott Walker chose a different and unique road to travel, to the end.

Climate of Hunter 1984 LP

249. Rawhide (Scott Walker)

Original release: *Climate of Hunter* 1984 LP

Rarely has an LP opened with a more prophetic line than *Climate of Hunter*: 'This is how you disappear.' Having waited six years for him to deliver an album, Virgin Records' business minds must have been nonplussed, to say the least. The LP is a short record, just 31 minutes long, comprising seven Walker originals and one cover version. None of the originals have literal or readily understandable lyrics, or any immediate hooks. Half the tracks do not even have titles. And none of them were, in anybody's wildest dreams, likely to become a hit single. The record did not sell, and no further Scott Walker LPs followed from Virgin Records. In some ways the LP can be seen as coming from the same place as the *Nite Flights* tracks, but in other ways it takes things in a different direction. Nothing on *Climate of Hunter* is as accessible as *Nite Flights*, or as urgent or as angry. *Climate of Hunter* is an acquired taste, but one that most Scott Walker fans (and some non-fans) will find is worth acquiring, if they can put up with the 1980s production style that mars the record. One of the chief rewards is of course Scott's voice, which unquestionably sounds as good as it ever did, but that is not to belittle its songs.

'Rawhide' starts with the lonely clanging of what sounds like a solitary cowbell. Then it is by turns spookily atmospheric, soaring, electronic, orchestral, as cold as steel and as warm as toast. It sounds simply like nothing else on earth and it is undoubtedly a highlight. What is it about? Well, it would be wrong to suppose that the lyrics on *Climate of Hunter* (or any of those that followed in his career) were born out of some random cut-up technique, or that they are meaningless. Of course, they have more in common with abstract poetry than linear pop-song lyrics, and their meaning is more evocative than literal. Scott historically was loath to accept invitations to explain his lyrics, on the grounds that to do so would be impractical, impossible, or would 'destroy the magic'. Nevertheless, there are some themes that are undoubtedly present, whether or not they are metaphors. 'Rawhide', from the title downward, is dominated by the theme of the herd. The words and phrases 'rawhide', 'shaggy belly', 'hindlegs', 'graze with them', 'sweeping tails' and 'the hooves all around' all play with the imagery of a herd of cattle. Perhaps the herd is something primeval or timeless that will always exist: 'Cro-magnon herders will stand in the wind,'[1] and perhaps the herd is something we cannot help but be a part of: 'as one of their own, you graze with them.' Further meaning is within the eye or the ear of the beholder.

250. Dealer (Scott Walker)

Original release: *Climate of Hunter* 1984 LP

With only three out of the seven original compositions on the album having titles, it's hard not to attach weight to those that do exist. Given the references in the song's lyric to 'ice', 'junkies' and 'tracks', and to death and numbness, it's reasonable to surmise that the dealer of the title is a drug dealer. Maybe the song is about the longing, insatiability and hopelessness of drug addiction, or maybe the drug dealer is a metaphor for one human being who is capable of taking over the soul of another: 'he climbs into your mouth, when the windows ring.' Either way the track is remarkable and eerily atmospheric, to the extent that one can almost feel the darkness even when listening to it in the daytime.

1984's Climate of Hunter – *a brave, interesting and, at times, brilliant record.*

251. Track Three (Scott Walker)
Original release: *Climate of Hunter* 1984 LP

Despite being the most hook-laden on the album, and even having what might pass for a chorus ('Rock of cast-offs bury me, hide my soul and sink us free') and a rock guitar solo, this song is seriously marred by its horrid 1980s production, all tiny shiny drums to the fore. Surprisingly, 'Track Three' features a harmony vocal from one Billy Ocean, of 'When the Going Gets Tough' fame, and the song was even released as a single. It was accompanied by a video, as odd as the song's lyric, which has dated in an even worse fashion than the track itself.[2] Needless to say, the single didn't chart.

252. Sleepwalker's Woman (Scott Walker)
Original release: *Climate of Hunter* 1984 LP

Side one of *Climate of Hunter* finishes with its most beautiful and, arguably, best track. 'Sleepwalker's Woman' is, simply put, the *132* 'Boy Child' of the album. Like 'Boy Child', it is more classical in origin. Mercifully drum-less and extremely touching, the song appears to be about a relationship, even a love song

155

born of gratitude. Is it autobiographical? Scott had used a little wordplay on *251* 'Track Three' (such as 'the shadow of the son'[3]) so, perhaps, despite Scott Walker's latter-day statements about his not writing autobiographical lyrics, it's not beyond the imagination to suppose that the title of this track might be a pun: sleep-Walker's woman (i.e. Scott Walker's woman). The song's references to returning from exile may be Scott's return to recording and to a public profile, following his self-imposed six-year exile. With or without this autobiographical interpretation, 'Sleepwalker's Woman' is an artistic peak, all the more remarkable in that the majority of its lyric seems to be sung from the female perspective of the relationship.

253. Track Five (Scott Walker)
Original release: *Climate of Hunter* 1984 LP

Side two of *Climate of Hunter* mirrors side one too closely to be anything but intentional. 'Track Five' mirrors *249* 'Rawhide' (both tracks begin with strange, lonely noises, both start quietly and build); *254* 'Track Six' mirrors *250* 'Dealer' (both are slower, more evocative pieces); *255* 'Track Seven' mirrors *251* 'Track Three' (both are more up-tempo pop/rock tracks, both featuring electric guitar), and even *256* 'Blanket Roll Blues' mirrors *252* 'Sleepwalker's Woman' (both are drum-less, a world away from the pop music of the day). Unfortunately, 'Track Five' is not the equal of 'Rawhide'. It starts well enough, from the line, 'It's a starving,' up until, 'we chew up,' where Scott sings almost *a cappella*, but thereafter it's dogged by the same early Eighties sound that mars 'Track Three'. There is also much less to hold the listener's attention than on 'Rawhide''s eclectic palette. The lack of a song title does not help make it any more memorable. Walk away from *Climate of Hunter* for a few days (or months, or years) and try to discuss the songs by the titles given on the record. You will find yourself thinking, well, which one was 'Track Six'? Which one was 'Track Five'? Scott's comment on these numerical titles, given in his uncomfortable interview on TV pop programme *The Tube*, was that the songs were complete and that titles might 'lopside' them or 'overload' them, presumably giving artificially undue weight to one line of the lyric over the others. All well and good, but the numeric titles come across as a wilfully obscure move. Thankfully, Scott did not feel the need to repeat the experiment on the records he eventually made after *Climate of Hunter*.

254. Track Six (Scott Walker)
Original release: *Climate of Hunter* 1984 LP

'Track Six' begins with the line, 'Say it got late,' and has the chorus (using the term loosely), 'The ceilings are rising and falling, the ceilings are shiny and slow . . .' Like *250* 'Dealer' on side one, it is eerily atmospheric, but even more so. The song's first part is slowed down to a crawl and the instrumentation on the second part is the aural equivalent of being attacked by a flock of angry birds. The lyric also mirrors that of 'Dealer', with its themes of desperation/yearning ('say it got late on that one, that life-giver one'), satiation/satisfaction ('taken up I could hold him, when all falls away'), hints of religious imagery ('Dealer' has 'psalms'; 'Track Six' has praying and the 'life-giver one') and the drug experience (walls appearing to 'breathe' during the psychedelic drug experience is too universal a phenomenon not to suggest itself). The track has Scott's shortest lyric on the LP, but it is also one of the best simply because so many themes, possible interpretations and emotions are crammed into so few words, without ever seeming to veer off into random obscurity. Undoubtedly the best track on side two, it was inexplicably not included on the *Five Easy Pieces* box set compilation, whilst most of the rest of *Climate of Hunter* was.

255. Track Seven (Scott Walker)
Original release: *Climate of Hunter* 1984 LP

Again for identification purposes, 'Track Seven' begins with the line, 'Stump of a drowner,' and has the 'chorus', 'Deserting your lead . . .' Like *251* 'Track Three', it is dominated and marred by its early Eighties sound. Even before we get to that incessant tinny foreground drumming, the beginning sounds a little reminiscent of Ultravox's 'Vienna'.[4] It doesn't add very much of interest to *Climate of Hunter*'s soundscape, least of all its technically proficient but noodling electric guitar solo.

256. Blanket Roll Blues (Tennessee Williams/Kenyon Hopkins)
Original release: *Climate of Hunter* 1984 LP

The only non-Scott Walker composition on the album, 'Blanket Roll Blues' is obscurity itself: the only song lyric ever written by playwright Tennessee Williams, as sung by Marlon Brando in the 1959 film *The Fugitive Kind*. Scott had this to say about it in the 1984 radio interview with Alan Bangs: '[It's] been . . . in the back of my mind for years and years and it was just finding a time and a way to use it, and I thought it's such a small song and I've never been able to put it anywhere and it seemed like the perfect sort of period at the end of all this.' Though clocking in at three minutes and sixteen seconds on *Climate of Hunter* (and therefore not its shortest track), the majority of that time is not taken up with Scott's voice, but with the unaccompanied bluesy guitar playing of Mark Knopfler of Dire Straits. Scott's description, 'such a small song', refers to the brevity of Williams' lyric, which is a mere two sentences long: 'When I crossed the river, with a heavy blanket roll, I took nobody with me, not a soul.' / 'I took a few provisions, some for comfort, some for cold, but I took nobody with me, not a soul.' It takes Scott only about a minute to sing it slowly. Coming at the end of the LP, the song is certainly apposite. Scott Walker, had he directed his career to that end, could have been a very rich and famous man in 1984. Instead, as he told Bangs, he had never received much money and lived on 'not a lot' between *Nite Flights* and *Climate of Hunter* – 'a few provisions', it seems, sufficed. Moreover, *Climate of Hunter*, in particular, and Scott's solo career since *Nite Flights* in general have been a unique and solitary journey – nobody, 'not a soul', has had a recording career like his. Arguably, Scott's desire not to repeat what he saw as the artistic mistakes of the past led him toward obscurity. That he took his post-*Nite Flights* manifesto seriously cannot be in any doubt. During the Bangs interview, he talked about his previous 'sentimentality' as if it was a crime and described his 'bad' records as 'sins'. *Climate of Hunter* can be seen as an exercise in overcompensation for these so-called sins; even *Tilt* has more straightforward lyrics. It nevertheless remains a brave, interesting and, at times, brilliant record.

Part of *Climate of Hunter*'s uniqueness is due to the fact that Scott released no records in its aftermath. Following the LP's poor sales, nobody at Virgin was rushing him back into the studio to record *Climate of Hunter Part Two*. And as things turned out, despite Scott telling Alan Bangs that he was sure he could record a follow-up LP 'fairly quickly', it remained his only record release of the 1980s.

Scott pictured in 1984, around the time of Climate of Hunter's *release.*

1993

257. Man from Reno (Scott Walker [lyrics]/Goran Bregovic [music])
Original release: France only CD single 1993
Most recently available: on *Five Easy Pieces* box set

The early Nineties finally saw the release of a decent Walker compilation in *Boy Child*, a selection of his best solo compositions. The only previous worthy compilations were *Fire Escape in the Sky* from 1981, compiled by Julian Cope and not widely available, and the 'does exactly what it says on the tin' compilation *Scott Walker Sings Jacques Brel* from the same year. Hot on the heels of *Boy Child* came the long overdue reissue of the *Scott* LPs, this time on shiny little compact discs. Encouraged by rave reviews in *NME* and other music publications, a new generation of Scott Walker fans was born. The long overdue critical praise for *Scott 4*, not to mention the royalty payments from the reissues, must have given him some satisfaction – even given his aversion to looking back. The early Nineties also saw Scott sign to Phonogram, ready to record again. This time the portents were good. Phonogram (Mercury/Fontana), the company who already owned most of the Walker back catalogue, were obviously aware of *Climate of Hunter*'s sales record and Scott's lack of commerciality, but they were happy to let him make the records he wanted to make. The first fruit arrived with a whimper rather than a bang – a CD single released only in France in 1993, which even the keenest Walker fan might have missed. It comprised two tracks featured on the soundtrack of Philomene Esposito's 1993 French language film, *Toxic Affair*, with music by Goran Bregovic and lyrics by Scott.

The Yugoslavian Bregovic had been an Eastern Bloc rock star during the Seventies and Eighties, before successfully reinventing himself as a composer of music for films. Reading Bregovic's biography from his website,[5] there are strange parallels with the story of Scott Walker. Bregovic variously grew 'sick and tired' of being a youth idol, was interested in philosophy, drawn to Paris (albeit under forced circumstances), retired from live performance for a long period and pursued a maverick mix of musical styles to critical acclaim. Perhaps the two men had found something in common. The tracks they created together were hardly going to set the world on fire, but they do make for interesting listening.

'Man from Reno' starts as an orchestral ballad, before turning into quite a funky little pop song. Scott's lyric is by turns amusing and disturbing. Of course, nothing is either linear or definite with a latter-day Walker lyric, but the wonderful line, 'I ain't no pussy with the blues' might be autobiographical – a reminder, if one were needed, that Scott Walker is no longer the sentimental romantic of old. The line 'man from Sarajevo' might be a reference to Bregovic, as that city was his birthplace.[6] The song also includes the splendid line, 'you got him by the balls,' which is a delight to hear Scott singing every time! Disturbingly though, its most recurring allusion is to the 'Zodiac Killer' – a real-life serial killer active in California in the Sixties and Seventies. He had a penchant for murdering young couples and sending letters and coded messages to the newspapers, saying how much he had enjoyed killing them. It's even more disturbing that the Zodiac verses are the most poppy on the record, complete with chirpy female backing singers repeating the lines. One might compare this to the beautiful orchestral passage from *245* 'The Electrician', which is bookended by lyrics about the electrician's sadism.

258. Indecent Sacrifice (Scott Walker [lyrics] / Goran Bregovic [music])
Original release: France only CD single 1993
Most recently available: on *Five Easy Pieces* box set

A lesser track than *258* 'Man from Reno', 'Indecent Sacrifice' grooves along quite nicely in a kind of sub-Steely Dan way. Scott's lyric is about someone moving on and leaving the past, metaphorically or literally, for dead: 'saying goodbye without warning'. The song's title, and the fact that its narrator 'took the murder weapon' and 'took you by the throat to drag you under', suggest a sequel to the serial killer references in 'Man from Reno'.

Tilt 1995 LP

259. Farmer in the City (N. S. Engel)
Original release: *Tilt* 1995 LP / CD

1995's Tilt *– a disturbingly compelling album and easily twice the record that* Climate of Hunter *is.*

Scott Walker's second post-*Nite Flights* solo LP, *Tilt* was finally released in 1995, some eleven years after *Climate of Hunter*. The album's release had been expected as long ago as 1992, and the CD booklet makes a point of mentioning that the majority of its songs were composed during '91 and '92. If anybody at the time of *Tilt*'s release had supposed that *257* 'Man from Reno' / *258* 'Indecent Sacrifice' gave an indication of its musical direction, they were in for a rude awakening. *Tilt* is a dark mix of the orchestral and the industrial, discordant sounds and spartan arrangements. Scott's fairly restrained vocal performance on 'Man from Reno' does not prepare you for his literal highs and lows. It becomes very apparent that his voice is different than it was. Of course, no one should expect a man in his fifties (as Scott was at the time of *Tilt*) to possess the same voice that he did as a young man. Scott's vocals on *Tilt* are decidedly more mature, more operatic, than anything that had come before. Unlike *Climate of Hunter*, nor is *Tilt* a short record – its pieces are, for the most part, longer than the three or four-minute norm, with most clocking in at over six minutes. Its lyrics are as deep and dark as its music and anything but easily accessible. *Tilt* is a serious record (although, paradoxically, it does contain traces of humour that don't really work), and requires patience and repeated listenings to get much from it (although there are elements which almost beg the listener not to bother with it). A bit like the man himself, *Tilt* is a contrary beast. So is it worth the effort one needs to expend in order to appreciate it? Yes. It is easily twice the record that *Climate of Hunter* is.

Tilt opens with 'Farmer in the City'. It is undoubtedly one of the best tracks and also one of the most accessible. Although comprised of different lyrical and/ or musical sections, like most of the tracks on the album, it is more of a continuous and cohesive whole. The music is dominated by the orchestra for the most part. The opening and closing might be gloomy, but there are no sudden changes of pace or abrasive sounds. Curiously, Scott appears to plagiarise himself by lifting the 'man from Reno/Zurich/Italy' section from 'Man from Reno', rewriting it as 'man from Rio/Vigo/Ostia' and dropping it in[7] with the strings of the Sinfonia of London behind it. It works rather better than it did in its original setting. An artist plagiarising himself typically suggests he's running out of ideas, but, given the obscurity of 'Man from Reno' and the resulting brilliance of 'Farmer in the City', Scott's reuse of material can easily be overlooked.

The lyrics to *Tilt* in general, and 'Farmer in the City' in particular, are opaque, and attempting a line-by-line exegesis doesn't really make sense. In interviews, Scott said that to do so would be impractical, and would 'cheapen' the words. Many of the lyrics have evocative rather than literal meanings, but there are definite clues to be found in the CD booklet and in interviews. 'Farmer in the City' is a case in point. The song is subtitled '(remembering Pasolini)', and Scott did say that the song is in some sense about his murder. Pier Paolo Pasolini (1922-1975) was an outspoken Italian intellectual and filmmaker. Ever controversial, a Marxist, and openly gay, he was found murdered in Rome on 2 November 1975. It has long been supposed that the official version of events (and the conviction of his alleged killer)[8] does not tell the true story. In May 2005, the police in Rome belatedly reopened their investigation of the case. Whilst there are oblique references to Pasolini in the lyric ('Paulo' is perhaps a misspelling; 'Ostia' is the suburb of Rome in which Pasolini's body was found; 'Ninetto' is presumably a reference to Ninetto Davoli, one of Pasolini's leading actors), the song is obviously not a linear telling of his murder and neither is it political sloganeering. Instead, we find that in addition to whatever it says about the murder of Pasolini, the song transcends its origins in this particular historical incident. The titular farmer in the city seems to work as an allegory for someone who finds himself in a world that is not his own (a world up for auction sale, perhaps, to evoke the song's opening and closing sections), a world in which he is not at home, or, more frighteningly, a situation which has gone too far and which he is no longer in control of (as Pasolini must have found at the time of his murder). The allegorical image of a farmer in the city is developed to a certain extent in the lyric, but we also find the same notion from the opposite point of view before the song's end – with the city dweller (the citizen) in the farm knowing nothing of 'the horses' or 'the thresher'. It is typical of a latter-day Walker lyric that there should be a number of different narrative voices (all sung by Scott, which doesn't aid comprehension). This is obviously true of some of *Climate of Hunter*, but it also goes back as far as *103* 'The Amorous Humphrey Plugg' – where some of the lines that Scott sings can be taken to come from Mrs. Plugg rather than Humphrey.

260. The Cockfighter (N. S. Engel)
Original release: *Tilt* 1995 LP/CD

In interview, Scott said that it was always the lyric that dictated how the track would go on to sound. Of 'The Cockfighter', he said that the song is in some sense concerned with a man having a nightmare.[9] True to form, the music is the stuff of nightmares. It starts with some inaudible words and discordant wailings that sound like the mumblings and moaning of the nightmare dreamer in his sleep. The listener is not advised to turn the track up to listen to these sounds, unless already prepared for an assault on the senses. 'The Cockfighter' is a discordant mix of percussion made into industrial sound, its clanging and wailing punctuated by quieter passages which only serve to make its return more oppressive. Scott's vocal too, on those sections of the lyric written in capitals in the CD booklet, is more akin to shouting than anything else he had hitherto sung on record.

As with *259* 'Farmer in the City', there are indications as to the lyric's origins to be found in the CD booklet and in interviews Scott gave. It includes extracts from two historic trials, those of Queen Caroline and Adolf Eichmann. Queen Caroline was tried for adultery in 1820, the charges being levelled rather hypocritically by her husband, King George IV of England. With public sympathy on her side, she was acquitted of the charge. In contrast, Eichmann was a Nazi war criminal, an SS officer who shared responsibility for the deaths of millions of Jews in extermination camps. When finally brought to trial in Israel in 1961, Eichmann claimed to have been just following orders – but, by all accounts, he carried out his part in Hitler's 'Final Solution' with dedication. He was found guilty of all the charges brought against him and executed in 1962. The reasons for including lines from these two trials seem to have been manifold. Scott said that the song was about 'an internal struggle within one man', and that the two trials were evoked to 'play with time' and to 'attack the ludicrous of the law', but also to 'talk about what can't be talked about'. Although he spoke in general terms about his lyrics as an attempt to 'say the unsayable', this is a specific reference to the Holocaust – the Nazis' attempt to destroy the Jewish race in Europe, in which they succeeded in murdering six million. It's a difficult enough subject to approach in conversation or prose, let alone poetry or song. But the lyrical strategy of 'The Cockfighter', its opaqueness coupled with the horror of its sound, do enable it to address the subject without lapsing into bad taste.

Easy listening it is not, but its aural and lyrical overload (in addition to all of the above, there are erotic images juxtaposed with the barbarism of the cockfight) make it the most powerful and fascinating track on *Tilt*.

261. Bouncer See Bouncer (N. S. Engel)
Original release: *Tilt* 1995 LP / CD

It is hard not to imagine that 'Bouncer See Bouncer' continues with the Holocaust theme found on *260* 'The Cockfighter'. The sheer bleakness of the track, for most of its nearly nine-minute running time, suggests this, but Scott all but spelled it out for us with the phrase 'halo of locust', which appears written thus in the lyric sheet. On each of the occasions it is sung, the word 'of' is hardly pronounced, leaving us with 'halo locust', a clear wordplay on 'holocaust'. Of course, nothing is literal about the lyric, and *Tilt*'s themes do not compartmentalise themselves neatly into individual songs. But other possible references to the Holocaust are suggested by the lyric. There are references to hair and to teeth – one of the most abiding and disgusting images of the Nazi death camps relating to how the victims' hair and gold teeth were perceived as valuable (whereas the human beings themselves were not), removed and stockpiled as a useful by-product of mass extermination. There are also references to the family made in the past tense, as though the family in question has been in some way destroyed. Additionally, one possible reading of the 'I've been spared' line is to see it as coming from the lips of a Holocaust survivor.

'Bouncer See Bouncer' is a remarkable track. For the most part the song's arrangement is spartan to the point of being horrific, comprising eerie rattling and wailing sounds against a relentless and monotonous pounding. There are also locust sounds heard at the beginning and the end, apparently courtesy of a hurdy gurdy.[10] Against this backdrop, Scott raises the dramatic pause to a high art form with his delivery of the lyric. The track also repeats what we might call *235* 'The Electrician'-trick. For in the midst of musical and lyrical bleakness comes a passage of the most beautiful music, against which Scott sings lines which begin, 'I love this season . . .', before the monotonous, pounding drum resumes and we are back where we started. The juxtaposition is just as startling as the musical beauty bookended by the lyrical beast on 'The Electrician'. If one does see 'Bouncer See Bouncer' as in some way coming from the point of view of a Holocaust survivor, then the 'I love this season . . .' section, and the fact that it's sited between such stark musical and lyrical bleakness, makes every sense. Such a person is, we imagine, going to feel glad to be alive at some point. But that feeling is likely to be forever tainted by the horror that the person has endured. This is one possible interpretation of course, but the fact that it can even suggest the emotional overload of the Holocaust survivor is testament to its powerfulness. It would be fair to call this track a work of art.

262. Manhattan (N. S. Engel)
Original release: *Tilt* 1995 LP/CD

If the whole of *Tilt* were as good as its first three tracks, then it might well be considered an unequivocal masterpiece. But flaws in its make-up begin to show to a greater or lesser extent on the next four, before the album finishes on two very strong tracks. Unfortunately, *Tilt* seems to sag a little in the middle. 'Manhattan' is its earliest composition, written, the CD booklet tells us, in 1987. It almost comes across as the missing link between *Climate of Hunter* and *Tilt* – on the one hand, we have a twisted take on traditional rock/pop instrumentation (drums, bass, guitar), and on the other, the out-there oddness (massive church organ and weird Eastern sounds) and more operatic vocal style of *Tilt*. The quasi-*Climate of Hunter* sound, however, isn't what spoils it. Rather, this otherwise strong track is marred by a section of its lyric, which, possibly in an attempt to lighten the mood, includes lines lifted from the African American spiritual, but now more children's sing-a-long, song 'Dry Bones'.[11] Thus we get (with some of it in 'Franglais'): 'le wrist is connected . . . a la collar bone connected . . . and hear the word of the lord . . . le jaw bone connected . . . a la ankles connected.' This might have been intended as light relief from the darkness of the album thus far, but it's counterproductive, as the rest of the album is so successful at building a seriousness and an intensity of mood that the last thing the listener wants is for it to be broken by an apparent attempt at humour. There is also the question of whether – for art's sake or not – this is pushing the boundaries of taste too far, given the sensitivity of the subject matter of the preceding two tracks, and the context of a lyric that addresses oppression and, in particular, imperialism and slavery. In 1689 the King of France, Louis XIV, passed a decree known as the *Code Noir*, containing the following among its articles setting out the rules of slavery: 'The fugitive slave who has been on the run for one month from the day his master reported him to the police, shall have his ears cut off and shall be branded with a *fleur de lys* on one shoulder. If he commits the same infraction for another month, again counting from the day he is reported, he shall have his hamstring cut and be branded with a *fleur de lys* on the other shoulder. The third time, he shall be put to death.'[12] The song is given the subtitle '*flerdele*' (a corruption of '*fleur de lys*') and the words appear in the lyric, along with abstract lines that suggest torture, and the line, 'it's on me all my life, on me all my life,' which suggests branding. Of course, the song is not just about the way the French or any other imperialists treated the people they made their slaves, any more than *260* 'The Cockfighter' is straightforwardly about the way the Nazis murdered Jews. True, there are references to Bengal and Somal, which were part of the French colonial empire, but the other place names mentioned in the lyric do not all neatly fall into this category. Also, there is the suggestion from the title and the modern American term 'Chief of

Police' that the song is juxtaposing modernity with the history of slavery (as 'The Cockfighter' juxtaposed the nineteenth century with the Eichmann trial). Nothing is straightforward in the world of *Tilt*, but the song addresses another way in which human beings have treated their fellows as worthless.

263. Face on Breast (N. S. Engel)
Original release: *Tilt* 1995 LP/CD

Like the track that proceeds it, 'Face on Breast' also includes an incongruous use of the familiar in its lyric. In this case, the lines in question are lifted from Lauren Bacall's often parodied dialogue from the 1944 film *To Have and Have Not*: 'You know how to whistle, don't you, Steve? You just put your lips together and . . . blow.' With which Bacall's character, a night-club singer, makes her availability pretty damn clear to Humphrey Bogart's character, Steve. As with the previous track, the effect of Scott singing the familiar lines in a deadpan delivery is distracting and mood destroying. This is a shame, because the 'swan section', which begins the track and is reprised at its end, is as intense as anything else on the album. Scott's delivery is almost painfully strained against a backing of discordant sound, whistles, feedback and a steady tapping of a bass drum, like the flapping of birds' wings in flight. We are definitely in the realm of abstract poetry, but the image of the swan from the song's opening line is both simple and effective: 'Swan you glide above the thrashing.' The swan appears to glide effortlessly as it moves across water, but beneath the surface its legs are a frenzy of thrashing. It's undoubtedly an allegory – the world appears civilised, but beneath the surface there are atrocities taking place. Man appears civilised, but beneath the surface there is seething sexual desire.

The rest of the track – with its more conventional backing and insubstantial content, consisting of the distracting Bacall dialogue and three other lines repeated over and over – makes for the slightest section of the whole album.

264. Bolivia '95 (N. S. Engel)
Original release: *Tilt* 1995 LP/CD

If repetition is a notable part of *263* 'Face on Breast', by the time we get to 'Bolivia '95' it really starts to be a problem. There are three words that anybody who has listened to it a few times will probably never forget: 'lemon bloody cola'. They are sung just nine times each, so perhaps it just feels like they go on ad infinitum. The problem is that hearing it for the nth plus one time doesn't become any more profound, interesting or enjoyable than it did for the nth time. The effect is merely grating. Also, 'lemon bloody cola' is apt to come across as a piece of nonsense. Might he as well be singing 'hatstand meringue artichoke' over and over, with feeling? Perhaps not – perhaps we can relate the grating repetition of the phrase, with its suggestion of American influence, to US involvement in South American politics. Or perhaps we can relate cola to cocaine, which has played such a significant part in Bolivia's history. But this aside, 'Bolivia '95' will forever remain, to its detriment, that 'lemon bloody cola' song.

The track itself is a dark and moody piece containing one of *Tilt*'s more memorable musical motifs (which echoes the 'gonna sponge you down' line), a wonderfully discordant rock sound on the 'save the crops . . .' section, and apparent contributions from a cimbalom (the national musical instrument of Hungary – a 125-stringed instrument played with mallets) and a bawu flute (a woodwind instrument from Southern China). Once again it shuns linear narrative, but the theme appears to relate directly to the song's title. Bolivia is a country with a troubled history – plagued by instability, revolution, military government, narcotics and human rights abuses. During the mid-Nineties Bolivia was responsible for growing the coca leaves used to produce one third of the world's cocaine. Apart from the possible cola/coke allusion mentioned above, we find references to 'C' (a slang term for cocaine), 'key' (an abbreviation for kilogram used in the narcotics trade) and the line 'opiate me' in the song's lyric.

265. Patriot (N. S. Engel)
Original release: *Tilt* 1995 LP/CD

If 'Bolivia '95' had its hard-to-love 'lemon bloody cola' repetition, then 'Patriot' follows suit with its '*Luʒerner Zeitung*' sections. They occur twice in the song, where each time the backing drops to a minimum of atmospheric sound and Scott intones, sounding for all the world like a drunk at chucking-out time, 'Oh the *Luʒerner Zeitung*, the *Luʒerner Zeitung*, never sold out, never sold out.' He's answered in places by a silly twiddle on the piccolo, and a crash on military drums and cymbal. The effect is grating, once again. Perhaps the intention is for Scott to evoke the toneless sound of a newspaper seller (the *Luʒerner Zeitung* is a Swiss paper), but even so, it's merely annoying and mood destroying.

Again, this is a shame because other parts of the track are compelling, especially its sombre beginning and the level of tension created by the string section immediately preceding the '*Luʒerner Zeitung*' section. The track is subtitled 'a single' – although it wasn't, but it's separated from the other tracks on the album, beginning and ending with a few seconds of silence. The subject matter appears to be established by the date given, somewhat cryptically, at the start and end of the lyric sheet: 17 January 1991,13 the start of the 1991 Gulf War. And although the usual caveats apply, other references to that conflict can be found: the song's title (the American missile defence system first used in the Gulf); 'hit the muezzin yells' (the muezzin is the crier who calls the Islamic faithful to prayer – it's estimated that over 20,000 Iraqis were killed in the conflict, in comparison to less than 500 coalition casualties), and references to the sale of arms (notoriously, some of the coalition countries, including the United States, sold arms to Iraq during the 1980s).

266. Tilt (N. S. Engel)
Original release: *Tilt* 1995 LP/CD

Along with *259* 'Farmer in the City', the most accessible piece on *Tilt* and the closest thing to a straight pop/rock arrangement. Of course, it is somewhat tilted. In interview, Scott described it as his satirical take on a 'country song'.[14] And in the lyric we find the image of a hero (perhaps riding into town) and a mention of stampeding buffalo. But it's anything but straight storytelling. And the guitars, especially the acoustic guitar that opens the track, drone as well as jangle (perhaps due to the use of newly invented chords that Scott mentioned in connection with this song[15]). The track lurches to a stop for its chorus, and later features wailing, feedback-laden electric guitar. The whole is, like the rest of the album, like pretty much nothing else on earth. In this case, it's also an unequivocally great track. Why 'Tilt' for the song and album title? Perhaps the attraction of the word was its multiple meaning. 'Tilt' can mean a bias, a slanting, a deviation from the horizontal (as *Tilt* is a deviation from the linear), and an attack or joust (as in the phrase 'tilting at windmills').

267. Rosary (N. S. Engel)
Original release: *Tilt* 1995 LP/CD

Tilt ends with an understated coda performed with just voice and guitar. Here Scott accompanies himself on a song written, the CD booklet tells us, after the rest of the material on the album. It is one of those rare occasions where we hear Scott's voice sounding very exposed and, in places, vulnerable.[16] The result is wonderfully emotive, although the lyric defies categorical interpretation. There are echoes of themes from the rest of *Tilt*: religious imagery (rosary beads), drugs (vein; 'gotta quit') and inhumanity and violence (bullets; 'wire of the snare'). But to try to force one of these ideas onto the song as its 'meaning' would seem to be the critical equivalent of mounting a butterfly. As Scott sings, 'And I gotta quit,' at the song's end against utter silence, it's a compelling end to a disturbingly compelling album.

1996

268. I Threw It All Away (Bob Dylan)
Original release: *To Have and to Hold* soundtrack album 1996
Most recently available: on *Five Easy Pieces* box set

Scott's next move after the release of the avant-garde *Tilt* was surprising, to say the least. Some 21 years since he had last released any cover versions (excepting Tennessee Williams' two-line poem *256* 'Blanket Roll Blues') or anything that might be described as easy listening, he contributed a vocal to the soundtrack of the 1996 Australian film, *To Have and to Hold*.[17] The song he sang was Bob Dylan's 'I Threw It All Away', which originally featured on Dylan's sentimental

1969 country album, *Nashville Skyline*.[18] It's a very good song, and the listener can't help but be amused by the possible sexual innuendo contained in the line, 'once I held mountains in the palm of my hand,' but Scott's version is surprisingly uninspiring. His post-*Tilt* vocal style doesn't really suit Dylan's song any more than his Walker Brothers vocal style suited Dylan's druggily poetic *15* 'Love Minus Zero' all those years ago. On both tracks Scott's vocal comes across as unduly pompous. Maybe Walker and Dylan just weren't meant to be a combination. Those unappreciative of Scott's post-1978 direction, who had been waiting years for him to 'sing something simple', might well have been left with a definite sense of anticlimax.

1999

269. Only Myself to Blame (Don Black/David Arnold)
Original release: *The World Is Not Enough* soundtrack album 1999
Most recently available: on *Five Easy Pieces* box set

Recorded for, but not featured in, the James Bond film *The World Is Not Enough*,[19] 'Only Myself to Blame' is a much stronger track than *268* 'I Threw It All Away'. Although the two songs are thematically similar (in each case the singer blames himself for lost love), Don Black and David Arnold's stylish and jazzily laid-back ballad suits Scott so much more. He had, of course, given great performances of Don Black's lyrics before, notably on *101* 'Best of Both Worlds'. Seemingly effortlessly, he proved that, even after all those years, 'that voice' could still send a shiver up the spine.

270. The Time Is out of Joint

271. Light

272. Meadow

273. The Darkest Forest

274. Never Again

275. The Church of the Apostles

276. Bombupper

277. River of Blood

278. Running

279. Closing

280. Isabel

Composition all tracks Scott Walker
Original release: *Pola X* soundtrack album 1999
Most recently available: on *Five Easy Pieces* box set

If Scott's contribution to *The World Is Not Enough* soundtrack was a marginal one, then his contribution to that of the film *Pola X* was much greater. *Pola X*, Leos Carox's 1999 French language film, was set in modern-day France but based on Herman Melville's 1852 novel *Pierre: or the Ambiguities*[20]. It is from an acronym of the French translation of the book's title, *Pierre ou les ambiguities*, that the film gets its own title – the 'X' standing for the number ten, which was how many

Scott Walker pictured in 1995, around the time of Tilt.

drafts the script went through, rather than a description of its one X-rated sex scene. The film divided critical opinion, either being loved or hated, hailed as both a masterpiece and a mess, in equal measure. In fairness, *Pola X* is neither. The film is lovingly well made, with a number of scenes that stay with the viewer. Its notorious bedroom scene is daringly graphic without coming across as pornographic. Where *Pola X* fails to convince is in the melodramatic manner in which its characters behave throughout. Like a production of Macbeth set on a London council estate, it is all too obvious that the characters and the plot are out of time. The film's other problem lies in the audience's likely lack of sympathy with the lead character, Pierre, who throws away an idyllic lifestyle, friends, family and fiancée to pursue an incestuous relationship with his semi-feral half-sister, Isabel, who turns up as if from his dreams, complete with two illegal immigrant family members in tow. Pierre's actions will also (directly or indirectly) leave most of the characters dead by the end of the film.

The *Pola X* soundtrack album included contributions from the groups Smog and Sonic Youth. It is technically not a Scott Walker album, but it was Scott who dominated the proceedings, contributing the majority of the soundtrack album's music. Music being the operative word – for, to the disappointment of those who might have expected otherwise, Scott's *Pola X* contributions featured no new vocals, and the only time we hear him singing is in an excerpt from *Tilt*. Instead, his music is partly orchestral and partly industrial/experimental. Three themes dominate – the *271* 'Light' theme, a beautiful piece of music performed by the Paris Philharmonic Orchestra used very effectively at the beginning of the film to accompany the idyll of château life; the more sombre *273* 'Darkest Forest'/*280* 'Isabel' orchestral theme used throughout the film, and the percussion-heavy industrial music, apparently played by the members of the artistic/paramilitary cult with which Pierre and Isabel hide out during the film's second half.

Elsewhere we hear a brief excerpt from *260* 'The Cockfighter', various excerpts of film dialogue (including at its start the Shakespeare quotation from Hamlet[21] that begins 'The time is out of joint,' being read out in French) and sounds from the film (including a motorbike, and dogs barking) and a rap track (one Sean Andrews is credited as the rapper) – making the track on which that appears *274* 'Never Again' the closest Scott Walker ever came to a hip-hop recording.

With no new Scott Walker songs, as opposed to instrumental pieces, and only one non-orchestral piece (*275* 'The Church of the Apostles') over a minute or two long, Scott's *Pola X* soundtrack contributions were probably for the dedicated only. Nevertheless, their inclusion on the *Five Easy Pieces* box set did afford them a wider audience, who could find Scott as natural creating orchestral music as he was creating industrial or experimental sounds.

2000

281. Scope J (sung by Ute Lemper) (N. S. Engel)
Original release: Ute Lemper album *Punishing Kiss* 2000
Later included on 2003's Scott Walker *Five Easy Pieces* box set.

The year 2000 saw Scott involved in two notable projects, curating the Meltdown Festival and contributing to Ute Lemper's *Punishing Kiss* album. Meltdown, an annual event held at London's Royal Festival Hall and organised by a different guest 'curator' each year, included the performance of his original piece 'Thimble Rigging'[22] on 17 June 2000. The collaboration with Ute Lemper resulted in two tracks, sung by Ms Lemper but subsequently brought into the Walker discography by their inclusion on the *Five Easy Pieces* box set. They are as much Scott Walker tracks as *142* 'Long About Now', with its Esther Ofarim vocal, and are therefore included here.

The album *Punishing Kiss* was something of a departure for German actress and cabaret performer Ute Lemper. Previously she had been best known for her interpretations of songs by the likes of Bertolt Brecht and Kurt Weill. *Punishing Kiss* saw her move into the arena of 'alternative rock', with an album of songs largely written for her by Nick Cave, Elvis Costello, the Divine Comedy, Philip Glass, Tom Waits and, last but not least, Scott. Of his two songs for Ms Lemper, only 'Scope J' was actually included on the album proper, *282* 'Lullaby (By-ByBy)' appearing on the Japanese edition as a bonus track. Perhaps this isn't surprising, given that both tracks clock in at over ten minutes long.

'Scope J' is, like a *Tilt* piece, composed of different sections — we have the gentle, piano-led section beginning, 'the Russians are going . . .'; the discordant, sirenlike section that starts with, 'fingered but I won't be soiled . . .'; the 'furside-skinside' sleeping bag poem section; a reprise of the piano section with different lyrics; a reprise of the siren section with different lyrics, and a further reprise of the piano section to end the song. Lyrically too, it is like a *Tilt* song in that it's more of an evocative poem than a literal narrative. At the same time, however, like some of *Tilt*'s lyrics, it does hint at a starting point: in the case of 'Scope J', the setting that suggests itself is the aftermath of conflict, an army retreating through arctic conditions, leaving scarred civilians and the dead in its wake — 'at the roadsides carts are piling up with corpses.' Perhaps the title refers in some way to a particular historical event, but if it does it's not obvious. There are sections of the lyric taken from Herbert Ponting's 'The Sleeping Bag Poem', which add to the feeling of desolation and cold.[23] Ute Lemper more than rises to the challenge of performing this idiosyncratic material, contributing a superb vocal performance.

Perhaps a little too much for some of *Punishing Kiss*'s buyers to take, to *Tilt* fans 'Scope J' is an easy track to love. In *MOJO* magazine at the time,[24] Scott described it as 'one of the best things I've written,' and in the same interview suggested that he planned to record his own versions of both the songs he'd given to Ms Lemper.

282. Lullaby (By–By–By) (N. S. Engel)
Original release: Ute Lemper album *Punishing Kiss* 2000 Japanese edition only
Later included on 2003's Scott Walker *Five Easy Pieces* box set.

At eleven minutes and six seconds, an even longer track than *269* 'Scope J', again *Tilt*-esque in its lyrical obscurity and sectional approach. The less accessible track of the two, the verse sections (for want of a better description) to 'Lullaby (By-By-By)' comprise eerie electronic noise punctuated by what sounds like a set of bagpipes being tortured and wordy (almost clumsily verbose[25]) lyrics. By way of contrast, the chorus (again for want of a better word) soars with an almost *Scott 4*-esque majesty. The overall feel of the track is strangely reminiscent of Joan Baez's original version of *172* 'The Ballad of Sacco and Vanzetti', a track with which it shares structural affinities.[26] Lyrically, Scott described the song as being 'about today'[27], presumably as opposed to the historical setting of 'Scope J'. Perhaps, then, the song is in some way a comment on the crassness and disposability that characterise the modern world, and what passes for modern culture, albeit a characteristically oblique one. Latterly, Scott added the more specific information that 'in a sense, in a very superficial sense, the song is about assisted suicide'.[28]

The Drift 2006 LP

283. Cossacks Are (Scott Walker)
Original release: *The Drift* 2006 LP / CD

Excepting the performance of 'Thimble Rigging' at the Meltdown Festival and the two Ute Lemper tracks, the 21st century had yet to see any new Scott Walker material until 2006.[29] On 1 March 2004, it was announced that Scott had signed a new record deal with 4AD, and that recording would start on a follow-up to 1995's *Tilt*. As an independent label with an exceptional history and a roster of critically acclaimed acts far from the mainstream,[30] 4AD seemed a far more appropriate place for him to pursue his post-*Tilt* muse than his previous label, Mercury (owned by the multinational conglomerate Universal Music Group). And on 8 May 2006 Scott's first 4AD album, *The Drift*, was released, giving the world 70 minutes of new, original Walker material, ten songs that disturb as well as compel. It came across as *Tilt* only more so – its soundscape is, if anything, more consistently nightmarish than its predecessor's and its lyrics more uncompromising. However, with Scott having less to prove than he did in 1995, and in a seemingly more relaxed and open mood (as evidenced in magazine interviews and his BBC2 television appearance at the time[31]), *The Drift* is ultimately a more 'user-friendly' record than *Tilt*. This may sound odd to those hearing its nightmarish tones for the first time, but *The Drift*, unlike *Tilt*, does contain a sense of humour that is playful as opposed to forced and stilted. It is also more romantic, albeit a morbid kind of romanticism (see *284* 'Clara', *291* 'The Escape'). And, sleeve notes aside, it is less wont to come across as wilfully pretentious in places. Whereas no particular tracks are obviously superior to the best of *Tilt*, as an album *qua* album *The Drift* succeeds better.

Like its predecessor, *The Drift* opened with its most accessible track. 'Cossacks Are' might even be described as catchy on repeated listenings. As he did with *Tilt* and would do with *Bish Bosch*, Scott emphasised that it was the lyrics that came first and dictated how the track would sound. This is reflected in the heavy percussion (percussionist Alasdair Malloy's effusive tambourine playing led to a profusely bleeding hand), with the pounding drums representing the charge of the Cossacks on horseback. Also in a minor break from the live / analogue recording ethic of the album, the track includes backwards guitar and vocal effects. This is a musical / lyrical pun, for a large part of the lyric is made up of quotations which Scott described as backhanded compliments, taken from critical reviews and other sources – one in particular comes from George W. Bush[32] – though none of them, according to him, came from reviews of his own records. Amusingly, one of the quotations is 'you could easily picture this in the current top ten,' which probably isn't the case!

Whereas, later in *The Drift*, ideas are more obviously conflated and lyrical themes drift between tracks, its opener does at least offer a more singular interpretation: to wit, that words can be as unthinkingly vindictive as fictional Cossacks crushing 'fields of white roses' with their charge.

284. Clara (Scott Walker)
Original release: *The Drift* 2006 LP/CD

The Drift's longest track, and something of a grand construction, comprising sound effects, musical minimalism, industrial noise, orchestrated strings, spoken word passages, and guest vocals from French chanteuse Vanessa Contenay-Quinones, as well as Scott's grandly operatic vocals. Subtitled 'Benito's Dream', a paragraph of historical explanation in the CD/LP booklet about the 1945 execution of Italian dictator Benito Mussolini and his mistress, Claretta Petacci, makes the subject matter unequivocally clear. Claretta, or Clara, chose to die with Mussolini rather than live without him, and was consequently shot and strung up by the heels next to his body, as a spectacle for the crowd. Such romantic subject matter (albeit a doomed romance), with only the possible exception of *252* 'Sleepwalker's Woman', had not graced a Walker composition since way back in 1970. The song is dreamlike in its construction – the latter-day Scott simply did not do literal narrative – but most of the lyric is clearly relatable to either Mussolini, Clara or their unceremonious deaths. Only the reference to 'what happen [sic] in America' seems extraneous to the subject; unless it refers to some historical event contemporary to Mussolini's execution, it may be a lyrical 'drift' from *285* 'Jesse', perhaps a reference to the 9/11 attack on the Twin Towers as contained in that song. 'Clara' drifts between Benito's dream and a nightmare, both musically and lyrically. Clara is clearly likened to a bird, a little swallow trapped in a room – the kind of romantic metaphor not seen since the end of the 'God-like genius' era of 1967-70. But there are nightmare images too: the skinned rabbit; the 'terrapin with its shell torn away'; the atheistic depiction of death, which also finds reflection elsewhere on the album. The living Mussolini and Clara were not, the lyric insists, 'cornhusk dolls dipped in blood', but the dead couple later in the song are exactly that – dead pieces of meat. As if to emphasise this, the track features a side of pork played as an unusual (to say the least) percussion instrument.

As well as being what is, according to Scott, 'in effect a love song', 'Clara' is also his attempt to keep the conversation about the past horrors of fascism alive, in the face of neo-Nazism in the modern world. On this level, it succeeds less well – the latter-day Scott did not do protest songs (arguably he never did[33]), but he was capable of producing deep, dark and compelling works of art.

285. Jesse (Scott Walker)
Original release: *The Drift* 2006 LP/CD

One of the earliest written tracks on the album, Scott composed 'Jesse' in October 2001, in the immediate aftermath of the events of 9/11 – when Al-Qaeda hijacked passenger aeroplanes and used them as missiles to destroy the Twin Towers in

New York. The track is subtitled 'September Song', a pun on the famous autumn-of-my-life song and an allusion to the events of 11 September 2001. But its literal twin subject is Jesse Garon Presley, Elvis Presley's stillborn twin brother to whom, as the CD/LP booklet informs us, Elvis used to talk to 'in times of loneliness and despair'. By way of a pun that manages to escape being painfully tasteless, the song is both about the Twin Towers and Elvis's dead twin.

Musically, the track begins with a deconstructed take on Elvis's 'Jailhouse Rock'. Prefaced by an ominous hum, the guitar part of the introduction is slowed down to a crawl, and the drumbeats are replaced by a spoken 'pow pow' – a representation of the planes hitting the towers. Another dream-like lyric follows, with mixed references to 9/11 ('tall tall tower', 'building', 'ruins', and the poetic description of the dead as having 'nose holes caked in black cocaine') and Elvis/Jesse. (Jesse is the 'six feet of foetus' – the man who never was; 'Jesse are you listening?' is clearly intended as the words of Elvis seeking a response from his long-dead twin, which never comes.) The track ends with Scott singing *a cappella* the repeated line, 'alive, I'm the only one left alive' – words which could come from Elvis (the only twin sibling left alive) or a 9/11 survivor (whose friends and colleagues have been killed). A disturbing end to an inspiring track.

286. Jolson and Jones (Scott Walker)
Original release: *The Drift* 2006 LP/CD

From this point on, *The Drift* starts to get stranger still. This track's repeated line, 'I'll punch a donkey in the streets of Galway,' has already formed the star piece of evidence in the case for the prosecution; in an early review, one reviewer likened this song to 'the random ravings of a madman'.[34] But 'Jolson and Jones' can no more be described thus than other works in the post-modern idiom, say the writings of James Joyce.[35] In fact, Scott encourages comparisons to Joyce with this track's references to 'brogue' (defined by the dictionary as 'a strong dialectal accent, especially a strong Irish accent') and Galway (not the Irish city most associated with Joyce, which was Dublin, but nevertheless the hometown of his wife and muse, Nora, as celebrated in his novella *The Dead*). Scott was an admirer of Joyce, commenting around the time of *Tilt* that he 'changed the rules for all of us'.[36] Joyce's books, with their stream of consciousness approach and defiance of literary convention, are not easily accessible, requiring effort on the part of the reader. They contain ambiguities of meaning which cannot – and need not – ever be explained away, along with puns, parodies and allusions that can, to an extent, be unravelled. If this sounds like it might also apply to *The Drift*, then it's intentional. An album that requires effort on the part of the listener in order to appreciate it is a rare thing, in an age that increasingly demands immediacy and disposability – especially in the area of pop/rock music.

'Jolson and Jones'' lyric is constructed of disjointed and seemingly unconnected ideas, more akin to a controlled collage than a set of 'random ravings'. One of its premises again appears to be a dream/nightmare, wherein of course ideas do get mixed together and the illogical can be taken for granted. The dreamer (a sleepwalker?) even at one point appears to wake and get up to go downstairs, accompanied by appropriate sound effects – the credits on the album cite Scott's co-producer Peter Walsh as 'man descending stairs'. The scenes that are juxtaposed in the song/dream are the nightmare vision of a 'bloodied head' and a 'tumour balloon'; perhaps a crime scene; perhaps a circus where girls become whores; perhaps a stately home where normalcy hides death; perhaps the Egyptian pyramids. As the song progresses, the titular Jolson and Jones come into play via lyrics taken from songs more than half a century old. Jolson is Al Jolson (1886-1950), the vaudeville singer best remembered for performing with a (politically dubious, with hindsight) blacked-up face in cinema's first real 'talkie', *The Jazz Singer*. The Jolson song quoted is 1928's 'Sonny Boy'. Jones is Allan Jones (1907-1992), the father of Scott's one-time favourite Jack Jones, and a successful singer and film star in his own right during the 1930s. The Jones song quoted is 1937's 'Donkey Serenade', from which the following words are taken: 'there's a song in the air, but the fair senorita doesn't seem to care,' and 'in her voice there's a flaw . . . e-e-aw, e-e-aw.' (The jokey lyric has the singer serenading his mule when his efforts fail to impress the young lady he wants to woo.) According to the interpretation offered by *The Wire*, the respective songs of Jolson and Jones become conflated and a 'tussle between these songs' ensues which 'mimics an actual confrontation on the streets'[37] – and therefore perhaps it's Jolson's Sonny Boy punching Jones' donkey in the streets. Either way, this strange ride is more than worth taking.

287. Cue (Scott Walker)
Original release: *The Drift* 2006 LP/CD

The track with the longest genesis. Scott began writing 'Cue' shortly after the completion of *Tilt*. More so than other tracks on *The Drift*, it has a *Tilt*-like sectional construction. It also has affinities with Scott's Ute Lemper tracks (*281* and *282*), not least in terms of its ten minutes-plus length. (Indeed, there are indications that a longer version may exist, as a working version of the lyric sheet gives additional lyrics that occur after the ending of the released version.) Subtitled 'Flugelman', even its author described it as 'odd'. Its nightmare vision actually begins with something of a joke: 'What do Seoul, Sudan have in common?' – then, whilst the listener is wondering what the capital of democratic South Korea and the authoritarian Republic of Sudan have in common, comes the answer: 'Both start with an S.' Thereafter, the horror is fairly unrelenting. Lyrically, the themes of religion ('Mary', 'Holy Ghost'), pestilence/disease ('deep as a virus', 'birth of a vermin', 'herpes to clit', 'tumour to breast') and the death-bringing flugelman dominate. The flugelhorn is an instrument similar to a trumpet but considered 'darker' in tone, its name apparently derived from the German word for 'wing', and the flugelhorn's use on the battlefield to summon the flanks, or wings, of the army into battle. In Scott's song, the flugelman appears as the harbinger of death, if not the bringer of plagues on a biblical scale. His arrival is heralded by an eerie flugelhorn and the words, 'BAM BAM BAM BAM,' followed by a gargantuan knocking sound achieved by hitting a specially constructed five foot by five foot wooden box with a cinder block. Elsewhere, the nightmare vision is enhanced by a string arrangement that is truly remarkable – preceded by a section of silence and *a cappella* vocals. At the point where the singer makes a plea for 'immunity', the strings enter with a sound as intense as it is frightening.

Perhaps it is possible to interpret the track as an attack on organised religion (the lyric suggests that the plagues have been ordained by the Holy Ghost), or at least a comment on the incongruity of Judeo-Christianity. How can one worship a supposedly merciful God who, on the evidence of the Old Testament, brought about plagues with an almost spiteful relish? How can one worship God in the face of breast cancer, or infant mortality? (The flugelman visits wards and nurseries.) But this is to risk oversimplification – the imagery in this powerful centrepiece to the album defies simple explanation.

288. Audience (AKA Hand Me Ups) (Scott Walker)
Original release: *The Drift* 2006 LP/CD

At the time, in 2006, television had undoubtedly changed greatly over the preceding few years, with the rise of reality TV dominating the populist end of the spectrum. Derivative reality TV shows appeared to follow each other *ad nauseam*, and it seemed that the term celebrity began to apply to anyone with the merest hint of fame, rather than someone possessing obvious talent. The clearest indication that 'Audience' is concerned with celebrity/reality TV is the lyric, 'twelve bunnies in a hutch for nine new weeks, the audience is waiting' – a clear reference to the programme *Big Brother*, which at the time ran for around nine weeks, with around twelve contestants prepared to give up all privacy and dignity in exchange for short-lived television fame. Scott's song extends the idea to nightmare proportions, with the character in the song prepared even to sacrifice his children in the cause of his own celebrity. Elsewhere the track includes images of brutality (an arrow in the eye, a stoning), culminating in a crucifixion ('I felt the nail driving into my foot while I felt the nail driving into my hand') – being perhaps both a description of the feelings of the 'celebrity', who has crossed the line into insanity, and a lyrical drift from the preceding track, *287* 'Cue'. It continues the nightmare feel of *The Drift*, complete with the sound of children wailing, and the obscure instrument that is the tubax – an outsize saxophone of which there are believed to be only two in the UK.

289. Buzzers (Scott Walker)
Original release: *The Drift* 2006 LP/CD

Apparently *The Drift*'s strangest track, 'Buzzers', at first blush, comprises the tale of a man being cooked and eaten to the accompaniment of minimal instrumentation, punctuated by a gently orchestrated passage, with some seemingly impenetrable lyrics about lengthening faces. But is it really so strange? Within the context of the album, not at all. The track opens with the sound of a radio being tuned and landing on a number of stations, which is not a new device at all – like the use of backward guitar and vocals in *283* 'Cossacks Are', it was the kind of thing the Beatles were doing in 1966/67.[38] The radio eventually lands on a station where a newsreader speaks of Serbian leader General Milosöeviç's lack of concern about whether Bosnia is recognised by the rest of the world, likening its relevance to the Roman emperor Caligula making his horse a senator. In fact the newsreader's words provide the clues to unravelling the track, the main part of which represents a fictionalised account of an atrocity from the Bosnian War, whilst the 'faces of the grass' section is about the evolution of the horse. Over time, horses' faces lengthened so that the animal could better survive – a longer face meant the horse could graze whilst keeping its eyes above the grass to watch for predators. The two ideas are conflated in the track, but this is actually one of *The Drift*'s less esoteric collages. The implication is logical, if not immediately transparent: why can't we humans evolve? Why do we not learn the lessons of history (Hitler's and Stalin's atrocities), but instead continue to treat other members of our species as completely worthless (cf. most of *Tilt*)? As a plea for peace it's hardly a straightforward protest song, but, as noted above, Scott Walker did not do those.

290. Psoriatic (Scott Walker)
Original release: *The Drift* 2006 LP/CD

The Drift track that, more than any other, conflates ideas drifting in and out of other tracks. 'Psoriatic' opens with the image of the thimble-rigger – the confidence trickster who hides a pea under one of three thimbles or shells, eventually fooling his audience into losing track of the pea and thereby their money. This idea drifts in from the unreleased 'Thimble-Rigging', as performed at the Meltdown Festival. The lyrical appearance of the thimble-rigger is prefaced by the sound of a giant pea rolling – an effect achieved with a bowling ball and a microphone inside the 'big box' constructed for *287* 'Cue"'s 'BAM BAM' percussion. The titular psoriasis ('psoriatic' is the adjectival form of 'psoriasis') appears in the 'scaling', 'red' and 'silver' of the lyric. Psoriasis is a chronic skin disease characterised by red sores and silvery scales, which is in some loose way a drift from the preceding track – as the album artwork states under the heading of 'Buzzers', the Bosnian city of Srebrenica[39] has a name literally meaning silver, juxtaposing this statement with another that informs us that, during the Middle Ages, people afflicted with psoriasis were known as 'the silver people'. The lyrical drift from *289* 'Buzzers' may be stronger than this, if we take the line, 'Donje is Donje in the spring' as referring to the small settlement of Donje Celo near Dubrovnik. But there is more of disease than psoriasis in the song: we have germs carried in the wind (psoriasis is a not a contagious disease), a mention of anthrax and, ultimately, the track seems to culminate in the final farewell of death. In common with *287* 'Cue', we have the religious imagery of Jesus and 'the Angelus begins' – the Angelus is a prayer concerning the Incarnation that mentions Mary and the Holy Ghost (indeed, 'Cue' might be seen as a twisted take on the Angelus – a song concerning the Incarnation of death as opposed to life). In common with *283* 'Cossacks Are', we find an apparent compliment that turns into a putdown: 'don't think it hasn't been fun, because it hasn't.' In common with *286* 'Jolson and Jones', the track borrows lyrics from a pre-war popular song, in this case Bob Carleton's 1918 'Ja-Da', from which the words, 'ja-da ja-da ja-da ja-da jing jing jing' are taken. With so many drifts coming in and out of the track (one could also say the reference to 'the king' might relate to Elvis and therefore *285* 'Jesse', or that it has a theme of death in common with, say, *284* 'Clara' and *292* 'A Lover Loves'), according to the man himself, the song deals with (amongst other things) being stranded without a past or a future. This notion can be related to the 'silver people' as medieval outcasts, the Balkan refugee, the dying, or even the pea lost or hidden by the thimble-rigger.

291. The Escape (Scott Walker)
Original release: *The Drift* 2006 LP/CD

With no let-up in the nightmare sound of the album, those of a nervous disposition may find that the worst is yet to come with 'The Escape'. For although the track is bookended with a dark take on Warner Brothers' *Looney Tunes* theme, played on the slide guitar, towards the end a demonic voice, sounding like it comes from the possessed child in *The Exorcist*, repeatedly intones, 'What's up, doc?', and the effect is truly horrific. Of this song, Scott was more reluctant than with the rest of the album to provide a foothold on its meaning, saying only that it addresses 'secrecy, and reception of conspiracy theories'[40] – hence the inclusion of language from the Kabbalah,[41] the esoteric system of Jewish mysticism, and the generally paranoid feel of some of the lyrics. But it is not secret societies or conspiracy theories that come across most strongly on listening to the track, but the theme of meeting one's own death. The first part moves at such a funereal pace that one might suppose that 'the car in front' may be part of the funeral cortege. Then the singer is hunted by angels, followed by the line, 'I wish I was in Dixie,' from the traditional American song incorporated into 'American Trilogy' – a nod perhaps to Elvis (and therefore *285* 'Jesse'), given that he recorded the most famous version, but also a telling inclusion in that 'American Trilogy' is one of the best known songs about facing death. After the first part of the track there is a moment of virtual silence, before a horrifically discordant string arrangement heralds the line, 'You and me against the world' – embodying a desperate sense of romance not heard in Scott's work since the 1967-70 era – but this is followed by the atheistic/solipsistic vision of death contained in the line, 'world about to end'. There is weary resignation in a gentle passage about a visitor whose eyes the narrator must look into (the flugelman? death?), before the demonic voice is heard. And isn't the title another indication, as death is the greatest escape of all? All in all this track is, like the rest of the album, truly disturbing, compelling and brilliant.

292. A Lover Loves (Scott Walker)
Original release: *The Drift* 2006 LP/CD

Resisting the temptation to follow through his take on the *Looney Tunes* theme by saying, 'Th-th-th-that's all folks!', Scott ends *The Drift*, as he did *Tilt*, with an understated coda. 'A Lover Loves' was recorded in a late-night single take with Scott accompanied only by his own acoustic guitar. The two-note guitar playing is almost childlike in its simplicity, but anyone expecting easy listening will be disappointed. Firstly, Scott interrupts his vocal with a hissed, '*Psst. Psst,*' at nearly every turn. The effect is unsettling and presumably intended to be, as if he were saying: you've come with me this far, so you can come a little further; there will be no gentle letdown. Secondly, there is the lyric, which is undeniably concerned with dying: 'corneas misted . . . colour high'. The lyric even announces that the song is a dance for the dead, by name-checking the dodo, the bird estimated to have been extinct since 1681, Bambi, the cartoon deer from the 1942 Disney film of the same name, Kaiser Wilhelm II (1859-1941), the Emperor of Germany until his forced abdication at the end of the First World War, Joseph Beuys (1921-1986), the celebrated German conceptual artist, Rosa Luxemburg (1870-1919), the Marxist revolutionary, and Tintin, the cartoon character from Hergé's books. The inclusion of the fictional Bambi and Tintin is perhaps a drift from the cartoon setting of *291* 'The Escape', but, more significantly, the dead are being likened to that which never existed in the first place.

2006

293. Darkness (Scott Walker)
Original release: Various Artists album *Plague Songs* 2006 CD

A mere five months after the release of *The Drift*, 2006 also saw the release of another new Scott Walker track in the shape of his contribution to the project by the arts organisation Artangel called the Margate Exodus. This involved commissioning ten 'plague songs' to represent each of the ten Plagues of Egypt from the Book of Exodus. Various artists contributed, among them Brian Eno and Robert Wyatt, Laurie Anderson and Rufus Wainwright. Scott's contribution was a song for the ninth plague: darkness. According to its author: 'I was given the darkness. In order to avoid purely passive reception, memory kicked in with an elemental lesson from childhood school days. This led to other disparate paths including slavery, corporate reach etcetera.'[42] That explanation, though, ironically sheds little light on the track's lyrics, which are minimalist and opaque (apart from the clue that the repeated line 'Threadbare little earth' might connote darkness via the fact that the first ever light bulbs relied on threads of carbonised cotton for their filaments).[43] The track itself is remarkable for its *a cappella* call and response vocals. Scott's vocal lines are answered by the shrill responses of a choir of eight, who elsewhere also provide chants that border on the funky.

At the end of the track, Scott delivers the spoken line 'Get your coat'. It's an interesting track worth seeking out and one on which Scott might be congratulated for coming up with something so different from the songs on *The Drift*, so soon after its release.

And Who Shall Go to the Ball?
And What Shall Go to the Ball? 2007 album

294. And Who Shall Go to the Ball?: 1st Movement (Scott **Walker**)

295. And Who Shall Go to the Ball?: 2nd Movement (Scott **Walker**)

296. And Who Shall Go to the Ball?: 3rd Movement (Scott **Walker**)

297. And Who Shall Go to the Ball?: 4th Movement (Scott **Walker**)

Original release: *And Who Shall Go to the Ball? And What Shall Go to the Ball?* 2007 CD

As if to confirm that the Scott Walker of the 21st century was not going to disappear from view following the release of *The Drift*, 2007 saw the fruits of his involvement in another project in the shape of his 25-minute dance soundtrack *And Who Shall Go to the Ball? And What Shall Go to the Ball?* This piece in four movements was used to accompany performances by the CandoCo Dance Company under choreographer Rafeal Bonachela in the UK and Europe during 2007. Scott met with Rafeal Bonachela a number of times to explain the concepts behind the soundtrack and advised on the production and lighting design before CandoCo, a company comprised of disabled and non-disabled dancers, took the show on the road. 4AD meanwhile released the soundtrack as performed with the London Sinfonietta on CD as a limited edition of 2,500, despite being easily available today. It is an entirely instrumental work; there are no Walker vocals to be heard and it certainly does not make for easy listening. Instead, in Scott's words, 'the music is full of edgy and staccato shapes or cuts'. There are scraping sounds and silence, bursts of mournful cello, discordant orchestration, huge clangings of a bell and insanely fast orchestral tempos. These techniques attempted to evoke concepts such as man against machine, a dysfunctional world and, again in Scott's own words, 'how we cut up the world around us as a consequence of the shape of our bodies,' and 'How much of a body does an intelligence need to be potentially socialised in an age of ever-developing AI?' [44]

2009

298. The Big Sleep (by Bat for Lashes) (Natasha Kahn)
Original release: Bat for Lashes album *Two Suns* 2009 CD

It might perhaps be stretching a point to give this track its own entry here, as it is a track by Bat for Lashes rather than Scott. However, it is one to which he contributed additional vocals and his voice can be unmistakably heard on the record, very much contributing to the atmosphere of the closing track on Natasha Khan's second and very successful album. (Bat for Lashes is Natasha Khan herself rather than being the name of a band.)

It also allows us to note how far from disappearance Scott Walker was during the period between *The Drift* and *Bish Bosch*. In 2008, he had been involved, albeit hidden behind a mixing desk rather than performing on stage, with *Drifting and Tilting* – a performance of Scott Walker's modern works by various artists at London's Barbican. As the writing process began for the album that would become *Bish Bosch*, he made the vocal contribution for Bat for Lashes. And, simultaneously with work on *Bish Bosch*, he composed an original score for the production of *Duet for One* (a work based on Cocteau's similarly titled monologue and performed 17-25 June 2011 at the Linbury Studio Theatre, Royal Opera House). That score did not receive (or has not yet received) a commercial release, so it doesn't get its own entry here, but 4AD have made a tantalising excerpt available on YouTube (search 'Scott Walker – An Excerpt from Duet for One (4AD)').

Bish Bosch 2012 album

299. 'See You Don't Bump His Head' (Scott Walker)
Original release: *Bish Bosch* 2012 CD/LP

2012's Bish Bosch - the final instalment in a 'kind of trilogy' that began with Tilt *and* The Drift.

Scott's fourteenth and what turned out to be his final studio album proper was released in December of 2012. The man himself saw *Bish Bosch* as the final instalment in 'kind of a trilogy' that began with *Tilt* and *The Drift*.[45] The 'kind of' qualification is an important one as Scott's don't-look-back philosophy and strict avoidance of listening to his own work once it was finished extended to *Tilt* and *The Drift*. This meant, as he freely admitted, that he had forgotten the detail of a lot of what had come beforehand as he approached *Bish Bosch*[46] and that this new record was in fact more a continuation of the style and the parameters of the other two modern Scott Walker records. *Bish Bosch* does, in some ways, echo *Tilt* and *The Drift*, and yet, in other ways, it is clearly very different. Of course, there was to be no turning back from uneasy listening to easy listening, nor any return to conventional song structures. The sectional approach and the use of repetition in place of choruses are carried forward from *Tilt*; the focus on songs being character-led and the harrowing feel of the whole is carried forward from *The Drift*. But *Bish Bosch* is very much its own record too, separated from its predecessors by the increased emphasis on playfulness with language. As with *Tilt* and *The Drift*, Scott's way of working remained in place. The lyrics came first, with a lot of time being spent on writing them, and those lyrics then dictated everything else that followed: the arrangement, the vocals, the instrumentation – however unusual that turned out to be – with everything leading to the realisation of Scott's vision in the studio. However, with those lyrics for *Bish Bosch*, there was no stripping back to the essence of the thing that Scott had spoken about previously in connection with writing lyrics. Instead, Scott even described the lyrics of *Bish Bosch* more accurately as 'verbal diarrhoea'.[47] And apparently that took in a literal emphasis on bodily functions. Much has been made of the farting in *300* 'Corps de Blah', but we also find the likes of 'piss', 'shit', 'buggers', 'coglione', 'fucked' and 'bollocks' scattered throughout the lyric sheet and a strand of scatological humour amongst the layers of lyrical ideas in *Bish Bosch*. And from the title downwards, words and expressions carry multiple meanings and connotations. As the album's official website[48] explained, 'Bish' on the one hand meant 'bitch' and 'Bosch' referred to the Medieval Dutch painter, and on the other 'bish bosh' as a whole meant 'job done, sorted'. Scott went on to imagine how the title could be envisioned as referring to 'a mythological, all-encompassing, giant woman artist' – Bitch Bosch, as it were. And the title was surely not without irony; the slang 'bish bosh' implies the completion of an easy task, whereas *Bish Bosch* was, like the other two modern Scott Walker albums, a work of obsession, years in the making, meticulously envisioned and planned. It could not really have been otherwise, with the expense of its studio time and the use of a sizable orchestra. *Bish Bosch* was not thrown together lightly. And like its immediate predecessors, it cannot be listened to lightly. Again, however, much like its immediate predecessors, it more than rewards the listener's patience. As complex as Hieronymous Bosch's most famous painting, *Bish Bosch*'s multi-layered garden of (un)Earthly delights is a unique record worth celebrating, as the almost universal critical acclaim it received on its release attested.

The album's first track, "See You Don't Bump His Head", opens with a rhythmic pounding, high on the beats for minute but a world away from anybody's conception of popular music. This industrial pounding continues throughout the song, overlaid with occasional electric guitar crunches and eerie hints at the kind of other-worldly orchestration that perhaps carries distant echoes of the haunting feel of the orchestration of *132* 'Boy Child'. But nothing is romantic or gentle here, and the track is dominated by Scott's almost aggressive delivery of the line 'While plucking feathers from a swan song' punctuated by the rest of the song's lyric. These words that open the album, 'While plucking feathers from a swan song', exemplify the so-called playfulness of language that *Bish Bosch* is said to embody. You can literally pluck feathers from a swan, but you can only pluck feathers from a swan song allegorically. Is it to suggest the album itself as the swan song? – Scott was pessimistically apt to think that every latter-day album he recorded might be his last.[49] Is it the feathers or the swan song that are for keeping? It might even be in keeping with the tone of the humour of *Bish Bosch* to point out that this is not a pheasant-plucking song, or indeed a pleasant fucking song. Elsewhere the lyric mixes the horrific, the poetic and the profane with obscure references to keep the listener guessing ('Scarpia' is the police chief in Puccini's *Tosca*; 'Rummy' must be former-US Secretary of Defense Donald Rumfeld; 'bdelloid rotifers' are microscopic freshwater creatures that survive without mating.) The track is also accompanied by one of the footnotes that Scott described as 'kind of fun'[50], in this case to explain the track's title: apparently being a line cut from the film *From Here to Eternity* said by Montgomery Clift's character of his dead friend and comrade then being loaded onto a truck. It's a line that, in the context of the movie, would have been meant sincerely, but one which would also have introduced a profound absurdness (why care if a dead man's head gets bumped? – he won't feel it). In fact, this sense of absurdity might indeed be a description that could be applied in a non-pejorative way to *Bish Bosch*'s arresting opening track.

300. Corps de Blah (Scott Walker)
Original release: *Bish Bosch* 2012 CD/LP

In stark contrast to *299* "See You Don't Bump His Head", the opening to 'Corps de Blah' replaces the background of incessant rhythmic pounding with silence. Scott's opening lines are sung *a cappella*, with *Bish Bosch*'s use of silence here and elsewhere adding constructively to its remarkable soundscape. This was deliberate, as both Scott and his long-term co-producer Peter Walsh separately explained in interview[51] that it was worth introducing an element of digital recording into the otherwise analogue ethic of the recording of Scott's work, so as to achieve a purer silence; that is, without tape hiss. There follows over 'Corps de Blah''s ten-plus minute running time a nightmare collage of lyrics and sound which seems a world away from anyone's traditional conception of a song. The opening to the lyric is pure surreal nightmare, the protagonist apparently making his way through chickens in the dark, feeling his teeth being burned and hearing owls being boiled alive. Then things get stranger. We get a myriad of obscure, disparate historical, medical and astrological references thrown into the mix, including lines that defy any logic other than that of alliteration ('Macaronic mahout in the mascon') and a couple of references to Native American chiefs ('Sachem' and 'Sagamore') which if they appeared in a different context might appear troubling – the Sachem is 'scabby' and the Sagamore is a 'wino' covered in 'ticks'. And then there's the common place: a joke remark about 'Earls Court' or the 'Embankment' being 'the sticks' and most notoriously the sound of farting that bookends the 'a sphincters tooting our tune' line – as Scott was keen to explain in his interviews that accompanied the release of *Bish Bosch*, the layer of absurdist humour included in the album was a necessary part of the whole 'to keep the interest going' and prevent it being 'dark, dark, dark'.[52] But strangely the effect isn't necessarily bathetic; whether or not one feels the temptation to give in to a schoolboy giggle midway through 'Corps de Blah', nothing feels out of place in the strange world of *Bish Bosch* where the sublime regularly rubs shoulders with the ridiculous. 'Corps de Blah' is a key track on the album – and one whose lyric includes the album's title, making it the closest thing there is to being a title track. Through its lyrics and sometimes literal sound collage, it paints an aural picture that is disturbing, evocative, intriguing, sublime and ridiculous, that evokes decay and even its associated bad smells and that ultimately ends, as we might expect it to, on a note of impending death ('Double-bladed axe poised over shoulder').

301. Phrasing (Scott Walker)
Original release: *Bish Bosch* 2012 CD/LP

'Phrasing' next offers up a shorter message of ultimate pessimism. It would be stretching the point to suggest that this is a song with a chorus, but it does have the line 'Pain is not alone' repeated in four separate lots of four. And each time the line is sung, it is sung differently; as a gentle lament, as a near shout, and with the emphasis being on different words in turn. The song's title might be taken to refer to these different emphases, indicated on the lyric sheet by the hyphenation of words ('P-a-i-n is n-o-t alone, Pain is not a-l-o-n-e'). And this is another example of *Bish Bosch*'s playfulness with language – do statements change their meaning if uttered gently or in anger, or if the emphasis is placed on different words? 'Pain is not alone' could be taken as saying you are not alone in feeling pain, *à la* R.E.M. saying that 'Everybody Hurts', but perhaps, more realistically, it refers to pain as just one of the many horrors one is likely to face in life. In the rest of the lyric these are said to come at us from the south, the east and the north – presumably we can take it that the listener is already in the west. And in the world of *Bish Bosch*, where history is not presented in terms of linear facts, those horrors can come from any time or place in the history of humankind. So, we get specific references to Khruschev's shoe along with the Klu Klux Klan – the former recalling Cold War tensions that could have ended in the nuclear obliteration of the world, and the latter referring to the white supremacist hate group. Then there's 'protein' used as a universal adjective throughout and the ultimate sinking of any potential solace contained in the 'chorus' as the song's ending repeatedly bids us, 'Here's to a lousy life' - all set against a mixed backdrop of heavy percussion, electronic effects and the deployment of guitars and near silence that are also found elsewhere on the album. This is also accompanied by what might be described as a section of nightmare-Calypso instrumentation, unique to 'Phrasing', which pre-echoes the nightmare Hawaiian instrumentation yet to follow on *303* 'Epizootics!'

302. SDSS1416+13B (Zercon, a Flagpole Sitter) (Scott Walker)
Original release: *Bish Bosch* 2012 CD/LP

Clocking in at over 20 minutes and so placed, it is hard not to see 'SDSS1416+13B (Zercon, a Flagpole Sitter)', which we'll call 'Zercon' for short from now on, as *Bish Bosch*'s centrepiece. It's a track where direct echoes from *Tilt* and *The Drift* can be felt, although these are taken to the next level here. In both *Tilt* and *The Drift*, songs were built around the juxtaposition of two people or things that shared neither time nor place but had one thing in common. *Tilt*'s *260* 'The Cockfighter' brought together the trial of Queen Caroline and the trial of Adolf Eichman. *The Drift*'s *285* 'Jesse' brought together Elvis's dead twin, Jesse, and the Twin Towers. And in *The Drift 283* 'Cossacks Are' built part of its lyric around one-liner put-downs (such as 'It's hard to pick the worst moment'). With *Bish Bosch*'s 'Zercon', the one-liners come thicker and faster, and the song is built on a bringing together of two things that are both in some sense cool brown dwarves. We can say this because 'Zercon' is one song – perhaps in part because of its length and the strangeness of its title – where Scott was willing to be fairly open with his explanations, both in interviews at the time of the album's release and with the series of footnotes that accompany the track's lyric. So, one of the cool brown dwarves is the titular SDSS1416+13B, a sub-stellar body (between a large planet and a small star in size), the discovery of which by astronomers was reported in 2010, and which was, physically, the coolest ever such object discovered to date. The other dwarf is Zercon 'a stuttering, lisping, Moorish dwarf jester' who entertained guests at a banquet put on for Roman envoys in the year 449 and who, according to the footnotes provided with *Bish Bosch*, became something of a 'living legend'. As Scott explained in his own words, as quoted on the album's official website, he was 'interested in this thing about someone trying to escape his situation – in this case Attila's wooden palace, which he [Zercon] regards as an immense toilet – and achieve a kind of spiritual sovereignty, and a height beyond calculation. As the song moves forward, he imagines himself at different stages of height. First he imagines that he escapes and finds himself surrounded by eagles; then there's the mention of St Simon on his pillar; then he jumps to 1930s America where it's become a flagpole-sitter...' and, '[a]t the end of the song he eventually becomes a Brown Dwarf, known as SDSS1416. As with the majority of my songs, it ends in failure. Like a Brown Dwarf, he freezes to death.'[53]

Further aspects of the lyric were explained by Scott in radio interviews. The silences (described as such on the lyric sheet) were explained as Zercon the jester being heckled by silence. The Roman numerals, sung as the closest thing 'Zercon' gets to having a chorus, were described as telephone numbers written on the toilet wall. Of course, history is not linear in *Bish Bosch's sui generis* universe, so it's not important that telephones weren't around in the year 449, any more than it's important that some of Zercon's one-liner put downs belong in the modern rather than the ancient world, including the likes of, 'You should get an agent, why sit in the dark handling yourself.' Of course, there are more historical points of contact too in Zercon's journey of ascension, from the ancient racism directed at Gauls and Greeks ('For grosse Gauls who won't leave our sheep alone' and 'For a Roman who's proof that Greeks fucked bears') to the ropes made of hair of the ancient Roman city of Aquileia (as explained in one of the footnotes that accompany the lyrics), to St Simon on his pillar (as mentioned by Scott in the quote above). St Simon here is the ascetic Saint Simeon Stylites who lived, near what is now Aleppo in modern Syria, for over thirty years on top of a small platform in the 5th century. Jump cut to the connection with 1920s and 30s America and the bizarre craze of flagpole sitting where most notably Albert 'Shipwreck' Kelly achieved fame at the time by sitting for days on end atop a small platform on a high pole. Kelly is actually pictured in *Bish Bosch's* CD booklet in a grainy photograph (in which he bears a passing resemblance to Scott Walker himself). As elsewhere on *Bish Bosch*, the lyric is, before it reaches its Brown Dwarf conclusion ('What if I freeze and drop into the darkness?'), multi-layered and complex. In 'Zercon', the one-liner put downs occur throughout. Some of these one-liners strike the listener as clichéd, others genuinely funny; some are poetic, whilst others are vulgar. Explained historical references mix with the unexplained, history jump cuts everywhere, and the poetic mixes with the horrific and vulgar ('reeking gonads' and 'Caesar's shrivelled coglione'). The instrumentation answers the highly-varied delivery of the lyric with the occasional negative space of silence, other times instrumentation whose oddness meets that of the lyrics (the tubax makes a return and we get rams horns too), and the whole is compelling in its epic strangeness.

303. Epizootics! (Scott Walker)
Original release: *Bish Bosch* 2012 CD/LP

An 'epizootic' is an outbreak of disease in an animal population. However, in interviews, Scott cautioned against attaching any weight to the literal meaning of the title. Rather, in keeping with the linguistic playfulness of the album, Scott chose the title because the word sounded a bit like hipster slag ('*Epi-ʒoo-tics!*'). If anything, 'Epizootics!' is stranger still than *302* 'Zercon'. With no footnote clues to guide the listener, the lyrics are an idiosyncratic mix of place, time and language. The hipster slang of the 1940s/50s brushes shoulders with both outdated and contemporary British slang in a suggestion of city street hustles, and bustles, then and now. There is plenty that could be taken to refer to drug deals as well as merely crowded busyness. But, of course, it wouldn't be *Bish Bosch* without the more ancient history too; we have references to Pope Julius and Michelangelo too. Sonically, we get a vocal that, at times, is more spoken than sung, including on the 'Take that accidentally in the bollocks for a start' line. We get a regular brassy five-note sequence that sounds like it might be at home prefacing public-service tannoy announcements in some nightmare future. We get Hawaiian steel guitars – in part courtesy of one B. J. Cole, who had played on Scott's 1970s albums – used here to create what Scott described as an 'Hawaiian nightmare'[54], finger-clicking to reflect the hipster slang, the tubax again, and, to end the track, Scott singing the line 'Sweet Leilani, heavenly flower' over a ukulele accompaniment.

'Epizootics!' was also accompanied by a short film – or official video – for which Scott had a say in its imagery but no hands-on involvement in its creation. It features the likes of a Hawaiian dancer with bad teeth, petals falling on white shoes, maggots in flowers and jive dancing in variously slowed down and speeded up black and white footage together with a colour interlude to accompany 'Epizootics!''s gentler middle section. It can be found on YouTube, where at the time of writing it has now received a remarkable 647,000 views.

304. Dimple (Scott Walker)
Original release: *Bish Bosch* 2012 CD/LP

The title 'Dimple' stems from Scott's discovery of the factoid that no matter how much a person's face changes over time, if they have a dimple, it will remain in the same place. Hence, fittingly, in 'Dimple' time is telescoped. It is 'November in July'. The distorted refrain from Jimmy Durante's 1930s song and signature tune, 'Inka Dinka Doo', rubs shoulders with the more contemporary references to a Dorgi and Lego[55]. It is 'hi there' and 'goodbye' in quick succession. (Playing with language again, some of the lyrics of 'Dimple' are in Danish, where '*hej do*' means 'hi there' and '*farvel*' means 'goodbye'.) That is as long as there is something rather than nothing ('*ingenting*' as sung in Danish) and you are alive. Ever the existentialist, Scott sings, 'If you're listening to this, you must have survived.' For elsewhere, despite Scott's assertions that his songs are not autobiographical, it is hard not to see 'Dimple' as being from the point of view of someone who knows they are relatively close to the end of their life. There is the 'I won't …' or 'I will not …' '… again' lines and the air of bodily decay carried in both the imagery of the rest of the lyric and the haunting soundscape against which it is presented.

305. Tar (Scott Walker)
Original release: *Bish Bosch* 2012 CD/LP

As if in answer to the end-of-life tone – if I am right – of *304* 'Dimple', 'Tar' turns its focus to religion and specifically 'contradictions in the Bible'. The lyric sets up competing claims against each other (say 'Jacob's offspring in Egypt totalled seventy' vs. 'Jacob's offspring in Egypt totalled seventy-five') for, with clear sarcasm, one to be embraced as the clear and obvious truth and the other to be dismissed as absolute nonsense, and carrying forward the telescoping of time that we find everywhere on *Bish Bosch* those dismissals vary from the archaic ('Hogwash!') to the modern ('GTFO!') As already noted in connection with *The Drift*, the latter-day Scott Walker didn't do straightforward protest or message songs, but with 'Tar', and even more so with the album's next track *306* 'Pilgrim', there is a clear message here. Of course, there's much more to the lyric of 'Tar' than invective against Christianity, or at least those who would pore over every line of the Bible as if it mattered, but invective might be right as in amongst the electronic effects that recall larger-than-life buzzing flies and other horrors, some of the percussion on the track comes courtesy of the sharpening of genuine machetes. These, as promotional footage for *Bish Bosch* attests, were not toys and as Scott recalled were 'three or four feet long'.[56] In any event, the song ends with a lyric 'There but for the grace of god goes God' that can only be taken to imply that it is happenstance rather than divinity that gave Christianity its place.

306. Pilgrim (Scott Walker)
Original release: *Bish Bosch* 2012 CD/LP

And then there follows the album's shortest and most direct track, 'Pilgrim'. As with *305* 'Tar', there is a message here, yet in contrast to all other pieces on the album where multiple ideas are bought together in the lyric, 'Pilgrim' is essentially about juxtaposing two items only: children torturing and killing bullfrogs by blowing them up with straws and scientists experimenting on mice. Again, it's not a straightforward protest or message song, but things are as direct as they get here in the Walker universe. The two horrific portraits are placed side by side - on the one hand the bullfrog whose eyes are studied just before it bursts and on the other the 'room full of mice' whose mutations are catalogued at the end of the song: 'No ear, two tails, one eye, three toes'. The instrumentation, along with the song's length and lyrical content, is stripped back too with the only credits being for drums, double bass and keyboards, and the overriding impression being of a mix of an ominous rattling, Scott's voice and dramatic points of silence that surround the bullfrogs' death.

307. The Day the "Conducator" Died (An Xmas Song) (Scott Walker)
Original release: *Bish Bosch* 2012 CD/LP

As with *Tilt* and *The Drift*, *Bish Bosch* ends on a track where the sole credit for instrumentation went to Scott Walker himself. However, in place of the voice and lone guitar approach and brevity of *267* 'Rosary' and *292* 'A Lover Loves', 'The Day the "Conducator" Died' adds percussion and keyboards to Scott Walker's credits and the song stretches out over nearly eight minutes. Like *302* 'Zercon', it's one of those tracks where a footnote with the lyrics provides a key to understanding those lyrics, about which Scott was prepared to open up in radio interviews too. The "Conducator" is a specific individual, and the 'Xmas' Day in the song's subtitle is a specific one. Nicolae Ceauşescu, who styled himself the Conducător (Romanian for 'Leader'), was the President of Communist Romania from 1974 until the overthrow of his regime in 1989. At the same time as other anti-Communist revolutions then occurring in Eastern Europe, rebellion came to Romania in the shape of an uprising that took Ceauşescu and his wife, Elana, captive to be tried and sentenced on Christmas Day, 25th December 1989. That trial was swift and its death sentence was quickly carried out. Nicolae Ceauşescu's cult of personality, which had been pervasive in Romanian life for nearly two decades, was brought to an abrupt end. Scott explained that it was that notion of cult of personality which inspired the approach of the lyric of 'The Day the "Conducator" Died' which largely takes the form of a personality test that might be found in a magazine with multiple choice answers to be given. The refrain 'Nobody waited for fire' was one Scott was drawn to because, whilst it might suggest multiple meanings or connotations, its meaning is actually quite specific. The Ceauşescus requested that their death sentence be carried out on them simultaneously together, to which their captors agreed, but the firing squad began shooting as soon as the two were in position against a wall. So keen were they to execute them that nobody literally waited for 'Fire!' As the song comes to its close, with a good dose of irony, as this is nobody's conventional idea of a Christmas song, the sleigh bells rhythmically ring out to be joined by a faltering rendition of a line of melody from 'Jingle Bells'. It's a fittingly blackly humorous end to an album like no other.

Soused 2014 collaborative album with Sunn O)))

308. Brando (Scott Walker)
Original release: *Soused* 2014 CD/LP

And there was more. Surprisingly hot on the heels of *Bish Bosch* came not quite a fully-fledged album but a collaborative album with Seattle experimental metal band Sunn O))). Sunn O))), in essence a duo, had pioneered drone metal in the early 1990s and been recording a series of experimental metal albums throughout the 2000s, often involving collaborations with other artists, including in one case Julian Cope. They had invited Scott Walker to work with them for their 2009 *Monoliths & Dimensions* album. He had declined, but clearly kept the offer in mind and later approached Sunn O))) to say he had written some songs specifically with them in mind. The results became *Soused*, a five-track album with a reasonably full-length playing time (all the tracks are over eight minutes long) jointly credited to Scott Walker and Sunn O))). However, it is fair to say it's more a Scott Walker album than it is a Sunn O))) album. Scott Walker wrote and, of course, sang all the songs. The album was recorded in London with Scott's long-term collaborator and co-producer Peter Walsh and with *Bish Bosch*'s musical director Mark Warman. And perhaps the curious thing is that, rather than the sum of the experimental Scott Walker and the experimental Sunn O))) equalling an ever more experimental whole, *Soused* is less of an experimental record than those beforehand by Scott and Sunn O))) individually. *Soused* does not out-weird *Bish Bosch*, and it is definitely a more accessible record than that masterpiece of strangeness. Thus, although *Soused* does yield four strong new Scott Walker tracks (and one re-recorded song), it feels a little anticlimactic in the wake of *Bish Bosch*. *Soused* harks backward a little to earlier modern Scott Walker records, and its final track – a re-recording of a 1999 Walker composition – does not feel out of place here.

The opening track 'Brando' opens with the latter-day Scott at his most melodic and operatic, recalling say *259* 'Farmer in the City' from *Tilt*, as he delivers the lines 'Ah, The Wide Missouri / Dwellers on the bluff / Across the Wide Missouri'. Guitars soar, crunch and drone, but the addition of Sunn O))) on this track won't come across as excitingly experimental at all to those who have been with the man through *Tilt*, *The Drift* and *Bish Bosch*. In keeping with the ethic of modern Scott Walker solo records, the aural tapestry reflects the lyrics. Here there's eerie whistling and the sound of bull whips cracking. The lyrics drop both clear and veiled references to Marlon Brando with the emphasis on him being somehow beaten – 'Wild One' requires no explanation; 'Johnny Friendly' is the union boss from *On the Waterfront*; 'Dwellers on the bluff' is the Native American meaning of 'Omaha', Brando's birthplace in Nebraska. We also get the marvellous and sado-masochistic lines 'I am down on my knees' and 'A beating would do me a world of good' contributing to the cinematic sweep of the track.

It's also the most accessible track on the album, and if albums like *Soused* had singles, this would be it, with 4AD releasing a video, or rather short film directed by Austro-French choreographer and filmmaker Gisèle Vienne to accompany the track (which, beautiful and strange in its own right, seems only loosely related to the song, if at all).

309. Herod 2014 (Scott Walker)
Original release: *Soused* 2014 CD/LP

With beheadings by the then-ascendant Islamic State making the news in 2014, 'Herod 2014' carries forward the technique from earlier modern Scott Walker records of juxtaposing disparate points of historical reference to create a horrific non-linear portrait. Here, reference to the Stasi (the East German secret police from the Cold War era) rubs shoulders with Biblical infanticide (the titular Herod and the repeated refrain 'She's hidden her babies away'), and the lines from a traditional Ojibwa Indian lullaby rub shoulders with images of pestilence from tsetse flies to lice to church mice. The lyric also gives us a reference to an obscure 17th century art debate where, with both artists having been dead for years, supporters of Peter Paul Rubens and Nicolas Poussin respectively argued over whether colour or drawing were most important. But really, the only thing approaching any moment of light relief is the utterly incongruous inclusion of a reminder, if one is needed, that this is not a song about favourite things that won't make you feel so bad ('No "Raindrops on roses" / "Whiskers on kittens"'). Otherwise, the bleakness and horror of the lyric are what stand out against a backdrop of instrumentation that, with its effective evoking of crying and groaning against an ever-ominous drone, mirrors perfectly the song's lyric.

310. Bull (Scott Walker)
Original release: *Soused* 2014 CD/LP

Here the distinctness of the collaboration with Sunn O))) is more strongly felt, as sections of 'Bull', including its opening, are among the most heavy, aggressive and noisy in the Walker canon. True, sections of *302* 'Zercon' were delivered angrily, but here the effect is more sustained, more metal, and as the maxim on the album's back cover advises, 'Maximum volume yields maximum results.' The track also features long instrumental passages where the droning and industrially creaking sound of Sunn O))), supplemented with a Moog synthesiser on this track, is given more of a centre stage. There are also distant vocals from voices other than Scott's to be heard here, including from Scottish singer/songwriter Dot Allison. Scott's lyric both recalls the stripping-down-of-the-thing-to-its-essence approach of *Climate of Hunter*, with its short and disconnected lines, and the bathos of *Bish Bosch*, where the down-to-earth and crude interrupt the flow ('Leapin' like a River Dancer's nuts' and 'Woke nailed to cross / Could not give a toss'). There's also the recurring theme of juxtaposing disparate time frames, as we both get a line of the lyric presented as text speak (and shown in a messaging speech bubble on the lyric sheet, 'Nite-nite') and part of the lyric presented in Latin – of which '*inquietum dolor*', meaning 'restless pain', is probably the most telling in terms of the lyric's overall meaning.

311. Fetish (Scott Walker)
Original release: *Soused* 2014 CD/LP

'Fetish' takes us further into a world of pain, with the obvious focus on the blade of a knife. 'Gleam away, little brute, gleam away,' sings Scott of the blade which the song title suggests might bring sado-masochistic pleasure as well as pain, and might, as the lyrics suggest, be used without restraint (on 'the body including the face'). There's bed and there's spunk and there's blood in the *mise en scène*. The archaic word 'bescumber' means to spray shit upon, or 'discharge ordure or dung upon' as the dictionary would have it, which brings fresh meaning to the then-71 year-old Scott Walker singing the song's most notorious line: 'Can't afford, but bescumber, our spunk-stiffened-tresses'. The line 'Acne on a leper' is also equally visceral and, to these ears, carries the possible meaning of the protagonist in the song already being so sick inside that the actual sadistic behaviour is just the superficial topping, or maybe it's to say that just when you think things can't get any worse, or behaviour can't get any darker, there's always that little bit further you can go. And once again here, the instrumental backing keeps pace with the subject matter of the lyric, from the agonised sound of the trumpet to music that evokes slashing, sawing and chiselling, with silence again creatively deployed *à la Bish Bosch* to complete the picture.

312. Lullaby (Scott Walker)
Original release: *Soused* 2014 CD/LP

Back in 2000, Scott had said that he planned also to record his own versions of the two songs he had contributed for Ute Lemper's *Punishing Kiss* album (*281* and *282*). Here, with Sunn O))) on board, he was true to his word in respect of the second of those songs, the one which only appeared on the Japanese edition of Ute Lemper's album. For Scott's version the '(By By By)' subtitle of the original is dropped, but there are no substantial lyrical changes between the two versions. (At one point, Ute Lemper sings 'autonomy' in one line where Scott sings the word 'dignity' instead, but the lyrical differences are at this level of detail.) In Sunn O))) and company's hands the backing is far more ominous than it is in Ute Lemper's version, and significantly more discordant in the chorus. Nothing, though, feels out of place, and the song is a fitting note on which to end the album, which, despite being perhaps less rather than greater than the sum of its two parts (that is, Sunn O))) and Scott), nevertheless gave us some strong new Scott Walker material much sooner than we would have come to expect following the release of his last album.

The Childhood of a Leader 2016 soundtrack album

313. Orchestral Tuning Up

314. Opening

315. Dream Sequence

316. Village Walk

317. Untitled

318. Down the Stairs

319. Up the Stairs

320. The Letter

321. Versailles

322. Cutting Flowers

323. Boy, Mirror, Car Arriving

324. Third Tantrum

325. Printing Press

326. On the Way to the Meeting

327. The Meeting

328. Post Meeting

329. Finale

330. New Dawn (Synth Layout for Cut Scene)

Composition all tracks Scott Walker.
Original release: *The Childhood of a Leader (Original Soundtrack)* 2016 CD/LP

The last physical Scott Walker record release of the man's lifetime, though, turned out to be his official soundtrack album for Brady Corret's acclaimed film *The Childhood of a Leader*. Given that Scott had admitted that dictators held a fascination for him – a fascination which, of course, found reflection in the likes of *284* 'Clara' and *307* 'The Day the "Conducator" Died' – it is perhaps unsurprising that he was drawn to a film that imagined the childhood of a dictator in the years following the First World War, and moreover was loosely based on a short story by the great existentialist himself Jean-Paul Sartre. The film, Corret's directorial debut, was released to positive critical reviews in July of 2016, closely followed by Scott's soundtrack album, which met with an equally warm, if not warmer, critical response. The review by Pitchfork even went as far as to say that it was one of his best works since *The Drift* (with which we might technically agree but be left wondering where that left the reviewer's opinion of the significance of *Bish Bosch*). The same review, less questionably, praised how 'like the composers this music most closely recalls (Edgard Varèse, György Ligeti, Bernard Herrmann) Walker manages to play his fully-sized orchestra like one huge, terrifying instrument here,'[57] – Herrmann of course being the composer of the seminal score for Hitchcock's *Psycho*. And fully-sized orchestra it certainly was; Scott, working with his now-usual collaborators co-producer Peter Walsh and musical director Mark Warman, engaged an orchestra where in Warman's words: 'The strings numbered 24 violins, eight violas, 10 cellos and four double-basses … [and] the brass comprised six bass trombones, five French horns and five trumpets, with certain players doubling on flugelhorns and tenor trombones.'[58] On the record, the wholly instrumental soundtrack's short overall running time of 30 minutes is split into 18 tracks, many only around a minute in length and with only the urgent, tension-building opening theme exceeding five minutes. The music by turns conveys calm foreboding and brooding aggression (especially on the *Psycho*-esque 'Third Tantrum' – the film is divided into three episodic tantrums – and on the epic 'Finale') but does – albeit rightly so in this case as it all works very effectively in the context of the film – find Scott playing a relatively straight bat in comparison to the altogether more *outré* world of *Bish Bosch* or, in purely instrumental terms, *And Who Shall Go to the Ball? And What Shall Go to the Ball?*

Contributions to the Vox Lux 2018 soundtrack album

331. Prelude

332. Night Walk

333. Opening Credits

334. Anthem

335. Yearning

336. Terrorist

337. C&A Walk

338. Dressing Room

339. Druggie

340. Finale

Composition all tracks Scott Walker.
Original release: *Vox Lux (Original Soundtrack)* 2018 digital streaming/download

For his second feature film, director Brady Corbet turned from historical drama to a musical drama that explored concepts of pop culture and modern celebrity. In *Vox Lux*, the main character (pop singer Celeste played as her older self by Natalie Portman) is rocketed to stardom after surviving a horrific school shooting and singing at the memorial vigil. Corman again turned to Scott Walker to compose the score, but this time additionally recruiting the enigmatic Australian singer-songwriter Sia to provide the pop songs to be sung by Natalie Portman as Celeste (and Raffey Cassidy as the younger Celeste). The resulting album, which at the time of writing is currently available only digitally, thus comprises a 56-minute soundtrack with the majority of the running time given over to Sia compositions sung by Natalie Portman and by Raffey Cassidy, and 22 minutes given over to Scott's score. Again, like his work for *The Childhood of a Leader*, it's all very effective in the context of the film as soundtrack *qua* soundtrack. Tracks such as 'Yearning' and 'Finale' carry forward the purely instrumental orchestral approach of *The Childhood of a Leader* score, but others add electronic sound and wordless male and female vocals; 'Druggie' even has a short lyric sung as though by children reciting a nonsensical nursery rhyme: 'All of the houses are out of doors / Standing in the rain'. Perhaps due to a number of factors (the fact of the film not being released in the UK until several months after the US, the distraction of the presence of Sia's contributions, and the lack of a physical record release) Scott's *Vox Lux* score has gone largely unheralded in the UK media and in the US even attracted somewhat negative reviews (on Pitchfork and from *Rolling Stone*). However, Scott's other product release of late 2018 attracted significantly more attention. In December 2018, Faber and Faber published *Sundog*, a book that collected selected lyrics from Scott Walker's career in print together for the first time. Unsurprisingly, the focus was on his modern work (from *Tilt* onwards) with only sparse inclusions from his early solo career and *Climate of Hunter*. And excitingly, the final chapter of *Sundog* headed 'New Songs 2016/2017' gave us the lyrics of six newly composed and never heard Scott Walker songs. The lyrics found Scott still at his esoteric and uncompromising best. We may never get to hear Scott sing, say, 'Hate-Fuck, Free Radio is saving the concaves / Brought to you courtesy of the Hate-Fuck, Free man' from new song 'The Boston Green Head'[59], but we can know that, like the *Luʒerner Zeitung*, he never sold out.

---

1. 'Cro-magnon' is the name of a genus of early man, falling somewhere between Neolithic and Modern man. 'Herder' is simply one who drives the herd.
2. It is hard to describe the video to 'Track Three'. It comes across as made by someone who quite liked the film *Eraserhead*, but whose idea of meaningful symbolism is to depict a rock being dropped into a puddle, and whose idea of excitement is to depict a man being chased by a Vauxhall Viva, slowly.
3. As opposed to the more obvious 'shadow of the sun'. Of course one has to be reading the lyric sheet to appreciate this.

4. Scott's *Nite Flights* tracks are often said to have been the inspiration for Ultravox's 1981 hit 'Vienna', so perhaps on 'Track Seven' he was returning the favour.
5. https://goranbregovic.rs/
6. Although of course there are a whole list of lines like this: man from Reno/Zurich/Italy, etc.
7. Or could this be the other way around? The *Tilt* CD booklet informs us that 'Farmer in the City' was written during 1991-1992. 'Man from Reno' was by all accounts written and recorded quickly, presumably in 1993. So could the 'man from . . .' section have been taken from 'Farmer in the City' for use in 'Man from Reno'? It seems unlikely, given that 'Farmer in the City' is obviously the more significant track. The most likely explanation seems to be that it was written in 1991 or '92 and amended to include the 'man from . . .' section before its release in 1995.
8. The official version of Pasolini's murder had him killed by his pick-up for the evening, a young male prostitute named Pino Pelosi. It now seems more likely that the murder was political and undertaken by a gang of men rather than one individual.
9. This, and other statements attributed to Scott Walker in these paragraphs, are taken from a CD pre-recorded by Walker and released to radio stations with a typed list of the questions asked in lieu of personal interviews to promote *Tilt*.
10. The hurdy gurdy is an unusual stringed instrument where the strings are sounded by a hand-turned wheel rather than a bow. It has been described as like a 'mechanical violin'.
11. Although originally a spiritual song, 'Dry Bones' would certainly seem to be more a sing-along or children's song in today's world; the religion-free version 'The Skeleton Dance' has, for example, enjoyed more than 62 million YouTube views.
12. This translation from the French is taken from https://en.wikipedia.org/wiki/Code_noir
13. The lyric as printed in the CD booklet has 'Ja 91' at its beginning and '17 aryanury [sic]' at its end; married together, the two give '17 January '91'.
14. Scott Walker interview, *The Wire*, May 1995.
15. In the above interview, Scott is quoted as saying, 'I structured the chords very carefully through the whole album and there are new chords, not used before. The chords in "Tilt" are meant to be like a yin and yang thing. David Rhodes is actually playing a major and a minor at the same time.'
16. In an absolutely unique piece of television, Scott appeared on the BBC's *Later with Jools Holland* programme to perform 'Rosary' live, accompanied only by his own guitar playing.
17. The soundtrack was otherwise the work of Blixa Bargeld, Nick Cave and Mick Harvey, a triumvirate whose bands respectively include Einsturzende Neubauten, the Birthday Party, Nick Cave and the Bad Seeds and Crime and the City Solution.
18. Those not familiar with *Nashville Skyline* might know its most famous track, 'Lay Lady Lay', a Top Ten hit for Bob Dylan on both sides of the Atlantic in 1969.
19. The track only appears as an instrumental theme in the film, but the song with Scott's vocal was included on the soundtrack album.
20. Nineteenth-century American author Herman Melville is best known for his *masterpiece Moby Dick. Pierre: or the Ambiguities* was the book that he wrote shortly after, which was so badly received on its publication that Melville did not write another novel afterwards.
21. *Hamlet*, 1.5.189-90.
22. According to *NME* at the time, 'Thimble Rigging' was a 'monkish medieval thrum with an almost industrial screen and drone' that featured 'the disembodied vocals of former Cocteau Twin Elizabeth Fraser and a five-string electric cello'. 'Thimble Rigging' was to some extent re-worked into *The Drift* track *290* 'Psoriatic' but this *Drift* track was a new recording and does not feature Ms Fraser's vocals.
23. Herbert Ponting was a photographer involved in the ill-fated 1910-13 British Antarctic expedition under Robert Falcon Scott. His sleeping bag poem was published in *The South Polar Times*, the expedition newspaper, in 1911.
24. *MOJO*, July 2000.

25. In particular the line, 'The most intimate personal choices and requests central to your personal dignity will be sung,' and variants of it

26. To wit, its extraordinary length, its sectional approach, its less melodic wordily written passages, its discordant sounds and its old-fashioned female vocal delivery. See *172* 'The Ballad of Sacco and Vanzetti'.

27. *MOJO*, July 2000.

28. https://thequietus.com/articles/16411-scott-walker-interview-sunn-o-soused

29. The only other Walker-related release of this period being the 2001 LP by British band Pulp, *We Love Life*, for which Scott is credited with production of the album and arrangements for a number of tracks.

30. The most celebrated 4AD acts past and present include the Pixies, the Cocteau Twins, Throwing Muses, This Mortal Coil, the Birthday Party, Lush, Wolfgang Press and Dead Can Dance.

31. Scott's first television interview in over a decade was broadcast on BBC2's *The Culture Show*, 30 March 2006. He also gave interviews for *The Wire* (May 2006) and *Q* (June 2006). A radio interview with Scott was also broadcast on BBC Radio 4's *Front Row* (26 April 2006). Scott's words of explanation regarding *The Drift* in this section of the book are taken from these and other sources.

32. 'There's also a quote from George Bush in the middle. I remember when Chirac was over in America recently, somebody asked in the press conference, "Are you going to take him out to your ranch, Mr. President?" And Bush said, "Well I'm looking for a good cowboy," and I thought I'll put that in 'cause that's a real backhanded compliment.' Scott Walker quoted in *The Wire*, May 2006.

33. The strongest candidates for a Walker protest song are *133* 'Hero of the War' and *134* 'The Old Man's Back Again', but even the political comment of these songs is no mere sloganeering.

34. *Q*, June 2006.

35. James Joyce (1882-1941), the influential Irish writer whose most important works include *Dubliners* (1914), *A Portrait of the Artist as a Young Man* (1916), *Ulysses* (1922), and the especially difficult *Finnegan's Wake* (1939).

36. Scott Walker, *Tilt* interview CD, see note 9 above.

37. Rob Young, *The Wire*, May 2006.

38. The Beatles used the sound of tuning a radio and landing on different stations in 1967's 'I Am the Walrus'. They first used backward vocals and guitar on their 1966 B-side 'Rain'.

39. Srebrenica was the location of the largest mass killing in Europe since the Second World War when, in July 1995, Serbian troops slaughtered 8,000 Bosnians – just one of the atrocities of the Bosnian War, a conflict that left over 100,000 dead, at least 8,000 women raped, and hundreds of thousands of refugees.

40. Scott Walker interview by Stefan Weidle for the 23 April 2006 issue of the German newspaper, *Frankfurter Allgemeinen Sonntagszeitung*, English version published online.

41. 'Serifot' and 'Kellipot'. Neither of these Kabbalah terms is easily explained concisely.

42. Scott Walker as quoted in *Plague Songs* CD booklet.

43. Information provided as a note in *Plague Songs* CD booklet.

44. Scott Walker as quoted on the 4AD website in an article published 5 September 2007.

45. Scott Walker 2013 radio interview with David Dye for World Café.

46. Ibid.

47. Scott Walker 2012 radio interview with Jarvis Cocker for BBC Radio 6 Music.

48. www.bishbosch.com

49. Asked by BBC2's *The Culture Show* in 2006 whether his next album following *The Drift* would be delivered in ten years' time, Scott replied, 'I probably won't be alive then.'

50. Scott Walker 2012 radio interview with John Schaefer for WNYC.

51. Scott Walker in radio interviews accompanying the release of *Bish Bosch*; Peter Walsh in interview with Paul Woods for the latter's book *The Curious Life and Work of Scott Walker* (Omnibus 2013).

52. Scott Walker 2012 radio interview with John Schaefer for WNYC.

53. Scott Walker as quoted by Rob Young https://www.bishbosch.com/biog/
54. Scott's words from the 2012 interview with Jarvis Cocker for BBC 6 Music.
55. The portmanteau term 'Dorgi' meaning a crossbreed of a Dachshund and Corgi is of relatively recent invention. Lego is, of course, a present day item, and is younger too in its invention than Jimmy Durante's song.
56. Scott Walker 2012 radio interview with John Schaefer for WNYC.
57. https://pitchfork.com/reviews/albums/22248-the-childhood-of-a-leader-ost
58. Mark Warman quoted by *Uncut* September 2016 (https://www.uncut.co.uk/reviews/album/scott-walker-childhood-leader-ost)
59. *Sundog*, Scott Walker (Faber and Faber 2018) pp.173-177

Afterword

The title of this work was not chosen entirely at random. Scott Walker was, it seems, always saying goodbye. In the Sixties, with the Walker Brothers, nearly every song he sang was concerned with the loss of love. If Scott was in misery, you were in for a good time. His solo career after the Walker Brothers said goodbye to his pop-star image. As late as 1969, Scott was complaining of people's expectations that he should be the person he appeared to be in the Walker Brothers. By the end of that year, his wish to no longer be seen as a pop star came all too true, when the record-buying public ceased to have any interest in him at all. Scott's brilliance endured through *Scott 4* and *'Til the Band Comes In*, but his audience did not remain with him. His commercial failure was to a large extent a product of the times. The music scene of 1969 simply had no room for someone who could release a pair of albums as different as *Scott Walker Sings Songs from His TV Series* and *Scott 4* within a few months. The Seventies saw Scott Walker temporarily saying goodbye to his muse and, for most of that decade, recording only the songs of others. Though no one would apply the 'God-like genius' tag to this period, this is not to say that he didn't make some good records. One or two pratfalls aside, Scott's self-styled artistic wilderness period does not altogether deserve the bad reputation the man himself gave it. The most visible and commercially successful product of this period was another rhyme of goodbye, a cover of a song about a relationship breaking up, 'No Regrets', which saw the reformed Walker Brothers back in the Top Ten a decade after their heyday. When Scott did return to writing songs in 1978, it was to say goodbye to pop music altogether, to sentimentality and to the mainstream. His albums since 1978 have been postcards from the edge, all of which are remarkable records. 1995's *Tilt* was remarkable not just for its content but for being such a significant defining moment so late in an artist's career. And the contrary brilliance of *The Drift* and *Bish Bosch* could not have been predicted even on the basis of *Tilt*. That loose trilogy of albums can be spoken of in the same breath as *Scott 1-4* as the peaks of a unique, influential, brave and beautiful recording career.

appendix

Unreleased Tracks

1. Unreleased Studio Recordings and the 'Bootlegged Three'

A long time ago, the fanzine *Walkerpeople* published a tantalising list of 29 unreleased Walker Brothers/Scott Walker tracks dating from 1966 to 1972, 19 said to be Walker Brothers tracks and ten to be solo Scott Walker tracks. Of these, 12 of the Walker Brothers tracks on the list were released in 2006 on the *Everything Under the Sun* box set, and three of the Scott Walker solo tracks did somehow unofficially escape, and are now well known amongst fans.[1] The titles of 'the bootlegged three' are as follows, and they are all remarkably good.

Free Again (Basile/Canfora/Colby/Jourdan)
Original release: not applicable, believed recorded 1967

'Free Again' is believed to be an outtake, albeit a perfectly finished one, from the *Scott* LP. Other artists, including Barbra Streisand and Nancy Wilson, have recorded the song, but never has it been more menacingly handled than in Scott's version. The lyric is an exercise in irony, with lines like 'free again, lucky lucky me, free again, back in circulation now, time for celebration now, time to have a party,' that the jilted narrator clearly isn't supposed to mean a word of. Against a haunting arrangement, Scott intones every line with vehement sarcasm. Chilling stuff, which might have made a more convincing inclusion on Scott than, say, *95* 'You're Gonna Hear from Me'.

I Get Along Without You Very Well (Hoagy Carmichael)
Original release: not applicable, believed recorded 1967

Also believed to be a *Scott* outtake. It would be fair to call this song a standard, recorded by a long list of artists including Billie Holiday, Frank Sinatra, Jimmy Dorsey and Peggy Lee. Scott's version is a welcome addition to the list. Like 'Free Again', it's an exercise in irony, with the singer declaring the song's title but then adding a list of circumstances in which he doesn't get along without you quite so well after all.

I Think I'm Getting over You (Roger Cook, Roger Greenaway)
Original release: not applicable, believed recorded 1967

The best of the three escaped outtakes, recorded for potential single release. What makes this song so appealing, in addition to its gorgeous tune, is the feeling of both sadness and hope it manages to impart – when Scott sings, 'and yesterday I saw the sun shining through,' it sounds like he really did. After all the songs of inconsolable heartbreak we've heard him sing, it's nice to hear him at least expressing some hope whilst at the same time acknowledging his pain. This is a wonderful track.

2. Scott Walker Sings More Songs from His TV Series

Okay, so there's no such album, and nor is there likely to be outside of a homemade or bootleg compilation. But, taking into account the two half-hour television specials that Scott recorded, as well as his six-part TV series proper, there are fifteen songs that didn't get included on the *TV Series* LP and don't appear anywhere else. These are not available in pristine release quality, but, courtesy of recordings made by fans from the television broadcasts, they can at least be heard.

Follow Me (A. J. Lerner/F. Loeure)
Originally broadcast: Scott Walker pilot show one – 16 August 1968

Appropriately enough, Scott opened the show with a musical invitation to follow him. The performance starts in ballad fashion, but builds into the big show-opening number you were expecting. Originally from the Broadway musical Camelot, which opened in 1960.

Days of Love (Rose/Webster)
Originally broadcast: Scott Walker pilot show one – 16 August 1968

A ballad from the 1967 film *Hombre*, with music by David Rose and words by Paul Francis Webster. Scott is quite gushing in his praise, describing it as a 'wonderful song' with 'very, very elegant' lyrics.

I'll Be Around (Alec Wilder)
Originally broadcast: Scott Walker pilot show one – 16 August 1968

Scott introduces Johnny Franz at the piano, to perform a standard written in 1943 and recorded by countless artists.

Passing Strangers (Mel Mitchell/Rita Mann)
Originally broadcast: Scott Walker pilot show one – 16 August 1968

Performed as a duet with Kiki Dee, one of Scott's guests on the first TV special. The song was a hit in the UK twice for the duo Billy Eckstine and Sarah Vaughan (in 1957 and 1969). And whilst Scott and Ms Dee's performance might conceivably have helped 'Passing Strangers' become a hit again, her appearance on his show didn't boost her career much – it would be another five years before she had a hit single, and she remains best remembered for her duet with Elton John ('Don't Go Breaking My Heart') rather than her solo records.

Gotta Travel On (Paul Clayton)
Originally broadcast: Scott Walker pilot show two – 30 December 1968

The second Scott Walker TV special yields three songs that don't feature on any of his records. The first of these was the opening number, 'Gotta Travel On'. Scott's version is big and brassy, but the song itself is apparently based on a nineteenth-century British folk song, a very folky version of which is performed by Bob Dylan on his 1970 LP *Self Portrait*.

And We Were Lovers (Jerry Goldsmith/Leslie Bricusse)
Originally broadcast: Scott Walker pilot show two – 30 December 1968

The love theme from the 1966 film *The Sand Pebbles*, starring Steve McQueen.

Tender Is the Night (Fain/Webster)
Originally broadcast: Scott Walker pilot show two – 30 December 1968

Originally from the 1961 film of the same name, performed with Johnny Franz at the piano. Scott describes this number as one of his and Franz's favourite songs.

In the Still of the Night (Cole Porter)
Originally broadcast: Scott Walker TV series show one – 11 March 1969

The big opening number for the first show in Scott's TV series proper, an up-tempo take on Cole Porter's classic song.

Why Did I Choose You? (M. Leonard/H. Martin)
Originally broadcast: Scott Walker TV series show one – 11 March 1969

The accompanied-by-Johnny-Franz-at-the-piano number from the first show in the series proper, a tune that really should have been included on the *TV Series* LP. An absolutely gorgeous song, as romantic as it's possible to be: 'And when I lost my heart so many years ago, I lost it knowingly and willingly to you, if I had to choose again, I would still choose you.' Beautiful.

There Will Never Be Another You (Harry Warden/Mack Gordon)
Originally broadcast: Scott Walker TV series show two – 18 March 1969

The opening number from the second show. Only two songs used as show openers were selected for inclusion on the *TV Series* LP, one opening each side. 'There Will Never Be Another You' dates from 1942 and was written for the film *Iceland*.

Alone (AKA We're Alone, originally Seul) (Brel/Shuman)
Originally broadcast: Scott Walker TV series show two – 18 March 1969

The spectacular closing number from the second show features Mort Shuman's translation of Jacques Brel's 'Alone' – which, like many of Scott's Brel covers, features on the *Jacques Brel Is Alive and Well and Living in Paris* soundtrack. Scott introduced the song with, 'This next song is probably my most favourite song to sing, I think. It's about loneliness of all kinds, loneliness happens to rich people, poor people, people of glory, fame.' Amazingly, given Scott's wonderful performance, the song remained unreleased – it could easily have fitted into *Scott 1-3*. A highlight.

Don't Rain on My Parade (Julie Styne/Bob Merrill)
Originally broadcast: Scott Walker TV series show three – 25 March 1969

The opening number from the third show, a song from the 1968 film *Funny Girl* that made Barbara Streisand a star. Scott's version is definitely enjoyable, but it's an odd choice of song for him to sing. It's weird to hear him sing, 'life's candy and the sun's a ball of butter,' or, even weirder, 'but whether I'm the rose of sheer perfection, a freckle on the nose of life's complexion, the Cinderella or the shine apple of its eye'! Uncharacteristically, Scott's enunciation is less than clear on these lines, probably out of sheer embarrassment at singing these words.

My Shining Hour (Arlen/Mercer)
Originally broadcast: Scott Walker TV series show four – 1 April 1969

The opening number from the fourth show, a song written by Harold Arlen and Johnny Mercer for the 1943 film *The Sky's the Limit*. Like many songs featured on the TV series, it was previously recorded by Frank Sinatra.

This Is All I Ask (Gordon Jenkins)
Originally broadcast: Scott Walker TV series show four – 1 April 1969

The accompanied-by-Johnny-Franz-at-the-piano number from the fourth show. Scott announces the song as being by 'my favourite American arranger, who's also a composer . . . Gordon Jenkins.' Very nice it is too, in a 'September Song' kind of way.

The Lady's in Love with You (Burton Lane)
Originally broadcast: Scott Walker TV series show four – 1 April 1969

Also from show four comes the last of the lost Scott TV songs, from the well-known 1959 film *Some Like It Hot*. Hardly the most essential Walker recording, but he did sing 'Big Louise' and 'Funeral Tango' on the same show.

3. Miscellaneous Live/TV Recordings

Unofficial recordings are also known to exist of the following songs, performed either by the Walker Brothers or Scott, that do not otherwise appear on any official release and which stem from miscellaneous TV or live appearances.[2] Original broadcast dates are in most cases hard to pin down. The list cannot be said to be exhaustive either, as both the Walker Brothers and Scott as a solo artist are known to have performed other songs live and/or on TV[3] of which recordings may exist somewhere.

He's Got the Whole World in His Hands (traditional), Slow Down (Larry Williams), Doo Wah Diddy (Barry/Greenwich), Promised Land (Berry), I'm a Loser (Lennon/McCartney)
Original release: not applicable, originally broadcast on the US TV show *Shindig* circa 1964

Unofficial recordings and video footage exist of the Walker Brothers performing the above songs on the US TV show *Shindig*, prior to the group's relocation to the UK. On the 30 September 1964 show (which at the time of writing can be found on YouTube in its entirety) the two-man Walker Brothers can be seen singing the traditional 'He's Got the Whole World in His Hands', along with all the other artists appearing on the show that week, and their versions of Larry Williams' 'Slow Down' and the Manfred Mann hit 'Doo Wah Diddy'. Other *Shindig* footage is also extant showing them perform Chuck Berry's 'Promised Land' and the Beatles' 'I'm a Loser'. The footage is really of historical interest only, for the sight of a pre-fame John and Scott performing with quiffed hair, matching outfits and smiling faces.

Saved (Jerry Leiber/Mike Stoller)
Original release: not applicable, originally broadcast on the TV show *Ready Steady Go* circa 1965

The Walker Brothers were regulars on the iconic Sixties TV show, *Ready Steady Go*, with an edition of the show devoted entirely to them. This reasonably well known number (lyric: 'I used to smoke, I used to drink, I used to smoke, drink and dance the hoochie coo . . . but now I'm saved.') features Scott on inessential lead vocal.

My Kind of Town (performed with rewritten lyrics) (Sammy Cahn/Jimmy van Heusen), Somewhere My Love (Francis Paul Webster/Maurice Jarre), What Now My Love (Becaud/Sigman/P. Delanoe)
Original release: not applicable, originally broadcast on the TV show *The Royal Gala* 4 December 1966 (filmed at the London Palladium on 29 November 1966)

Songs from the Walker Brothers' second televised London Palladium show. 'My Kind of Town' is the song made famous by Frank Sinatra. Chicago was Sinatra's kind of town, but the Walkers perform the song with a completely different lyric, written by person or persons unknown, concerning the delights of London. The resulting performance is cheesy. 'Somewhere My Love' is much more enjoyable. Also known as 'Lara's Theme', or the love theme from the film *Dr. Zhivago*, it is, as John announces, 'a very beautiful song'. Scott and John again take turns on lead vocal. 'What Now My Love' is probably best known from its version by Andy Williams, and is here given an almost marching-style orchestral backing and another shared vocal.

Send for Me (Ollie Jones)
Original release: not applicable, originally broadcast unknown Walker Brothers TV appearance

A recording from an unknown source, possibly one of the Palladium shows, of the Walker Brothers performing this song most associated with Nat King Cole.

Something You Got (Chris Kenner)
Original release: not applicable, originally broadcast unknown Walker Brothers TV appearance

Another recording from an unknown source, this time of the Walker Brothers performing a song by 'Land of 1,000 Dances' writer Chris Kenner.

More (Nino Oliviero/Riz Ortolani/Marcello Ciociolini, English lyric by Norman Newell)
Original release: not applicable, originally broadcast on *Billy Cotton's Music Hall* TV show circa 1967/68

A Scott Walker solo TV appearance and an up-tempo song performed with a big brassy arrangement. The kind of number with which Scott could have opened an episode of his own TV series, it's the theme to the cult 1962 Italian film *Mondo cane* ('world of the dog'!).

Let It Be Me (Gibert Becaud/Mann Curtis)
Original release: not applicable, originally broadcast on *The Dusty Springfield Show* circa 1967/68

Audio survives of Scott performing this song as a duet with Dusty Springfield on her TV show, and it's absolutely gorgeous. It's just a shame that this is not available to be heard in pristine quality. The song would have been familiar to British TV viewers at the time, as it had been a Top Twenty hit for the Everly Brothers in 1960.

What Would I Be (Jackie Trent)

Original release: not applicable, originally broadcast on the TV special *Mr and Mrs Music* 11 March 1969

Scott Walker sings Val Doonican! Well, almost. It's a recording, from the Tony Hatch and Jackie Trent TV special *Mr and Mrs Music*, of Scott singing the Trent song Doonican took to Number Two in the British charts in 1966. Colour video footage of this appearance is also known to survive.

Once I Loved (Antonio Carlos Jobim/Ray Gilbert/Vinicius de Moraes)

Original release: not applicable, unknown Scott Walker TV appearance

Often mistakenly referred to as 'When Loves Goes Away', there are unsourced recordings of Scott's version of this Antonio Corlos Jobim song in circulation. This melancholy number sets the reuniting of two lovers against a gentle Spanish guitar arrangement, while Scott sings, 'from my infinite sadness you came and bought me love again/I will hold you close, make you stay, because love is the saddest thing when it goes away.'

Main Street Mission (Jerry Fuller)

Original release: not applicable, performed live by Scott Walker at Coventry and other venues

Some live recordings exist of Scott performing this Jerry Fuller (who also wrote 'Lines', recorded by the Walker Brothers in 1976) song, and recorded by O. C. Smith (of 'Son of Hickory Holler's Tramp' fame, also a guest on Scott's TV series). The recording of this Coventry performance is enlivened by Scott's ad-libs to his excitable fans.

---

1. The remaining titles from the Walkerpeople list of unreleased tracks, some of which might see the light one day, are: the Walker Brothers' 'Are You Ready for Me', 'Don't Forget about Me', 'In the Evening Time', 'Where's the Man I Used to Be', 'Our Time', 'I Can't Help Myself ' and 'Are You Ready Now'; and Scott Walker's 'I'll Only Miss Her', 'When Am I Going Home' (AKA 'When Am I Ever Going Home'), 'For All We Know', 'There's a Feeling', 'Love Hurts', 'The Desperate Ones' and 'Lovers'. 'The Desperate Ones' is the Brel song. 'Lovers' is believed to be a Scott Walker composition and not the Mickey Newbury song of the same name recorded by the Walker Brothers.

2. The audio quality of these recordings varies tremendously (some of them being homemade recordings by fans) from good to very poor. Audiophiles beware.

3. For example, *A Deep Shade of Blue* mentions a Walker Brothers performance of the Beatles' song 'We Can Work It Out' on Ready Steady Go (p.76), and a Scott Walker live performance of 'The Long and Winding Road' (p.163).

Acknowledgements

I remain indebted to the following people who helped with the original edition of *The Rhymes of Goodbye*: Sue Walton for being expert on all matters Walker and who was good enough to read and comment upon an early version of the manuscript; David and Mark Boon, Lynne Tookey and James Aldred for their generosity in providing me with audio material I might not otherwise have heard; Margaret Waterhouse and especially Arnie Potts, collector of Walker memorabilia without equal, for assistance in providing material to illustrate the book; Paul Woods (now author of *The Curious Life and Work of Scott Walker*); and Sandra Wake and all at Plexus.

Index of Songs